NEW APPROACHES TO THE STUDY OF CENTRAL-LOCAL GOVERNMENT RELATIONSHIPS

New Approaches to the Study of Central-Local Government Relationships

edited by

G. W. JONES

London School of Economics and Political Science

Gower

Published by
Gower Publishing Company Limited,
Westmead, Farnborough, Hampshire, England

British Library Cataloguing in Publication Data

New approaches to the study of central-local
    government relationships.
    1. Local government - Great Britain - State
    supervision
    2. Great Britain - Politics and government -
    1964-
    I. Jones, George William
    354'.41'083   JS3137

ISBN 0 566 00332 5

Printed by
Itchen Printers Limited, Southampton

Contents

The contributors

Patrick Dunleavy, Lecturer in Government, London School of Economics and Political Science.

Royston Greenwood, Lecturer in Organisational Analysis, Institute of Local Government Studies, University of Birmingham.

John Gyford, Lecturer in Town Planning, University College, London.

K. Isaac-Henry, Principal Lecturer in Public Administration, City of Birmingham Polytechnic.

Bob Hinings, Professor of Organisational Studies and Associate Director, Institute of Local Government Studies, University of Birmingham.

Mari James, Research Assistant in Central-Local Relations, University College, London.

G.W. Jones, Professor of Government, London School of Economics and Political Science.

Martin Laffin, Staff member, Centre for Organisational and Operational Research, Tavistock Institute of Human Relations.

Howard Machin, Lecturer in French Government and Politics, London School of Economics and Political Science.

P.J. Madgwick, Reader in Political Science, University College of Wales, Aberystwyth.

Edward Page, Lecturer in Politics, Centre for the Study of Public Policy, University of Strathclyde.

Brian C. Smith, Senior Lecturer in Public Administration, University of Bath.

J.D. Stewart, Professor of Local Government and Administration, and Director, Institute of Local Government Studies, University of Birmingham.

Adrian Webb, Professor of Social Administration, University of Loughborough.

Gerald Wistow, Research Fellow in Social Administration, University of Loughborough.

Vincent Wright, Official Fellow, Nuffield College, Oxford.

1 Introduction

G.W. Jones

'It has long been evident to careful observers of English political
institutions that central control over local government has been
increasing rapidly not only in a positive or legal sense but also as
an influence. The events of the past year are, however, particularly
significant from this point of view and may be said without exaggeration
to constitute a new and ignoble chapter in the history of local
government in England.'(1) These words of William Robson written in
late 1932 would have been an appropriate dirge from those fearful of
'central domination of local government' on many occasions before then,
even throughout the nineteenth century when in many towns bitter
wrangles raged between localists and centralists.(2) At national
level, too, advocates of the rival philosophies of Sir Edwin Chadwick
and Joshua Toulmin Smith competed to influence legislation and
administrative action.(3) But Robson's lament could also have been
uttered many times after 1932, and is being heard in 1979 when once
again local government is said to have come to a crossroads, and now
faces a choice of becoming an agent of central government or of
maintaining a significant measure of autonomy.(4)

This latest bout in the battle between champions of localism and of
centralism has occurred because of the crisis of resources. Up to
about 1974 both centre and locality could march roughly in step: the
centre provided the money for local government to provide the services
that both it and the centre desired.(5) But from 1974 the resources
to finance this expansion of public functions were squeezed. The
centre felt it necessary to restrain and even cut its grants to local
government, while local government found it had not the cash for
achieving both its own priorities and those of central government. If
local authorities were not to be branches of central departments they
felt that either the centre should provide more money to finance both
central obligations and their own choices or else the centre must
reduce its plethora of controls, statutory and administrative, which,
they argued, compelled local government to perform certain duties in
certain ways. Central-local relationships in 1979 have been dominated
by this issue. Local authorities have sought to convince the centre
that proposed reductions in grant will provoke damaging cuts in local
services, redundancy amongst staff and politically intolerable
increases in rates.(6) And they have pressed the centre to remove
some of their statutory obligations(7) and to reduce the 'thousand and
one bureaucratic controls' over their activities.(8) The centre
responded with an offer to reduce about three hundred.(9)

For a century and a half localists have deplored the increase of
centralisation, and yet the trend seems inexorably against them. If
their own rhetoric is believed then central government has steadily
curbed local autonomy. This development is welcomed by the champions
of the centre. Sceptical of such merits of decentralisation as the
diffusion of power, the promotion of democratic participation and the

1

provision of efficient, effective and coordinated services in response to local circumstances, they regard the national government as the guardian of the wider public interest. Local authorities are seen as narrow in their vision, inefficient, extravagant, and oppressive to their citizens, while the centre, responsible for the national economy, is keen to stimulate efficiency, to ensure high national and uniform standards in services, to eradicate waste and to protect local inhabitants from maladministration by local officials and councillors. Michael Heseltine, Secretary of State for the Environment, told local authorities: 'I have to make it clear to you that as the sponsoring Minister for local government I am not only the sponsoring Minister for the rate spenders and the rate collectors but in the last resort for the ratepayers as well.'(10)

   Whilst there has been a considerable amount of assertion and counter-assertion from both local and central government, and from academics who have attached themselves to one side or the other, there has been little impartial scholarly investigation of relationships between central and local government, either to plot their historical evolution or to analyse their contemporary patterns. The interconnection between central and local government is clearly a topic of importance: it influences the provision of major public services and the expenditure of huge sums of public money. Yet since J.A.G. Griffith's Central Departments and Local Authorities in 1966(11) no single book has concentrated on central-local relations nor has there been much research directly concerned with such linkages.(12) Academic interest in the subject was stimulated in the 1970s by two government inquiries. The Layfield Committee's report on Local Government Finance in 1976 argued that the relationship between central and local government was confused and ambiguous, and that the main responsibility for local government expenditure and its financing should be moved clearly to either the central or local government.(13) In the following year the Central Policy Review Staff surveyed central-local relations and was critical of the inconsistent guidance issuing from central departments. It urged a more corporate and coordinated central approach to local government.(14) In 1978 the Social Science Research Council, recognising the need for systematic academic inquiry into this field, set up a Panel on Central-Local Government Relationships to develop a programme of research focussed on the interactions between central and local government. In 1979 the panel recommended support for six projects, which the SSRC accepted.(15)

   The panel's report contains details of the projects. It explains why the panel adopted their focus, a concern with organisational interactions and the process of implementation, and how the projects cohere together within a particular analytical framework.

   The panel argued that central-local relations raised issues that were relevant for two fundamental questions about industrial and post industrial society: 'to what extent may such societies be ungovernable and to what extent can government in them be accountable?'(16) In its discussion of ungovernability the panel noted that as government had undertaken more and new functions, penetrating deeper into society, so new forms of institutions and processes had emerged. Government had become organised complexity, with not only the traditional institutions of central departments and local authorities, but also ad hoc agencies of various kinds at national, regional and local levels and new bodies

2

set up to mediate between them. Institutions became increasingly interrelated and, as the processes of government became more inter-twined, more dependent on each other. This organisational inter-dependence gave rise to the major problem of implementation. One organisation finds that its aims are not achieved and blames others for impeding the realisation of its objectives - by failing to follow its guidance and direction or by erecting restraints and obstacles. As government intervenes more in society, discretion is increasingly conferred on low level officials or on other organisations, who thus have more scope to act in ways that may frustrate the goals of the initiators. They tend to respond by devising mechanisms of control to curb discretion and cramp the implementators. Thus exasperation for each is stimulated by the paradoxical combination of both growing discretion and increasing controls. Further, increasing governmental interdependence and a more complex organisational environment make the formulation and implementation of public policy more hazardous, since it becomes more difficult to trace clearly the connections between goals, policy proposals, measures to achieve them, and outputs and outcomes.

Organisational interdependence also produces a problem of account-ability. An increasing number of decisions on public policy are taken not within organisations that are clearly responsible to the public through elected representatives, either ministers or councillors, but in networks of mediation that link organisations and as a result of interactions between them. It, thus, becomes difficult to identify who is responsible for a decision, since responsibility is so often shared and diffused. This blurring of responsibility inevitably weakens the public's capacity to call decision makers to account or to influence them. Public frustration with this situation is intensified by the crisis of entitlement, that is the arousal of public expectations as a result of government promises or intervention which, however, do not produce services of the quality or quantity desired. This policy failure helps to generate further demands for further intervention, which is equally ineffective, and so the vicious circle spins.

The panel, therefore, felt that there was more to the study of central-local relations than investigating whether and how central government was controlling local government. They were seen to inter-penetrate in complex and subtle linkages, which required analysis. So the panel set about devising an analytical framework, a systematic inventory of elements to sensitise researchers to crucial aspects. The main characteristics of the framework are that central-local relation-ships should not be viewed along only one dimension. The linkages are multiple, and arise from the possession by each organisation of certain powers or resources, for instance, constitutional and legal, financial, professional and administrative, and political.(17) Organisations differ in the amount of such resources each possesses and in their skills in deploying them. Interdependence between organisations arises because no one organisation alone can perform its functions, provide services or accomplish its tasks without at some stage requiring resources controlled by another organisation. Accordingly it will attempt to acquire the needed resources, and cooperation, and to do so will employ various strategies. This process of exchange between organisations is regulated by rules of the game, and by how members of the organisations perceive their roles and the environment. Thus the assumption is that each organisation with its own views and interests to promote will seek to mobilise its own and others' resources to achieve its goals. Much of the variation in the relationships between levels of government arises from the possession of varying amounts of the different resources, from differences of skills in using them and from differential capability to compensate for deficiency in one resource by exploiting strength in another - all influenced very much by historical experience. The product of the interplay between resources, strategies, skills and rules of the game is discretion in the choice and implementation of goals.

The panel felt that this framework offered a useful and practical approach for analysing the organisational complexity of central-local relationships. They adopted it for their six projects and commended other researchers to use it. They felt it went some way in providing a conceptual language in which to form and develop models and theories about central-local relations. A fuller version of the analytical framework was published in the panel's report as Appendix I, 'Research into Central-Local Relations in Britain: A Framework for Analysis', by R.A.W. Rhodes. He had been commissioned by the panel to review the literature on central-local relations and on inter organisational relations, and to devise an analytical framework based on this literature. His survey, which includes an extensive bibliography and an elaboration of the framework, is published as the companion volume to this present collection of essays, entitled The Rationality of Ambiguous Consensus.[18]

The panel also commissioned a review of the literature on the process of implementation, to clarify the concept and draw together conclusions from previous research. Michael Hill and his colleagues from the School for Advanced Urban Studies at Bristol University produced 'Implementation and the Central-Local Relationship', which was published as Appendix II of the panel's report. The essence of the idea of implementation is that public policy is carried out or mediated by actors or agencies who are not themselves involved in formulating the policy. An implementation problem arises when the intentions and goals of central policy makers are subverted, transformed or reinterpreted at the periphery. This process, however, may be viewed disparagingly as a source of loss of control or more constructively as a source of adaptation and flexibility, indeed of innovation. Implementation is commonly used to describe the mediation of policy within a wide range of organisational and interorganisational relationships, and in the context of central-local government relationships very different implementation issues arise, depending on the characteristics of different policy areas, of different implementing agencies and of different external environments.

The analytical framework and the notion of implementation provided the intellectual guidelines for the panel's six projects, which, the panel hoped, would contribute to further development of the framework and of understanding the process of policy making. The SSRC's grant of £260,000 is distributed to the following:-

1. A study of policy implementation as an aspect of central-local relationships, which will examine the operation of discretion, explore the complex of relationships in the manpower policy field and develop theory about policy

4

implementation;

2.   A study of policy planning systems as a means of relating
     central and local government, which will examine how the
     introduction of such systems, in this case Transport
     Policies and Programmes and Inner Area Partnerships and
     Programmes, reshapes interactions between centre and
     locality, whether the relationships vary with the type
     of planning system and the extent to which planning
     systems produce different patterns of relationships
     compared with policy areas not organised in such a
     programmatic way;

3.   A study of the local authority associations and other
     central institutions of local government that act as
     intermediaries between central and local government,
     which will analyse the changing roles of the associations
     since 1974 and assess whether they have an effective
     capability for manging their relationships with central
     government;

4.   A study of the nature, extent and consequences of party
     political linkages between central and local government,
     which will focus on central and local government party
     politicians and investigate their activities in party
     headquarters, parliamentary party groups, party groups
     in the local authority associations, party local government
     conferences, party groups on individual local authorities
     and party organisations at local, regional and area levels;

5.   A study of local government professions as linkages
     between central and local government, which will examine
     their roles in policymaking and implementation, and
     investigate their relationships with other professional,
     administrative and political actors in central and local
     government;

6.   A study of the influence of central grants on central-local
     interactions, which will examine how to assess the extent
     to which key elements of grant shape the decision making
     processes of central and local government and the
     characteristics of the interactions between central and
     local government.

Although the panel were able to publish with their report the papers
by Rhodes on the analytical framework and by SAUS on implementation,
they were not able to publish some other papers that helped shape their
thinking and provided essential background for their projects. This
present book of essays contains some of the papers commissioned by
the panel and subsequently revised by the authors for publication. Some
of them relate specifically to the panel's projects and explain their
academic context.   Others relate to research that might be carried out
in the future and represent the panel's intention to maintain the
momentum of the SSRC's initiative and encourage further research both
within the framework adopted by the panel and within other frameworks.
Some of the essays were not commissioned by the panel but were written
independently and submitted for the panel to consider. In total they

comprise some of the latest academic thinking about central-local relations and the directions research should take.

The first three essays provide background about research projects on which the authors are currently engaged. They explore critical resources that are the bases for linkages between central and local government: the financial, the professional and the party political. John Stewart seeks to devise an appropriate research strategy with which to explore the effects of central grants. His objective is to outline the main characteristics of grant and to plot their impact on central and local decision making, and on interactions between central and local government. He wants to move discussion about the effects of grant beyond assertions that it does or does not encourage central control.

Professional linkages are the focus of Martin Laffin's chapter. His concerns are to examine the nature of local government professions, the factors that influence them and the interactions between them. His objective is to analyse the relationships between professionals in local government and their counterparts and other staff in central government, as well as in their professional organisations and local authority associations. His research strategy suggests that different professions with varying characteristics will operate through different networks of relationships and exercise differential influence.

John Gyford's essay is about party political linkages, outlining the different arenas in which party political contacts between central and local government are maintained and in which different strategies and tactics might be employed.

The next two essays explore the changing context in which central-local interactions take place. K. Issac-Henry contributes the first account of the local authority associations since J.A.G. Griffith's book in 1966.[19] He provides an introductory survey of their structure, functioning and influence. Bob Hinings examines new policy planning systems. He explains the theory behind them, their characteristics and possible impacts on central-local relations. His chapter is essential for an understanding of the research project, sponsored by SSRC, on which he is now engaged.

The next essay focusses on a policy area, the personal social services. Adrian Webb and Gerald Wistow illustrate how the analytical framework of the panel might be applied to a particular policy area. They depict the networks of complex interactions, financial, professional and political, fusing together over policy, technical issues and resources. They also show that academic study of central-local relationships can have practical implications for both central and local government, when they make recommendations to the Department of Health and Social Security about how to secure more effective implementation. They reveal limits on the use of certain central instruments of so-called control. This study of the personal social services might provide a model for other researchers to adopt in other policy areas, such as education or health, in which the panel hoped to stimulate future research.

The next two essays also survey a range of central-local linkages, each in the context not of one service but of many services in a territorial division of the country. Edward Page examines central-local relationships in Scotland. He shows how different they are from those in England, both in formal aspects of the structure and more informally in process. He also investigates the impact of grant on the outputs of local government, adding a further dimension to John Stewart's essay by using regression analysis to trace the consequences of alterations of different elements in the financial arrangements.

Central-local interactions in Wales is the subject of the chapter by Peter Madgwick and Mari James. As in Scotland they note the significance of proximity between local authorities and their superintending department. They emphasise financial factors, including the importance of the block general grant, the influence of politics and of bureaucratic cultures. They plot the network of central-local interactions as the consequence of a host of conflicting pressures in which consultation and control are blended in a subtle mix, producing not clarity of responsibility but an ambiguity that enables each side to bargain and negotiate with the other.

The next two chapters address themselves to advice for researchers in central-local relations. Patrick Dunleavy contributes a survey of a variety of other possible approaches to the study of central-local relations, including the literature on community power and Marxist, neo Marxist and structuralist frameworks of analysis. The panel wanted to encourage those who did not fully accept their own approach to develop alternatives and show how they could be applied to develop theory. Dr Dunleavy's essay provides some ideas that the panel hoped would stimulate competition in the research community to devise research projects that went beyond the panel's approach.

Brian Smith's essay also suggests an alternative approach. His concern is with the concept of decentralisation, its causes and consequences, and its relationship to the idea of autonomy. He formulates his conclusions as sets of hypotheses that further research should prove, refute or refine. His framework, like that of the panel's, is not simply of relevance for this country. It has potential for comparative application.[20]

The final two essays look abroad. Royston Greenwood examines the financial dimension of central-local relations in Sweden, extending discussion of John Stewart's theme of the consequences of grant. His inquiry shows how commonly-held British assumptions about the implications of block and specific grants are not apparent in practice in Sweden. Specific grants may well operate to limit the ability of central departments in Sweden to influence certain local authority decisions on expenditure, while block grants may work in the opposite direction.[21] His chapter also indicates one advantage of examining other countries: it helps to refine the analysis of a specific country.[22]

To encourage researchers to look beyond the shores of Britain and at some illuminating literature on central-local relations, the panel commissioned Howard Machin and Vincent Wright to survey recent French work on central-local interactions and explain the various schools of thought who are engaged in interesting debates about the nature of central and local power and the interactions between them.[23]

This book then is a report of some of the work that the SSRC panel commissioned and encouraged, which they felt should be made more widely available to the research community. It helps to explain a number of research projects already under way, and it should be of service to and stimulate other researchers. In 1979 the SSRC set up a new panel on central-local government relationships. Its purposes are to monitor and coordinate the first wave of six projects and to draw up a second wave. The hope of the new panel is that this book of essays, the companion volume by R.A.W. Rhodes and the report of the first panel will encourage the research community to come forward with constructive ideas for new projects which, after years of neglect, will advance the scholarly study of central-local relations. In addition, the approach and framework outlined here have a wider relevance for the study of British government. Their insights offer useful ways to explore the organisational complexity and interdependence that constitute British government today.

NOTES AND REFERENCES

(1)   W.A. Robson, 'The Central Domination of Local Government', The Political Quarterly, Vol. IV, No. 1, Jan-March 1933.

(2)   Derek Fraser, Power and Authority in the Victorian City, Basil Blackwell, Oxford, 1979.

(3)   S.E. Finer, The Life and Times of Sir Edwin Chadwick, Methuen, London, 1952; R.A. Lewis, Edwin Chadwick and the Public Health Movement, Longmans, London, 1952; R. Lambert, Sir John Simon, 1816-1904 and English Social Administration, MacGibbon and Kee, London, 1963; W.H. Greenleaf, 'Toulmin Smith and the British Political Tradition', Public Administration, Spring 1975, pp. 25-44.

(4)   The arguments of both central and local government over the events of 1979 can be seen in Municipal Journal, Local Government Chronicle, Municipal Review and County Councils Gazette for May, June, July and August 1979. Also see Tyrrell Burgess, 'Rates - safeguard of democracy', The Observer, August 12 1979.

(5)   This picture emerges from the Layfield report, Committee of Inquiry into Local Government Finance, Cmnd. 6453, HMSO, London, 1976.

(6)   See note (4).

(7)   Notably the Association of County Councils. See Municipal Journal, 13 July 1979, p. 730, and Local Government Chronicle, 13 July 1979, p. 741.

(8)   Review of Central Government Controls over Local Authorities, by the Association of County Councils, Association of District Councils, the Association of Metropolitan Authorities, London Boroughs Association and the Greater London Council, February 1979. The 'thousand and one' total appears in County Councils Gazette, April 1979, p. 9 and was referred to in the press after the report was published, e.g. Financial Times and Daily Telegraph, 6 March 1979.

(9)   Department of the Environment, Central Government Controls over Local Authorities, Cmnd. 7634, HMSO, London, 1979.

(10)   Speech to the Annual Meeting of the Association of County Councils, 25 July 1979. Department of the Environment Press Notice, No. 314.

(11) J.A.G. Griffith, Central Departments and Local Authorities,
      Allen & Unwin, London, 1966.
(12) Anthony Barker, Central-Local Government Relationships in
      Britain as a Field of Study: A Commentary and Research
      Register, Social Science Research Council, London, 1979.
      This study was commissioned by the SSRC's Central-Local
      Government Relations Panel.
(13) See note (5).
(14) Central Policy Review Staff, Relations Between Central
      Government and Local Authorities, HMSO, London, 1977.
(15) Central-Local Government Relations, a Panel report to the
      SSRC's Research Initiatives Board, SSRC, London, 1979.
(16) Panel report, p. 6.
(17) This approach was touched on in G.W. Jones, 'Intergovernmental
      Relations in Britain', The Annals of the American Academy
      of Political and Social Science, Vol. 416, November 1974,
      pp. 186-189, and developed in G.W. Jones, 'Central-Local
      Relations, Finance and the Law', Urban Law and Policy, Vol. 2,
      March 1979, pp. 25-46.
(18) R.A.W. Rhodes, The Rationality of Ambiguous Consensus, Saxon
      House, Farnborough, forthcoming.
(19) J.A.G. Griffith, op. cit., pp. 33-49. R.A.W. Rhodes is now
      engaged on a SSRC sponsored research project on the local
      authority associations.
(20) The SSRC is currently supporting Dr Smith to test his hypotheses
      in Nigeria.
(21) This point is touched on in A.R. Prest, Intergovernmental
      Financial Relations in the United Kingdom, Centre for Research
      on Federal Financial Relations, Australian National University,
      Canberra Research Monograph, 23, 1978, p. 86, and developed
      in Richard Jackman, 'Calling the Tune', Times Educational
      Supplement, 22 July 1977.
(22) Dr Greenwood is now engaged on a SSRC sponsored project inquiring
      into the effects of central government influence on the
      budgetary processes of local authorities in Britain.
(23) A recent book which adopts a comparative approach to British
      and French local government, and contains insights into
      central-local relations in the two countries, is Jacques
      Lagroye and Vincent Wright, eds., Local Government in Britain
      and France, Allen & Unwin, London, 1979.

2   Grant Characteristics and Central-Local Relations

J.D. Stewart

Introduction

The relationship between certain grant characteristics and the extent
of local autonomy has been the subject of assertion and counter
assertion in the literature on central-local relations. This essay
argues that research on this topic is still required but, in order
to carry out that research, the nature of the relevant grant
characteristics must be clarified and hypotheses as to the impact
on the actual behaviour of governmental institutions should be
formulated in place of assertions and counter assertions.   Rhodes[1]
has set out both the 'conventional wisdom' that as local authorities
have become 'increasingly dependent upon central government grant it
has led to centralising tendencies' and the 'conventional critique'
which challenges this contention. The publication of the Layfield
Report on Local Government Finance[2] renewed the debate. The report
argued that the increasing proportion of grant reinforced pressures
for central government intervention in local government decisions.
Cripps and Godley challenged the Layfield argument: 'In our view there
is a fatal confusion in Layfield's argument in that this supposes
local autonomy to derive uniquely from its power to raise local taxes,
thereby ignoring the autonomy that derives from a grant that is not
hypothecated.'[3]

   This topic, about which there are marked differences of view, is
central to the debate about the recommendations of the Layfield
Committee. Yet it is surprising that so little research is undertaken
by advocates of the differing views.[4] It may be that each side of
the argument sees the proposition as so obvious as not to require
research. That may be because some of those arguing that grant
characteristics have or do not have an effect on local autonomy rest
their arguments on the formal characteristics of either our
governmental system or the grant. For example, the formal accountability of central departments to Parliament for expenditure raised by
taxation is said to fuel their desire to control local authorities.
Alternatively advocates of the view that level of grants has no impact
rest their argument on the formal freedom of local authorities to spend
the grant as they wish. The arguments put forward can be regarded as
logical deductions from formal principles.

   Formal principles can be misleading as a guide to research. The
phrase local autonomy, suggesting formal principles, can itself mislead
unless clarified. In the end what must be researched are not formal
principles but the impact of certain characteristics of the grant
system on the actual behaviour of governmental institutions, influenced
or not by such principles.

Once one departs from the language of formal principles it is by no means clear that apparently opposed positions are as sharply opposed as has been suggested. Thus, whereas Cripps and Godley suggest that the Layfield Report saw the level of grant as the unique determinant of local autonomy, the Layfield Report did not actually say that. Its argument is not merely about the level of grant but about the tendency of the level of grant to increase - a topic relatively neglected in the literature. It does not assert a direct connection but rather that in a situation in which there is a complex of pressures operating these features of the grant tend to support the pressures for greater central government control. 'While it is not possible to demonstrate a direct connection between the proportion of grant and the extent of government intervention we are satisfied that the amount of grant and, more importantly, the fact that total grant was increasing to make development of services possible, powerfully reinforced the political pressures for government intervention.'(5)

Research into this area has been limited, in part because much of the literature has tended to take the form of assertions or counter assertions about a general relationship based on formal principles rather than detailed propositions about the nature of the relationship and above all the processes that lead to that relationship. Clarification of both the assumed independent variable (grant characteristics) and the assumed dependent variable (the impact on the behaviour of governmental institutions) and the relationship between them is a necessary preliminary to research.

THE RESEARCH AREA

The research area is the influence of the main structures and characteristics of grant on central-local relations. The justification for the research is that this topic is identified in the literature as a key issue for debate. A concern for such research does not mean that the research is testing the hypothesis that the main structures and characteristics of grant are the only influence on central-local relations. The hypothesis to be tested is that it is a significant influence.

In examining the nature of that influence this essay distinguishes between

(a)   System characteristics of central-local relations: describing the main characteristics of the organisational network linking central government and local authorities.
(b)   The decision making process in central government.
(c)   The decision making process in local government.
(d)   System outputs: the policy decisions (or expenditure levels deriving from those policy decisions) made by central government or local government.

The debate in the literature is about the relationship between grant characteristics and (a), (b) or (c). It is not about relations between grant characteristics and (d), although the limited research that has been done is about the relationship between grant characteristics and (d). This literature asserts that grant characteristics influence the

extent of central government intervention (area (b)); or the extent of
local accountability (area (c)); or the dependence of local government
on central government (area (a)). It is likely that if these influences
are present they will have an effect on area (d), but that is not the
main argument of the literature. Any research designed to test the
propositions in the literature should concentrate on areas (a), (b)
and (c) which are the main concern of that literature.

THE STRUCTURE AND CHARACTERISTICS OF GRANT

That the amount of grant influences decisions in a local authority is not
in dispute. Given that (after allowing for various balancing factors)
Expenditure (E) = Grant (G) + Rates Income (R) + Income from Charges
(C), or put another way G = E - (C + R), then a change in grant (or
perhaps more significantly a change in grant from expectation) must
imply a decision to change expenditure, rate income or income from
charges or some combination of them.

We do not know sufficient about the nature of that influence, e.g.
whether a change in grant has a greater effect on E, R, or C or what
determines the circumstances in which it has that effect. These are
important issues.

They are not, however, the issues mainly discussed in the literature.
The assertions in the literature are about the effect of the structure
and characteristics of grant. Structure and characteristics in the
British system can be distinguished in a variety of ways.

Structure

    (1)   General structure of grant:-
           general; specific; supplementary. (6)
    (2)   Breakdown of general grant:-
           needs element; resources element, domestic element. (7)
    (3)   Form of grant:-
           percentage or block;
           closed or open ended, distinguishing between whether
           closed to local authorities as a whole or to the
           individual authority. (8)
    (4)   System of distribution:-
           whether based on
           formula; local authority estimates; policy plans.
    (5)   Type of authority to which grant is paid:-
           shire district; shire county, etc.

Characteristics

    (1)   Scale of grant in relation to total local authority
           expenditure.
    (2)   Frequency and size of change in scale of grant in
           relation to total local authority expenditure.
    (3)   Stability of system of distribution.

The strategy proposed is to concentrate on the first and second
characteristics as being the main issues raised in the literature,
although noting the range and importance of the other characteristics

and structural features. As far as is possible research should cover
all these issues, but not at the expense of studying what has been
identified in the literature as the key characteristics:- the relative
scale of grant and changes in that relative scale.

SYSTEM CHARACTERISTICS AND DECISION MAKING PROCESSES

The general hypothesis to be investigated is that grant characteristics
have a significant influence on system characteristics of central-local
relations and/or on the decision making processes of central government
or local government or both.

   There are many system characteristics or features of the decision
making processes which it would be possible to investigate.

   1.   Intensity of the system:-
        number of communications between local authorities and
        central government.
   2.   The complexity of the system:-
        variety of forms of communication and the degree of
        variation in the points of communication.
   3.   The tone of the system:-
        the degree of conflict or cooperation shown in
        communications in the system.
   4.   Dependence relations within the system:-
        not merely the relative resources available to the
        different elements in the system, but also the effective
        use of those resources.

   Equally it is theoretically possible to investigate key decision
making processes in either central departments or local authorities.
For example it would be possible to investigate the budgetary
processes of local government and study such elements as

   (a) The distribution of influence in the budgetary process:-
        the actors mainly involved and the extent to which those
        actors determine the outcome.
   (b) The assumptions of the main actors about how the budgetary
        process operates and how it should operate.
   (c) The degree of formal rationality in the decision making
        process.
   (d) The relative priority given to decisions on expenditure
        or to decisions on rate levels in the budgetary process.

   In both system characteristics and the budgetary process there are
many elements to be examined. The problem within the complex of
features to be investigated is to select the key ones for inquiry.
Since the principle underlying the strategy is to test the issues
raised in the literature one should presumably be guided by the
literature. The difficulty is that much of the literature - both
that asserting a relationship and that denying it - is set at such
a high degree of generality that the guidance it gives is uncertain.

   The literature has used phrases like 'central government
intervention','sense of accountability', 'local government autonomy'

13

and 'control' to formulate general hypotheses about the influence of
grant characteristics. It is not always clear whether these phrases
are meant to describe system characteristics or to describe processes
of decision making either in central or local government. In
particular little or no indication is given about the mechanisms
bringing about the assumed influence. In order to determine a research
strategy, one has to proceed beyond such general statements to more
detailed hypotheses, setting out the possible nature of the relationship between grant characteristics and system characteristics, decision
making processes and the mechanism that brings about the relationship.
Such hypotheses would - and this element is crucial - set out not
merely the relationship but the intervening variables. The lack of
such hypotheses has held up research.

POSSIBLE HYPOTHESES

Grant characteristics could in principle have a direct influence on
system characteristics or decision making processes. The hypotheses
to be tested here assume that the main influences are on decision
making processes and only upon system characteristics through that
influence, i.e. grant characteristics →characteristics of decision
making processes ⟶ system characteristics.

   It is necessary to distinguish between hypotheses which set out the
effect of grant characteristics on the processes of decision making
at national level and those which set out the effect on the processes
at local level. The national hypothesis does not exclude the local
hypothesis nor does the local hypothesis exclude the national
hypothesis, but in principle they could be independent of each other.

   Possible local hypotheses and one national hypothesis are explored
below. They are examples to indicate possible areas of research.

Set of local hypotheses 1

This set, which could be described as the decline in local accountability hypotheses, is based on characteristic 1 above.

   1a. As the grant increases as a percentage of a local authority's
       expenditure there is a greater tendency for changes in grant
       levels to determine expenditure levels as opposed to rate
       levels (because of the gearing effect - as the grant percentage
       increases so does the proportionate adjustment in rates required
       to replace a given proportion of the grant). As the change in
       grant levels shows a greater tendency to determine expenditure
       levels the budgetary processes of local authorities change.
       The processes tend to give greater emphasis to the grant
       settlement or to predictions about the grant settlement as
       the starting point for decisions on expenditure. The budgetary
       process in local authorities tends to become grant led, rather
       than expenditure or rate level led.

          As these changes take place, there is a growing reluctance
       to take decisions on changes in expenditure except when
       initiated by changes in grant level.

1b. As the grant increases as a percentage of a local authority's
    expenditure so does the likelihood of grant settlements requiring
    major alteration in local authority expenditure plans (because
    of the greater dependence of expenditure plans on grant).

    As the percentage of grant increases there is therefore a
    tendency for a local authority to take expenditure decisions
    mainly as a result of grant settlement. The budgetary process
    tends to become grant led.

2. A tendency for the budgetary process to become grant led
    reduces the motivation for local authorities to pursue their
    own policies on expenditure.

    This development leads to a greater emphasis in the local
    authority budgetary process on central government's advice
    and it is more readily followed.

Set of local hypotheses 2

The set concentrates on the impact of changes in the frequency and
scale of grant (characteristic 2 above).   It covers the predominant
tendency up to 1975 for grant to increase in real terms. Different
hypotheses would be required for a decrease in grant in real terms.

1. The amount of increase in grant in real terms is the major
    influence on the amount of increase in expenditure in real
    terms of a local authority – the rate level being held
    relatively constant in real terms.

2. The main decision makers in the local authority tend to
    assume that grant is the major determinant of expenditure
    increases.

3. As this assumption is increasingly made, central government
    guidance is increasingly followed (conversely when grant
    decreases there is a lessening in the tendency to accept
    central government guidance).

Set of local hypotheses 3

This set could be described as the dependence hypotheses. They make
direct use of the assumptions of the main actors.

1. As the grant increases as a percentage of local government
    expenditure, leading officers and councillors see increased
    legitimacy and importance in central government advice and
    guidelines.

2. Greater information is provided in the budgetary process on
    central government advice and guidelines. There is greater
    reluctance to take independent local action.

Set of national hypotheses

This set is the increase in central government intervention hypotheses.
It is a hypothesis in terms of pressures.

1. As the grant increases as a percentage of local government
    expenditure so will the pressures for intervention in local
    authorities increase. Those pressures come from

    (a) Local authorities themselves, individually and
         through the Associations;
    (b) Pressure groups;
    (c) MPs.

2. As the grant percentage increases ministers and civil servants
    become involved in discussion about the expenditure plans of
    particular authorities (because the grant has become critical
    to the expenditure plans of local authorities).

3. These factors increase the number of occasions for ministers
    and civil servants to become involved in dealing with the
    expenditure of particular authorities.

4. These factors increase the number of occasions for ministers
    and civil servants to consider interventions.

5. Increasing grant creates expectations of intervention.
    Civil servants and ministers more and more operate in a
    climate of widespread expectation of intervention.

6. There are pressures in government both for and against
    intervention. The increasing grant percentage is seen
    as giving strength to arguments for intervention. The
    rationale for intervention is strengthened.

7. These tendencies tend to lead to greater intervention by
    central departments into local government activities.

CONCLUSION

The hypotheses go beyond general assertions about possible relationships. They explore the processes that lead to those relationships.
In that way they give fuller, but alternative, meanings to the general
statements. Through the development of such hypotheses a basis for a
major research study can be laid. The immediate priority is an
exploratory study to develop such hypotheses.

NOTES AND REFERENCES

(1) R.A.W. Rhodes, 'Research into Central-Local Relations in
       Britain: A Framework for Analysis' in Social Science
       Research Council, Central-Local Government Relationships,
       SSRC, London, 1979, Appendix I, pp. 3-6.
(2) Committee of Inquiry into Local Government Finance (Layfield)
       Report, Cmnd. 6453, HMSO, London, 1976, pp. 64-71. Hereafter
       referred to as the Layfield Report.
(3) Francis Cripps and Wynne Godley, Local Government Finance and
       its Reform, Department of Applied Economics, Cambridge, 1976,
       p. 11.
(4) This is not to deny the importance of the research carried out

by such studies as Noel Boaden, <u>Urban Policy-Making</u>, Cambridge University Press, London, 1971, or Douglas Ashford 'The Effects of Central Finance on the British Local Government System', <u>British Journal of Political Science</u> (4), 1974, pp. 305-22. But as will be argued later, such research is directed at studying policy outcomes (often in the form of expenditure levels). The assertions in the literature about the effect of grant characteristics are not, however, assertions about policy outcomes or expenditure levels. Such research does not directly test therefore the assertions.

(5)   Layfield Report, p. 66. para. 7.

(6)   cf. Layfield Report, p. 211, para. 5.

(7)   cf. Layfield Report, pp. 217-218 (needs element and resources element);
and pp. 161-163 (domestic element)

(8)   An open ended grant is a grant which increases with the amount spent or raised in tax by the local authority, a closed grant is fixed irrespective of the expenditure or rating decision by the local authority.

3   Professionalism in Central-Local Relations

Martin Laffin

Although the importance of local government professions has been widely acknowledged, attention has been limited to the activities of professional officers within individual local authorities. This essay opens up a neglected perspective on local government professions as significant forces in the relationship between central and local government. A framework for analysis of professionalism in the context of these relationships will be set out as a guide for future research and a pointer to relevant policy related issues.

The framework takes a local government profession to be a group of organised individuals intervening between central and local government. It assumes that this group is engaged in the attainment of its own objectives through the deployment of various resources and strategies. In deploying these resources and strategies members of a profession have to sustain accounts of their claims to expertise that are convincing in terms of the values and perceptions of other strategically placed actors and retain an occupational identity meaningful to themselves. A profession's occupancy of key administrative positions will face it with possible challenges and supports emanating from groups articulating other social and political interests.

As government has grown enormously in size, complexity and functional specialisation, so interest groups, especially those based upon occupation, have proliferated within and on the fringes of government, giving rise to what Beer terms 'technocratic politics' which refers to a state of affairs in which 'pressures and proposals tend to arise within government and its associated circles of professionals and technically-trained cadres'.[1] Thus policies are increasingly initiated, formulated and implemented without the effective participation of elected representatives. Such a thesis of technocratic or professional dominance at the local level has been advanced by a number of commentators, although it remains controversial.[2] A related feature of modern government is the emergence of new professions based within government, whose development has been nurtured by those within government, usually in conjunction with institutionalised pressure groups; whereas local government began by recruiting officers from professions existing outside government. A recent example is social work whose emergence as a single profession with its own local authority department is largely the result of the Seebohm Report. The membership of this Committee appears to have rendered its conclusions almost a foregone conclusion, as Sinfield notes:

> 'The public and private reaction of the vested interests to
> the Seebohm Report cannot but heighten anxiety that a major

function of the report has been to strengthen the position
of the profession and of administrators. The Committee
itself consisted essentially of the various vested interests
particularly from the National Institute of Social Work
Training, the staff college of the social work profession'.(3)

Thus, a profession can be seen as negotiating claims to expertise in
the development and implementation of certain public policies, but
negotiating within the context of changing problem perceptions among
strategically placed actors within government. Those termed
'strategically placed actors' include senior civil servants, ministers
and leading members of the local authority associations. A profession
will attempt to manage the emergence of these problem perceptions to
lead these other actors to conceive of the services of the profession
as essential in handling certain problems of social significance. So
professionals will tend to modify or reinforce their accounts of
professional practice in accordance with their perceptions of the
challenges and supports offered by these other actors. Professionals
may broaden and re-orient the boundaries of their profession in order
to appear competent to cope with new, emerging problems. They may
develop sub specialisms to cope with aspects of a problem beyond the
apparent capability of the core professionals. Again, professionals
may cooperate with other professionals on problems which demand the
services of more than one profession.(4)

Furthermore, it seems likely that professionals will attempt to
manage the distribution of decisions between the central government
and the local authorities. We may hypothesise that on certain issues
professionals will attempt to persuade central government to give local
authorities discretionary powers in the belief that their members will
enjoy increased discretion; while on other issues they will attempt to
persuade central government to make measures statutorily binding on
local authorities similarly in the belief that the hands of their
colleagues will be strengthened within their authorities. This
attempted management will be performed by the relatively few leading
professionals who have gained access to national level policy arenas.

The presence of other professions within government is significant
for a particular profession as members of other professions may be
strategically placed to affect its fortunes and may offer competition.
A profession already well-established at both levels of government or
indeed in the wider society frequently resists any potential threat
from an emerging profession by defining new occupational tasks as
simply extensions of its present tasks and by pointing to the dangers
of permitting the 'unqualified' to perform such tasks. An example is
the resistance town planning encountered from the engineering and
surveying professions to its emergence as a distinct profession.(5)

A further, much less clearly defined, group of actors also demand
consideration. In recent years there has been a mushrooming of groups
claiming a voice within government, as well as a weakening of citizens'
trust in government, both developments likely to change the premises of
the professions' case. Thus, the professions find themselves
increasingly in competition or in cooperation, usually tacitly, with
groups representing other social and political interests such as
tenants' associations, amenity groups and parent teacher associations.

Of importance too is the profession's maintenance of public trust in itself; it is compelled to shift its 'operating ideology' to remain in line with public opinion.(6)

So far, the term 'profession' has just been accepted as the description of themselves provided by those occupational groups within local government. However, in the extensive literature on the sociology of the professions, two approaches to the analysis of professionalism are discernible.

The first approach is concerned with the definition of professionalism and the debate over which occupations should be recognised as professions. Consequently its exponents have sought to delineate the essential attributes of an ideal type of profession. The best example of this approach is Moore's.(7) He sets out six major ideal typical attributes in the form of dimensions along which any given occupation can be located as more or less professional. The dimensions are: 1) the necessary condition that the occupation be full time; 2) a calling, that is the acceptance by practitioners of appropriate norms, standards and identification with professional peers and the profession as a collectivity; 3) an organisation, meaning the mutual identification of interests as distinctly occupational rather than as a result of common employee status interests (i.e. unionism); 4) a high standard of educational attainment amongst practitioners; 5) a service orientation incorporating rules of competence, of conscientious performance and service to the client; 6) autonomy or the absence of anyone else capable of challenging the professional with his own field.

Such ideal types have been widely criticised, not least because they direct attention away from relations between a profession and other power groupings.(8) These relationships, rather than simply the internal characteristics of the professions, appear to be crucial to the emergence and development of professions.(9) Indeed, the formation of the internal characteristics in large measure represents a profession's manoeuvrings in the negotiation for support and deflection of challenges from other power groupings. Any list of attributes, then, must tend to vary among professions and as the social and political circumstances of any given profession change. Thus, the major fault of studies like Moore's is that they do not go far enough. Nevertheless, they are of value as indicators of what the professions themselves have come to regard as essential attributes.

A more fruitful approach is to focus on the relationship between a profession and other power groupings rather than simply on its supposed attributes.(10) The local government professions are involved in a political process of maintaining and enlarging on the acceptance by others of their claims to expertise in certain areas of social concern. The relationship between a profession and other powerful actors may be conceptualised as power-dependent to stress their reciprocal nature, a profession being dependent upon those actors who influence recognition of these claims while, in turn, those actors depend upon a profession for information, policy implementation and advice. (11)

Although a great deal is known about the older professions, such as medicine and law, much less is known of the professions that work within government.(12) Consequently, the framework for analysis must draw heavily on studies of professions which, for the most part, work outside government. For the purposes of analysis some tentative hypotheses will be advanced, treating a profession as if its members all act as a single, rational actor. The following resources, then, may be hypothesised as significant in the emergence and maintenance of successful claims to expertise by a local government profession:

1. possession of a distinct and systemised body of knowledge and skills;

2. presence of a public service orientation;

3. presence of members of that profession at strategic positions;

4. existence of other organised social and political interests supporting the professional claims.

RESOURCE 1

Typically, a profession argues that it possesses a distinct body of systematised knowledge and skills which are scientifically well-founded. This body of knowledge is presented as unified to resist the usurpation by other occupational groups, or indeed lay people, of any of the profession's tasks as well as to reinforce the common identity of the membership against the tendency, exhibited by many professions, to fragment into sub specialisms. At the same time, a profession maintains barriers between itself and others, whether lay people or other occupations. Obviously, the technical components of its work will act as a barrier but professionals frequently raise this barrier by engaging in mystification - obscuring their reasons for decisions in technical jargon. However, this strategy may prove counter productive if it simply alienates lay people, for a profession is dependent upon some minimum cooperation from them if it is to retain its influence.

Certain professions experience difficulties in gaining acceptance as they lack a core of knowledge and skills in the eyes of lay people. Housing management, for example, has difficulties in creating a convincing rationale upon which to base its claims to expertise, since its existing occupational tasks are frequently seen by lay people, especially councillors, as simply commonsense. While, in contrast, a profession like civil engineering does not face the same difficulties, as lay people generally accept that its occupation tasks involve the application of a large and complex body of knowledge.

A profession, too, endeavours to control the transmission of its knowledge and skills to ensure their exclusiveness. By no means all professions control training and qualification to practice but they all have a strong influence on these entry processes. A profession attempts as well to increase its status by raising entry requirements to recruit the highly educated. Finally, it is usually actively engaged in refining and extending the professional knowledge base by the promotion of research and the diffusion of the findings amongst its members.

RESOURCE 2

A profession usually argues that its occupational tasks constitute
important services to the 'public good' or to the assistance of weaker
members of the community. This argument is probably not as convincing
as that based on knowledge, but many professions which find it difficult
to sustain knowledge claims will fall back on some type of service
based claims. A profession will have to orientate itself towards those
values, the attainment of which other powerful actors regard as
important. Such a requirement creates considerable tensions within
some professions. One instance is social work: many social workers
believing themselves to be serving values they reject.(13)

   Part of the service orientation is the stress placed on their
'neutrality' by the local government professions. Local government
officers within authorities are careful to avoid becoming associated
with a political party or even a 'politically motivated' pressure group.
For a great strength of professionalism lies in the trust that others
place in what is seen as an independent source of expertise.

RESOURCE 3

The previous two sections refer to resources which are of the type
regarded as typically professional. However, local government
professionals also occupy strategically placed positions within local
government, central government and organisations between the two levels
of government. Within local authorities, certain professions have
acquired their own professional departments headed by a chief officer
drawn from their ranks. It may be speculated that some professional
departments have emerged because of the acceptance by central and local
government of arguments of the sort outlined above, while others may
have emerged in response to the demands of essentially administrative
tasks. Housing management, for example, may have grown up to manage
the very large housing stocks which authorities accumulated rather than
because of professional claims to knowledge or service. Indeed, that
several housing departments are headed by officers without a housing
management qualification suggests that some councillors are not
convinced by the profession's arguments. It can be said also that
those professions whose members hold few or no chief officer posts as
well as lacking status vis a vis other actors will be under a serious
handicap in national level negotiations in which officers below the
top tier cannot easily become involved.

   There are substantial variations in the extent to which the local
government professions are represented in the central departments.
Planners and engineers occupy posts at the highest levels within the
Department of the Environment, while other professions are not
represented at all or only on the periphery of departments. So some
strategically placed actors are themselves members of the professions,
and are often active members; the chief planner (a deputy secretary)
in DOE, for instance, is a former President of the Royal Town Planning
Institute. Contact between professionals in central and local
government may be quite extensive and, although the published evidence
is sparse, it has been argued that officers use these contacts in
winning resources for their authorities.

Professional officers are involved too in the work of organisations which lie between central and local government. The major organisations are the three local authority assocations which the Layfield Report identified as 'the main channel of communication between the government and individual local authorities'.(14) Attached to their committees the associations have officer advisers appointed in consultation with professional associations. Although the advisers have no right to vote, 'their views are, of course, of great persuasive force'.(15) There are other organisations such as the Council for Local Education Authorities, the Housing Consultative Council and the Consultative Council on Local Government Finance in which professional officers are involved and again presumably influential.(16)

Finally, the professional associations themselves are directly consulted by the central departments. Little is known about the matters on which the professional associations' views are sought, but it is probable that more technical issues will be referred to them, though there is a likelihood of tension between a profession and central government over what should be defined as 'technical'.

RESOURCE 4

The activities of other organised social and political interests which are pressing their own policy demands on government are likely to affect the success with which a profession is able to realise its claims. These interest groups may support or challenge a profession's account of its practice in accordance with their own interests and values. Support is usually incidental rather than a conscious decision to cooperate with a profession; the activities of environmentalist groups may assist the claims of environmental health officers but none of them probably is in coalition with the officers. Nonetheless, members of a profession may be active in groups with interests similar to that profession. But there is the danger of a profession losing its reputation as a group of independent experts if it becomes too closely associated with these interest groups. Challenges are often implicit rather than part of an interest group's platform, although tenants' associations, for example, have quite explicit views on housing management. There are three possible strategies a profession can adopt faced with such groups: it can orientate its account of professional practice to attract support from them or to reduce the relevance of their criticism; it can attack and attempt to persuade those in government to ignore them; or it can simply do nothing, probably viewing the threat as insubstantial or transient.

Until now, it has been accepted as an analytically useful device to treat a profession as if it were a group of people displaying a remarkable degree of solidarity.(17) In fact, professions are more typically fragmented into sub groups or segments. The members of each sub group tend to accept similar accounts of professional practice, of the relative importance of the various occupational tasks and of the profession's relationships to other fields, as well as being affected by similar events which may have different consequences for others in the profession.(18) Thus, it may be supposed that changes in the external relations of a profession will both reflect and be reflected in changes in relations among these sub groups.

The considerations sketched out above are intended as provisional guides for research which, in turn, should generate further, more satisfactory hypotheses. Other factors which may prove important include the changing fiscal policies of government and the market for a profession's skills. At times of financial stringency the local government professions are under pressure to dilute professional standards, to accept rising unemployment in their ranks and less promotion.(19) Those professions, like architecture and surveying, with an extensive membership outside government may find it easier to resist governmental supervision of their internal affairs than those entirely or largely dependent on government for work.

The central objective of research should be to shed light on whether the local government professions are truly technocratic in that they constitute autonomous sources of influence and of policy initiatives or whether they are simply vehicles for the implementation of centrally determined policies.(20) The answer to this question will probably vary depending upon which policy areas are investigated.(21)

Research into this question must be concerned with disentangling the complex interactions between the two levels of government in which professionals are involved. The ideas of network building and management have been developed to analyse such complex interactions.(22) They suggest that there are, within each profession, leading members who manage the linkages between their profession and other strategically placed actors. Research should aim at specifying the paths of linkage, whether through professional organisations, the local authority associations or other channels; the character of these linkages, frequency of use, formality or informality, the direction of information flows and density of linkages; and those points which are linked, chief officers with fellow professionals in central departments or with administrative civil servants. The leading professionals can be seen as promoting or resisting changes in these patterns of linkage in line with their policy objectives and perceptions of other actors, such as councillors, civil servants and other professional groups; though it must be borne in mind that these actors will, too, be attempting to manage the same and overlapping networks.

The management of these networks must be understood as part of the implementation of a profession's policy objectives. These objectives should be analysed both at the level of an individual's 'appreciative system'(23) and at the collective level where individuals as members of a profession are engaged in evolving a shared self image. Tensions between the individual and the collectivity are revealing of how a profession responds to changes in its objective situation.(24) The related concept of a 'professional ideology', although frequently used as an 'explanation' of professionals' behaviour, has been little analysed sociologically;(25) further research then should assess the analytic usefulness of the concept.

This essay argues that the local government professions should be studied not merely within particular local authorities but also as independent forces acting on both levels of government. If indeed professions are such forces, then we cannot rely solely upon local authorities to counteract professional syndicalism; it may be that we have to search for new forms of accountability or new ways to control

the professions.[26] Research along the lines set out here should
contribute to our understanding of the dimensions of the accountability
problem and the possible remedies. In Mosher's words, 'How can we be
assured that a highly differentiated body of public employees will act
in the interests of all the people, will be an instrument of all the
people?'[27]

NOTES AND REFERENCES

(1)   Samuel H. Beer, 'The Adoption of General Revenue Sharing: A Case
        Study in Public Sector Politics', Public Policy, 24, 2, Spring
        1978, p. 158. See also his 'Federalism, Nationalism, and
        Democracy in America', American Political Science Review, 72,
        1 March 1978, 9-21. Although Beer is writing of the American
        case, it is arguable that his thesis is truer in UK.

(2)   In particular, J. Gower Davies, The Evangelistic Bureaucrat,
        Tavistock, London, 1972; Norman Dennis, People and Planning,
        Faber, London, 1970, and Public Participation and Planner's
        Blight, Faber, London, 1972. These studies are primarily
        concerned with planners; for a more general statement of the
        thesis of officer dominance see R. Buxton, Local Government,
        Penguin, Harmondsworth, 1973, Ch. 2. Kenneth Newton
        criticises this thesis in Second City Politics, Clarendon
        Press, Oxford, 1976, Ch. 7.

(3)   Adrian Sinfield, 'Which Way for Social Work?' in The Fifth Social
        Service, the Fabian Society, London, 1970, p. 41. Similarly
        Phoebe Hall describes how a 'small group of distinguished
        people' concerned with social work pushed successfully for the
        Seebohm Enquiry, Reforming the Welfare, the Politics of Change
        in the Personal Social Services, Heineman, London, 1976, 23-25.
        Seebohm and the 1970 Social Services Act meant a rapid
        improvement in social work career prospects including the
        doubling of top salaries; significantly Seebohm departments
        had to be imposed on some reluctant authorities, see Jef
        Smith, 'Top Jobs in the Social Services', in K. Jones (ed.),
        The Yearbook of Social Policy in Britain 1971, RKP, London,
        1972, p. 17 and p. 20.

(4)   These points are suggested by Frederick C. Mosher, 'Professions in
        the Public Service', Public Administration Review, 38, 2,
        March/April 1978, 144-150. The article concludes a stimulating
        series of articles on 'The Professions in Government', in that
        edition and in Public Administration Review, 37, 6, November/
        December 1977, 631-686.

(5)   G. E. Cherry, The Evolution of British Town Planning, Leonard
        Hill, London, 1974, 165-169. Brian McLoughlin detects a
        challenge to town planning in the emergence of corporate
        planners as an occupational group, 'The Future of the Planning
        Profession', in P. Cowan (ed.), The Future of Planning,
        Heineman, London, 1973, 69-92. See also W. Coode,
        'Encroachment, Charlatanism and the Emerging Profession:
        Psychology, Sociology and Medicine', American Sociological

Review, 25, 1960, 902-914.

(6) L.J. Sharpe, 'Instrumental Participation and Urban Government', in J.A.G. Griffith (ed.), From Policy to Administration, Allen and Unwin, London, 1976.

(7) Wilbert E. Moore, The Professions: Roles and Rules, Russell Sage, New York, 1970, 6-22. Cf. R. Pavalko, The Sociology of Occupations and Professions, Peacock Press, Itasca, Illinois, 1970, 17-27, who adds a model of professionalisation. But the most cited example of this approach is E. Greenwood, 'Attitudes of a Profession', Social Work, 2, 3 July 1957, 44-55.

(8) Terence J. Johnson, Professions and Power, Macmillan, London, 1972, Ch. 2.

(9) Eliot Freidson, Profession of Medicine, Dodd, Mead, New York, 1970, and M.S. Larson, The Rise of Professionalism, Berkeley, University of California Press, 1977, are two impressive examples of this work.

(10) The classic statement of this approach is E.C. Hughes, 'License and Mandate', Men and Their Work, Free Press, New York, 1958. See too, P. Elliott, The Sociology of the Professions, Macmillan London, 1973; E. Freidson, 'Professions and the Occupational Principle', in E. Freidson (ed.), Professions and Their Prospects, Sage, Beverley Hills, 1973, 19-38; Johnson, op. cit.; K. Prandy, Professional Employees, Faber, London, 1965.

(11) Cf. R.A.W. Rhodes, 'A Framework for Analysis', Central-Local Government Relationships, SSRC, London, 1979, 14-17.

(12) But see Frederick C. Mosher, Democracy and the Public Service, Oxford University Press, New York, 1968, Ch. 4,; and Mosher, op. cit. For an introductory discussion of professions in British government see Michael Hill, The State, Administration and the Individual, Fontana, London, 1976, Ch. 5 and 6.

(13) For a discussion of this tension in social work see Brian J. Heraud, 'Professionalism, Radicalism and Social Change', in P. Halmos, Professionalisation and Social Change, Sociological Review Monograph No. 20, Keele, 1973, 85-102.

(14) Committee of Inquiry into Local Government Finance, Report, HMSO, London, 1976, (Cmnd. 6453), p. 82.

(15) J.A.G. Griffith, Central Departments and Local Authorities, Allen and Unwin, London, 1966, p. 39.

(16) For a detailed account of the involvement of local government accountants in the Consultative Council on Local Government Finance see R. Harris and P. Shipp, Communications between Central and Local Government in the Management of Local Authority Expenditure, IOR, Coventry, 1977.

(17) W. Goode considers professions are just this, 'Community Within a Community: The Professions', American Sociological Review, 22 April 1957, 194-200.

(18) This account relies heavily on R. Bucher and A.L. Strauss, 'Professions in Process', American Journal of Sociology, 66, 1961, 325-334; and R. Bucher and J.G. Stelling, Becoming Professional, Sage, Beverley Hills, 1977, esp. Ch. 1.

(19) For a discussion of the fiscal pressures on professionals in government at the local level see Michael Lipsky,'The Assault on Human Services: Street-Level Bureaucrats, Accountability, and the Fiscal Crisis', in Scott Greer, Ronald D. Hedlund and James L. Gibson, Accountability in Urban Society, Sage, Beverley Hills, 1977, 15-38.

(20) In Kaufman's study, for example, the professional institutions
      are portrayed as promoting the control of the centre over the
      periphery, Herbert Kaufman, The Forest Ranger, John Hopkins
      Press, Baltimore, 1960.
(21) Technocracy may manifest itself as dominant professions in
      government impeding social change or at least those changes
      not promoted by themselves as John B. McKinlay claims, 'On the
      Professional Regulation of Change', in Halmos, op. cit., 61-84.
      How this claim is tested remains another question.
(22) Notably by J.K. Friend, J.M. Power and C.J.L. Yewlett, Public
      Planning: The Inter-Corporate Dimension, Tavistock, London,
      1974; and John Friend and Peter Spink, 'Networks in Public
      Administration', Linkage Three, July 1978, 18-22.
(23) Cf. Rhodes, op. cit., p. 23.
(24) Michael D. King discusses such tensions in, 'Science and the
      Professional Dilemma', Julius Gould, Penguin Social Sciences
      Survey 1968, Penguin, Harmondsworth, 1968.
(25) But for a stimulating analysis of differences among occupational
      ideologies see Vernon K. Dibble, 'Occupations and Ideologies',
      American Journal of Sociology, 68, 2 September 1962, 229-34.
(26) As Nevil Johnson argues, in the modern 'service state', '......
      traditional modes of accountability whether political or
      legal/financial become less relevant, though retaining their
      value for some purposes and on some occasions .... What is
      then missing are effective means of monitoring and (usually)
      of ensuring that the recipients of the services can gain
      sufficient access to the service providers to ensure that
      the latter remain responsive to changing needs and attitudes
      in Society.' 'Defining Accountability', Public Administation
      Bulletin, 17 December 1974, 3-13.
(27) Frederick C. Mosher, Democracy and the Public Service, p. 4.

4 Political Parties and Central-Local Relations

John Gyford

THE NATIONALISATION OF LOCAL POLITICS

In the wake of the growing involvement of political parties in local
government, it has become increasingly common to talk of the nationalisation of local politics in contemporary Britain.(1)   The term may
sometimes be used to refer simply to national partisanship in local
elections - the increasing tendency for such contests to be dominated
by the major political parties. Approximately two thirds of the local
authorities in England and Wales may in this sense be regarded as
having had their local political system nationalised.

However, this nationalisation may also be regarded as having extended
beyond the electoral arena into other aspects of local politics. It is
then to be seen as

> 'a process through which local political arenas are increasingly
> subordinated and integrated into a single national political
> arena ..... its agents are the great national parties, and its
> results are the gradual ironing out of autonomous local
> characteristics, styles and behaviour.'(2)

If this use of the term is adopted then it is possible to see
nationalisation as a process which starts with central (national)
partisan penetration and control of the local parliamentary arena
(constituency electioneering and representation), moves on to similar
penetration and control of municipal elections and representation, and
thereafter encompasses the between elections local politics of policy
making and administration. The perception that this form of
nationalisation has occurred, or is occurring, then gives rise to the
fear that the ideal of local self government is in danger of being
subverted, as the policy of local councils comes increasingly to be
dictated by the central organs of the major parties: rule from the
town hall is replaced by rule from Westminster.

However, things may not necessarily be quite as simple, or as
sinister. As already indicated, the term 'nationalisation of local
politics' may refer to partisan contests or to the imposition of
uniformity of policy across the board. Between these two points there
must lie a range of positions. Four possible points on the nationalisation continuum might reasonably be expected to exist, in theory
if not always in practice.

First, there is the minimal position, the partisan contest. Here
local election candidates certainly carry party labels. They may well
display party colours in their election literature, and employ

propaganda material produced by party headquarters - inevitably of a rather generalised and rhetorical kind. However, it is not a necessary corollary that the actual programmes on which they fight the election should in any way be other than the product of local party decision. Local policy statements in the election addresses could well be the outcome of purely localised party discussion with no input from central office. The possibility must be allowed that possession of, say, the Labour label and a red rosette imposes no more obeisance on local matters to a central office party line than would possession of a Democratic label and a donkey symbol in a US mayoralty election.

Second, once elected the partisan councillors are clearly in the business of making decisions, and of seeking advice to help them make the best decisions. One possible source of advice is party head-quarters. From this source there may be offered advice on legal requirements and obligations, on new techniques or on financial questions; access may also be afforded through party headquarters to the experience of other local authorities of similar partisan persuasion. Nationalisation has proceeded beyond the mere utilisation or national partisan electoral labels to the provision from central office of advice and assistance to those councillors who have been elected under the partisan label.

Third, as well as offering advice and assistance, whether in response to requests or gratuitously, party headquarters may go further and encourage its local councillors to adopt particular courses of action. Certain policies or schemes already in operation may be commended as models of their kind, well in tune with party principles. New ventures may be encouraged as the next steps in translating ideology into action. Local authority cooperation with the central government of the day may be called for, or alternatively discouraged, according to its political complexion. The electoral attractiveness or otherwise of particular policies may be stressed, whether in terms of their appeal to particular groups in the community, or of their contribution to the general public image of the party. Here nationalisation has proceeded beyond advice to exhortation.

Finally, there is a more active role of monitoring and instruction. Party headquarters would have clear ideas as to what it wished to see done by its local councillors. It would circulate its instructions and monitor councillors' performance in the light of those instructions. If it were truly serious in this role then it would also presumably need to possess a mechanism for preventing the re-nomination of party councillors who failed to carry out instructions.

The progession or continuum outlined above represents a move from an almost passive role in local politics by central office to a highly active one. The exact point along the continuum occupied by any one party may prove to be related to resources, ideology and constitution, though precisely whether the relationships were cause or effect would require investigation.

In the case of resources, for example, little demand might be made on these if the central office role were confined to one of electoral support. The party label costs headquarters nothing to bestow, and the production of leaflets and posters for local elections need not loom over large in the general publicity budget. In 1976-77, for instance, of the twenty five publicity leaflets produced that year by the Labour Party, only four were directed to the local elections of May 1977.(3) However, if the party were to adopt a more activist role, the greater would be the demands on its resources. The giving of useful advice and the issuing of effective exhortation demands adequate staff, as well as material resources, which would clearly be even more true of any role which involved instruction followed by monitoring.

It is possible to identify two ways in which party ideology may influence central office involvement in local politics. There is first the matter of whether or not the party ideology contains any significant bias towards or against the notion of local autonomy, which presumably could affect its willingness to take an active central oversight of local political decision making. Second, there is the question of whether, given an inclination towards some form of central office intervention, the party has any clear perception of exactly what the role of local authorities, as distinct from national government, should be in translating ideology into practical policy in the various functions of local government responsibility.

The third, constitutional, factor would presumably be of significance in the context of a highly activist role for central office. If local politicians are to be instructed on policy issues and their performance monitored and thereafter rewarded or punished, the party constitution must contain sufficient powers or sanctions to enable leaders at headquarters to secure the removal from office of those local politicians who are seen to have defaulted on their partisan obligations.

There are two further points which need to be added at this stage. It often seems to be assumed that party headquarters is the sole central agency involved in nationalising local politics. It would however be wrong to overlook the role possibly played by other elements in the parties at the centre, for example MPs and Ministers (or their Shadows). Similarly it is easy to assume that the objects - or victims - of any nationalisation are simply the local councillors, thus overlooking other locally based figures such as members of regional and area health authorities.

Implicit in much of the critical comment on party intervention in local politics is the idea that it is essentially a one way process with the local being subordinated and integrated into the national through the agency of party headquarters. However, the possibility exists that there may be some two way traffic, whether of information, experience, opinions, ideas or demands, and even that the national party may be influenced by local pressures.

Once partisan intervention has become established in local politics then both local and national politicians may share common character-istics such as the ideals, the language, the loyalties and the symbols of their party. This bond may well facilitate communication between politicians at the two levels. Local politicians may harbour national aspirations; conversely national politicians may have served a local apprenticeship. Such an informal career structure within the party, with shared aspirations and experiences, may further encourage mutual interaction between local and national politicians, including both

those of the latter who are concerned with the operation of party
headquarters and those who are involved in ministerial or legislative
roles.

As to the content of such interaction, one possibility stems from the
rather different roles of the two types of politician. National
politicians are primarily concerned with legislation and party policy
rather than with day to day administration. Local politicians,
through the local government committee system, are more deeply
involved in the working out in practice of national statutes and
policies. It would therefore not be surprising if their views were
sought and/or proffered as to how various national policy initiatives
were working out in practice at the grass roots. The same might
equally apply to views on the likely local outcomes of proposed
changes or new departures in national policy.

Another source of interaction generated locally might be that derived
from local initiatives or experiments. A local problem may emerge
which is not covered adequately by current national policies. Local
politicians may then bring this problem to the notice of their national
colleagues in the hope of securing new or amended legislation or a
change of policy, especially if they learn that other localities share
their predicament and support their initiative.

Some local authorities may be imaginative enough to pioneer
particular experiments of their own, offering new solutions to old
problems. Even within the limits provided by the doctrine of ultra
vires councils can experiment to some degree, especially in applying
new professional techniques or new administrative practices. If
successful the local politicians concerned may be eager to spread
the good news throughout the party in the hope of making their
innovations standard practice across the nation.

It would of course hardly be surprising if some local politicians
took advantage of their contacts at national level simply to lobby on
behalf of their own local authority. In this case, instead of
providing feedback on the operation of national policy, or publicising
some local municipal advance, the objective would simply be to secure
from national government some special consideration or dispensation
for their locality.

The intervention of national parties in local politics, therefore,
need not necessarily entail a simple one way relationship from the
top (or centre) down to the bottom (or locality). There may also occur
a flow of information, ideas and demands from locality to centre,
stemming from local experience and local needs. Thus the party based
nationalisation of local politics may have been accompanied, whether
in greater or less degree, by what might be termed the localisation of
national politics - by the alteration and amendment of national
legislation and/or party policy in the light of local experience and
locally based lobbying.

The tone of the argument advanced thus far has been speculative;
inevitably so, for it serves to indicate the limitations of our present
knowledge of party political linkages between centre and locality. We
know something of the internal constitutional linkages between centre
and locality within the parties, as expressed in their formal structure

and informal operation. But we know little of the internal linkages within the parties between those charged with evolving and carrying through party policy at the national level and those charged with the same tasks at the local level. As should now be clear, we do not know specifically:

(1) Just how active and extensive central party involvement is in local politics - the degree of nationalisation;

(2) In what ways any degree of nationalisation is related to resources, ideology and constitution;

(3) How far nationalisation by the central party is counter balanced by localisation from below;

(4) What changes have occurred over time in respect of the above, and for what reasons.

Other, related, questions are also at present unanswered. Local government carries out a variety of functions. Some of them may be more prone to partisan controversy than others and thus of greater partisan significance. Housing and education seem more likely to fall into this category than the library service or the fire brigade. We do not yet know:

(5) Whether the nature of the interaction between centre and locality varies in some way depending on the local authority functions at issue.

Moreover, the operations of local government may be conducted in varying ways, both politically and managerially. We do not however know:

(6) The extent of central party advice on the conduct and organisation of local authority members.

A further unexplored area is that of the impact of being in or out of power. Majority and minority groups on local authorities may see their relations with the centre in different lights. In addition, if a party is in power nationally the particular role of central office vis a vis local politicians may be affected by partisan control of the various relevant ministerial positions, which could provide an alternative, or supplementary, channel for central-local interaction. Thus we need to discover:

(7) How central-local interaction within a party is affected by that party being in or out of power, locally or nationally.

Finally, and perhaps most important, it would be desirable to know:

(8) What are the consequences and outcomes of such central-local interaction as does take place?

Answers to these questions would throw light on the evolution and implementation of central and local government policy. They could also add an important dimension to our understanding of the inner workings of the political parties, traditionally assumed to be fairly centralised institutions.

THE AGENCIES OF INTERACTION

There are a number of agencies which might be used for interaction between local and national politicians.

In the eyes of some commentators perhaps the most important are the headquarters of the political parties, which are seen as the chief beneficiaries of the nationalisation of local politics.(4) The term 'headquarters' is slightly misleading since it obscures a possibly important distinction between the paid staff and those politicians who operate through the central office. Thus both the Labour and Conservative Parties employ full time officials to handle local government affairs at Smith Square, and, in addition, each possesses an advisory committee on local government containing local and national politicians.

On the Labour side, despite references to a 'Local Government Department' being 'initiated at the beginning of May 1936',(5) the staff working in this field have in fact formed part of a larger department covering several fields. For many years, the work fell within the Research Department: it now lies within the National Agents' Department, as the task of a separate Local Government Section. At Conservative Central Office the Local Government Department was first set up in 1946 as one of a number of departments under the Director of Organisation, but is now autonomous.

· The functions of the local government staffs at the party head-quarters would appear, outwardly, to have much similarity. The Conservative department 'exists to advise on all local government matters and encourages the two way flow of information between the department and Conservative members of local authorities ..... (It) is purely administrative and is not concerned with the formulation of policy'.(6)   At Transport House, one of the most important functions 'is to be a clearing house for information to and from our Ministers, the NEC, the Parliamentary Party, the 500 Labour groups and 9,260 Labour Councillors.'(7) It would be interesting to know more about the nature of the two way flow of information in and out of headquarters - how it is generated, how it is received, what impact it has. This inquiry would cover not only regular publications such as Labour Councillor, Local Government Brief and Centre Forward but also the various circulars, briefing leaflets and other documents which circulate within this two way flow.

With the political committees at headquarters there are again apparent similarities of function. On the Conservative side the National Local Government Advisory Committee exists 'to advise (i) the Executive Committee of the National Union (of Conservative and Unionist Associations) on Local Government questions (ii) Central Office on the conduct on Local Government elections (iii) on Party Policy covering local Government Services'.(8) It is also charged with securing maximum Conservative representation in local government, arranging conferences and meetings, providing information and advice to Conservative Group Leaders, and coordinating local government,

Parliamentary and Central Office activity. A sub committee in the form of a Policy Liaison Group has particular responsibility for this last coordinating task. The Advisory Committee itself is a fairly large body dominated, numerically, by local politicians. There are 54 leaders of specified Conservative Groups plus 11 representatives of Area Local Government Advisory Committees: parliamentary politicians number less than a dozen.

The composition of Labour's equivalent committee provides a contrast. The NEC's Regional and Local Government Sub Committee contains an almost equal balance of parliamentarians and councillors (about 13 of each) plus a number of coopted experts.(9) The sub committee reports to the Home Policy Committee of the NEC on policy matters and to the Organisation Committee on organisational issues: it is also empowered to receive resolutions on local government matters from District and County Parties and, if it wishes, to refer them to the relevant Standing Committee of the NEC. In recent years, it has worked on draft policy statements on a number of local government issues. It would clearly be interesting to know the reasoning behind the contrasting make up of the two different party committees, and whether the contrast is reflected in the way they see and perform their role. The committees could serve merely as sounding boards for ideas generated elsewhere, or they could, more actively, initiate new departures in policy.

A further vehicle for interaction is the Local Government Conference organised annually by the headquarters of each of the two major parties. The Conservatives were the first to make it a regular feature of their political calendar, initially as an adjunct of the Annual Conference, but now as a totally separate event. The format of the conference, too, has changed over the years and may include addresses by Ministers or front bench spokesmen, the presentation of papers and discussion in open forum. No formal resolutions are normally taken since the conference is not confined to delegates from Conservative Groups, but is open to all interested party members; it has been described as a 'sounding board of opinions' within the party.(10)

On the Labour side, regular Local Government Conferences began in 1956, almost a decade later than the Conservatives' initial venture into this field. In the early years, the conferences concentrated on a single theme or topic each year but more recently the practice has been for much of the time to be devoted to working groups exploring a variety of different topics. The conference itself is composed of representatives from both Labour Groups and District and County parties.

The Annual Party Conferences have been the subject of some academic investigation but even so little is known of how far councillors feel bound, or influenced, by annual conference opinion on issues about local government. Local Government Conferences remain largely unexplored in terms of their impact on the parties at different levels of policy making, through both their official proceedings and the informal contacts and consultations which always take place at such events.

Local government departments, advisory committees and annual conferences are three aspects of the interaction of the national party

organisations with the world of local politics. They stem from the
'Smith Square' wing of the national parties. Some mention must now be
made of the purely parliamentary wing and its relations with local
politics.

Within the parliamentary parties there exists a structure of subject
groups (Labour) or committees (Conservative) catering for backbench
MPs interested in particular areas. The exact number of these, and
their breakdown by subject, tends to vary over time. In both parties
formerly separate provision for local government has now been replaced
by bringing the subject within the remit of the Environment Group/
Committee of each party.

The main focus of this backbench work is essentially parliamentary -
providing members for Commons Committees, bringing pressure to bear on
Ministers or their Shadows and discussing impending legislation, both
amongst themselves and with outside experts. There may be some
overlapping membership between these backbench organisations and the
party committees in Smith Square: indeed on the Conservative side
provision is explicitly made for the Chairman of the Parliamentary
Committee to sit on the National Advisory Committee. However, there
seem to be few formal links directly with the world of local politics.
The chairman of the former Planning and Local Government Group of the
PLP thought that direct contact between his group and local Labour
groups 'would be regarded as rather improper,' since it would challenge
the 'correct' link which lay through Transport House and the NEC
committee structure.(11)

With the ministerial side of the parliamentary wing, there is the
problem of divorcing the partisan and the departmental roles of a
Minister. One would imagine that most direct contacts between
Ministers and local politicians come in the line of departmental duty,
receiving deputations, visiting local authorities, addressing
conferences, attending the Consultative Council on Local Government
Finance. However, there are at least four possible sources of contact
between ministerial and local politicians in a partisan context. One
of these, the Local Government Conference, has already been referred
to in terms of both its formal business and its informal contacts.
Another source is the ad hoc meeting to discuss particular issues of
party or government policy. Thus Labour Council leaders met with the
Secretary of State for the Environment to discuss the expenditure cuts
of July 1976, and with the Secretary of State for Transport to discuss
the Transport Bill in early 1978.(12)

A third possible chanel of contact is provided by the ministerial
political advisor. Since one of his functions is often to keep his ear
to the political ground on his master's behalf, the political advisor
may well serve on occasions as a channel of communication between party
councillors and a particular Minister. A fourth source of contact was
represented by the establishment of a panel of representatives of
minority Labour groups to meet Ministers in the recent Labour government for discussions on policy. At these meetings - held on a
quarterly basis - panels made up of three minority group representatives
from each Labour Party region met the Secretary of State for the
Environment plus Ministers from, at different times, the Department of
Education and Science, the Department of Health and Social Security
and the Department of Transport. A Minister-Majority Group meeting

may well be as much departmental as partisan, but a provision for meetings with minority groups seems clearly a party venture. In fact, the project was financed from a fund launched by the Labour Groups on the three national local authority associations.(13)

All three local authority associations contain organised party groups and are run on party lines, as is the London Boroughs Association. Cecil Dawson has claimed that he introduced party politics into the associations during his term as Local Government Officer at Conservative Central Office from 1963 to 1974.(14) However, there appears to have been a Labour Group in existence on the County Councils Association as early as 1932, for in that year it was invited to act as an 'advisory panel' to the then Local Government and Social Services Sub Committee of the NEC Policy Committee.(15)

Whatever the historic origins of these groups, their contemporary role would seem to be important. Their primary concern is with the business of the three associations and their various committees. In this context the groups act much as do their counterparts on individual local authorities, discussing agendas at group meetings and taking decisions as to their stand on matters of partisan dispute. It would be wrong however to regard this activity as the sole important function of these groups.

Each of the groups contains senior party councillors from the three types of local authority and thus constitutes a unique forum of party opinion on local government issues. It is understandable that they should concern themselves with a wide range of issues over and above those which happen to be on the immediate agendas of the associations. Thus during the period 1974 to 1977 the (minority) Labour Group on the Association of County Councils discussed papers on devolution, health service reorganisation, the water industry, and members' allowances. In addition through its officers and executive committee, meetings took place with Ministers from the Department of the Environment to discuss issues such as local government finance, devolution, bus subsidies, transport policy, members' allowances, and direct labour. From time to time representatives of the Group met with their opposite numbers from the Labour Groups on the two other associations to discuss mutual concerns; these included financial support for local government work at Transport House, the desirability of a Local Government Section on the NEC, and the issue of industrial democracy in local government. In addition, the three group leaders held a meeting with the Prime Minister which was intended to be the first of a regular series.

Clearly this sort of activity suggests that, on the Labour side at least, these groups may regard themselves very much as spokesmen for the whole body of local politicians within the party.(16)

The importance of the groups now seems to be firmly established in the eyes of the national parties. The Conservative National Advisory Committee includes the Conservative leaders on the local authority associations, whilst the Labour leaders (or their representatives) are coopted onto the NEC Regional and Local Government Sub Committee. In addition, Transport House and Conservative Central Office both provide administrative and secretarial support services for their respective association groups through the two local government departments.

It would thus seem that these groups stand in a pivotal position,
linking the two worlds of local and national politics within the
political parties. A systematic investigation of their activities
would reveal just how they exploit this position and with what results.

Once our attention moves away from Smith Square, parliament and the
local authority associations towards the localities, the picture
inevitably becomes patchy and diffuse. There are several hundred party
groups on local authorities and from time to time any one of them may
seek or be offered the attention of national politicians or of the
national party in some way.

A majority group, acting as it were on behalf of the authority which
it controls, may of course take up an issue with a government
department, whether by writing or by deputation. Such an exercise
however is likely to be conducted as an exchange between two public
authorities, with the politicians on each side briefed, and perhaps
accompanied, by their respective officials. In these negotiations the
partisan roles of the politicians involved may be obscured by their
roles as representatives of national and local governments. However,
majority group politicians may well seek the ear of the Minister in
less formal and more partisan settings, such as the bars and lounges
of party conferences.

For a minority group however the party channel may well be the only
one available if it wishes to lobby for support at Westminster: so,
too, for the Opposition party at Westminster, which, denied the
departmental route, can only deal with any of its own local party
groups, majority or minority, through party channels.

The channels for this partisan lobbying may include the constituency
MP, if he is of the appropriate party. The frequency of contact
between local authority groups and local MPs is a subject on which
little is known.(17) Another possibility, if neighbouring local
authorities share a common problem, is that of pursuing the matter
through the regional groupings of MPs in each parliamentary party,
although not all parts of the country are currently covered by such
groupings.

Away from parliament, a third channel for such lobbying could be the
Area (Conservative) or Regional (Labour) organisations of the parties,
and the County coordinating committees (Conservative) or County
Parties (Labour). These channels permit some concerted local party
opinion to be expressed to those MPs and party officials most directly
involved.

The exact nature, frequency and effectiveness of lobbying for
parliamentary support by local groups is unknown. Nor do we know
whether or not, in addition to lobbying in time of crisis, there are
also regular consultations between groups and MPs, singly or severally.
In studying the effectiveness of such lobbying and consultation, it
would also be interesting to discover whether the behaviour of MPs
(and indeed, of Ministers) engaged in these interactions is in any
way influenced by whether or not they themselves have had previous
experience of serving on a local authority.

SUMMARY: TOWARDS A RESEARCH INITIATIVE

The first section of this essay identified eight major unanswered questions about party political linkages between local and central government. The second section identified some agencies of linkage which might prove worth investigating and thereby identified some further questions. Three possible research strategies are now suggested, focussing respectively on the centre, on the locality and on issues common to both centre and locality.

Research at the centre would examine the work of the local government departments and the advisory committees at the party headquarters and of the relevant backbench groupings of parliamentarians. It would also investigate individual ministerial and backbench reaction to and involvement with local government issues and local politicians. A further subject for research at the centre would be the party groups on the local authority associations: a knowledge of how effectively they function within the associations would, in itself, advance our understanding, but we would here also want to examine their role within the parties as well as their role as 'central' representatives of the localities.

At the local level a clear candidate for research is the party group itself and, perhaps, its associated local party organisation. An exploration of such possibly party links as lobbying or transmitting information or advice between these local elements and the centre would probably have to rely on some form of sample survey, given the large number of local bodies who could potentially be involved.

The third focus of research is that of issues or policies in which centre and locality share an interest and over which some party based interaction might be expected to take place: in education over comprehensivisation and selection, or over housing finance and council house sales. Other suitable topics might be innovations such as the Kent educational voucher experiment, or the campaign for greater powers for the larger district councils, or the fate of Labour's report on local government conduct, or the Conservative desire to abolish the rates.

These three strands of investigation could be interwoven. The focus on issues or policies could provide a specific means of linking up investigations of the centre and the localities. Another interweaving might appear in the course of investigation if certain key individuals seem, either simultaneously or over time, to occupy positions of consequence at both central and local level (e.g. ex councillor MPs, or councillor members of central office committees).

The latter interweaving, however, also serves to remind us that the party provides a potential avenue for breaking down any rigid central-local dichotomy (though in whose interests it remains to be seen). The distinction between central and local loyalties may be overshadowed by by loyalty to the party. Accordingly any research would need to see its field of concern as being intra as well as inter organisational.

NOTES AND REFERENCES

(1) R.W. Johnson, 'The Nationalisation of English Rural Politics: Norfolk South West, 1945-1970', Parliamentary Affairs, vol. 26, 1972, pp. 8-55; M. Schofield, 'The "nationalisation" of local politics', New Society, 28.4.77.
(2) R.W. Johnson, op. cit., p. 53.
(3) Labour Party Annual Conference Report, 1977, p. 31.
(4) cf. Q. Hogg, The Case for Conservatism, Penguin, Harmondsworth, 1947, p. 66.
(5) Labour Party Annual Conference Report, 1936, p. 83.
(6) Conservative Central Office, Local Government and the Party Organisation, 1971, p. 8.
(7) Ed Miller (then Local Government Officer, Labour Party), quoted in Labour Councillor, March 1975, p. 3.
(8) Rules of the National Local Government Advisory Committee, Conservative Central Office, n.d. (1975)
(9) The figures are for the year 1977-78 (some of the parliamentarians and experts are former councillors): Labour Party Annual Conference Report, 1978, p. 15.
(10) Conservative Party Annual Conference Report, 1958, p. 185.
(11) Arthur Blenkinsop, MP: Interview.
(12) Ed Miller: Interview.
(13) Labour Party Annual Conference Report 1977, p. 17.
(14) Cecil Dawson: Interview.
(15) Labour Party NEC Minutes, April, 1932.
(16) The account of the activities of the ACC Labour Group from 1974 to 1977 is based on personal knowledge as a member of the Group.
(17) L.H. Cohen, 'Local Government Complaints: The MP's viewpoint', Public Administration, Vol. 51, 1973, pp. 175-183.

5   The English Local Authority Associations

K. Isaac-Henry

Local Authority Associations are essentially a nineteenth century
development, created to protect and promote the interests of the
particular type of local authority they represented. Before April 1974
there were four main Local Authority Associations.(1) County, rural
and urban district councils had separate organisations to look after
their interests. The County Councils Association (CCA) was responsible
for protecting county councils' interests. The two types of districts
were represented respectively by the Rural District Councils
Association (RDCA) and the Urban District Councils Association (UDCA).
The Association of Municipal Corporations (AMC), unlike the others,
represented two main types of authority - county boroughs and non
county boroughs.(2)

The 1972 Local Government Act affected most of the Associations in
important ways. County boroughs were abolished. The distinction
between non county boroughs and the urban and rural districts was
removed. With the demise of county boroughs and non county boroughs
the AMC ceased to exist. Its successor, the Association of Metropolitan
Authorities (AMA), speaks not only for the metropolitan counties and
their districts but also for the Greater London Council (GLC) and the
London boroughs.(3) The RDCA and UDCA have been replaced by the
Association of District Councils (ADC) representing non metropolitan
districts. County councils were the least affected by the Act. The
majority of traditional counties are still recognisable in areas,
functions and names. There was little need for the CCA to undergo
change. It merely altered its name to the Association of County
Councils (ACC).

Many observers who have commented on the role of the Associations
have ascribed to them power and influence 'which would have made them
the most powerful pressure groups in the British Isles'.(4) J.A.G.
Griffith has argued that it would be difficult to exaggerate their
importance in influencing governments and in acting as coordinators
and channels of local authority opinion.(5) Some observers, however,
point to weaknesses of the Associations. The Redcliffe-Maud Report
saw in their separate existence the reason for their failure to
influence government policies.(6) Others suggested that their failure
to agree on fundamental principles and to present a united front to
governments caused an onward rush of central control over local
government.

This chapter considers the role and activities of the Associations as
well as their strength and weaknesses in their attempt to influence
government policies. Reference will be made principally to the AMC and
CCA as well as the ACC and AMA. The inclusion of the now defunct AMC

and CCA is because the AMA and ACC have retained the basic functions, activities and characteristics of their predecessors.

STRUCTURES AND ORGANISATIONS OF THE ASSOCIATIONS

Pressure group theorists often point to the structure, the policy and the attitude of governments as the most important determinants of group behaviour.[7] It would be a mistake, however, to ignore the organisation and structure of a group as determinants of its behaviour. R.D. Coates believes that just as the organisational characteristics of a group cannot fully explain its behaviour so neither can the structure, policy and attitude of the government.[8] He suggests that explanation of a group's behaviour will be a combination of these factors. The structure, organisation and membership of the Associations are important in the way they affect the groups' reaction to the government. For example, the response of the AMC to governmental initiative was conditioned by its representation of two types of member authority with different political interests and connections. On the reform of local government, which dominated the Associations' thinking between 1945 and 1972, these interests were opposed. The AMC was inevitably subject to internal conflict. This possibility of a clash of interests led to each type of authority in the AMC setting up its own organisation to protect its particular viewpoint. The Non County Boroughs Committee and the County Boroughs Association worked under the umbrella of the AMC. Added to the problems of speaking for two types of authority, the AMC represented members with major differences in population and resources. It spoke not only for 'the major cities lying at the heart of the conurbation but also for many of the smallest towns'.[9] This diversity added greatly to the problems of the AMC whenever reform was discussed.

The constitution of the AMC attempted to minimise conflict in a number of ways. First, on the most important organs of the Association parity of representation between non county and county boroughs was maintained. Second, on all committees, except General Purposes, the six members with the largest populations were included. Third, the management of the Association was not entrusted to a meeting of all the members, where the non county boroughs would have outnumbered the county boroughs by over three to one. Rather the Association was managed by a council which had restricted membership and parity of representation between the two types of member. Fourth, the constitution provided that where there was a clash of interests between the two types of authority, which could not be resolved, the AMC was to refrain from further discussion or taking any action on the subject. Thus between 1947-49 the AMC under this rule was prevented from discussing or making any proposals on local government reform at the crucial time when the Local Government Boundary Commission was sitting.

The successor to the AMC, the AMA, has inherited the problem of representing more than one type of authority. It represents three main types. Since it was realised that there would be clashes of interests in the relationship between the metropolitan counties and their districts, the AMA constitution provides that where one type of authority cannot agree with the decision of the Association, that type of authority will be allowed to speak for its own specific interests,

41

while the AMA will speak for the rest of the members.(10)

The ACC, like its predecessor the CCA, represents one type of
authority. Although differences of opinion existed in the CCA, they
were not as pronounced as those in the AMC, and the former Association
escaped the clashes that wracked the AMC over the reform of local
government between 1945-72. In the ACC it is recognised that there
may be differences of interests between the English and Welsh Counties.
Thus the ACC's constitution provides that where the Welsh county
councils dissent from a decision of the Executive Council of the
Association, the dissenting views will be recorded and, with the
decision of the Association, presented to appropriate bodies. The
constitution also provides that where a matter is mainly or exclusively
concerned with Wales, the Welsh counties, through a Welsh Committee,
should deal directly with government departments without going through
the Association.(11)

Eckstein argues that pressure groups tend to structure themselves
along similar lines to the organisation they seek to influence.(12)
If it is accepted that Local Authority Associations seek to influence
the government and its departments, then the Associations are an
exception to this generalisation. Their organisation resembles that
of their member local authorities rather than that of government
departments. As with local authorities, each has a council (or meeting)
which has the overall responsibility for controlling the organisation.
Each has a well developed committee system through which most of the
work of the Association passes. Each has a secretariat with a chief
officer, i.e. the Secretary of the Association.

In the former AMC, membership of the Council was decided partly by
nomination and partly by election. The size of membership and the
existence of different types of authorities in the Association made the
use of these two methods necessary. With a membership of nearly 400
authorities, if all members were represented on the Council, it would
have been unwieldy. Membership was therefore restricted. County
boroughs served on a rota, while non county boroughs were elected
regionally.(13)

The AMA has a membership of only seventy-seven. As a result there is
no need to restrict membership of the management body. It has, in fact,
dispensed with a Council. The Meeting of the Association has the
responsibility for managing the organisation. Each member authority
can send up to three representatives to a Meeting but only one is
entitled to vote.

All fifty eight county councils (in 1972) were allowed to send four
representatives to a council meeting of the CCA. However, only one of
these representatives could vote. The constitution and procedure of
the ACC differ in this respect. Each of the forty five non
metropolitan county councils is represented on the Council of the ACC
but the number of representatives each may send, and the number of
votes to which each is entitled, depend on the population size of the
authority. County councils with populations below 500,000 may send up
to three representatives; those with populations between 500,000 and
one million may send up to four and those with over one million may
send five. Most significantly each representative has one vote.(14)

This provision has a number of implications. First, whereas on the CCA member counties rarely sent the full quota of representatives to council meetings, all counties now endeavour to do so in order to utilise their maximum voting strength. Second, by allowing voting strength to be determined by size, the Association has met one of the main criticisms levelled at the CCA, namely that the small counties should not have a voice equal to that of the largest counties. Third, it was the practice of some county councils to allow a member from the opposing party groups to be one of the representatives sent to the Council of the CCA. Here such members could speak but not vote. The person responsible for voting would be from the majority party. With each representative being allowed to vote on the ACC's Council, this practice has been reduced, since the majority group on a county council is usually reluctant to select opposition representatives who may vote against its declared policy at Council.

Management of the Associations by the Councils (or Meeting) amounts, in reality, to the Council considering, and for the most part, accepting the recommendations coming from the various committees. The potential size of the council or meeting and their infrequent meetings suggest that they are not initiating bodies. C.A. Cross examined the recommendations of committees to the Council of the AMC in 1953 to determine how many were rejected. Of 679 recommendations 669 were accepted in the form presented. Another five were accepted after amendments.[15] An examination of committees' recommendations to the Meetings of the AMA in 1977 reveals that only one clause of a report was referred back to committee.

It is commonly held that committees are the life's blood of local authorities. This view can also be held of committees of the Associations. Committees are established to reflect the major functions of member authorities.[16] In keeping with local government practice, committees consist of councillors and officers from member authorities. The officers are included to proffer advice but are not allowed to vote. The primary committee of the ACC and AMA is the Policy Committee. This committee deals with all aspects of the Association's work, even those for which specialist committees have been set up.

Examination of the activities of the Associations and relationship between the formal management body and the committees leads to the conclusion that the decision making powers lie, in the main, with the committees. Although in each Association the constitution stipulates that the management body has to give approval before the Association can be bound by a decision of a committee, in practice committee proposals are rarely rejected, and the rule about approval by the Council or Meeting cannot be strictly applied. The structure and procedures of the Associations ensure that other organs, as well as individuals, have at times to take decisions which bind the Associations without prior approval from their Councils. Such actions are usually carried out by tacit agreement between the various organs within each Association. Committees are beneficiaries of such agreements. But the influence of the Meeting and the Council is not nugatory. They influence policy to an important degree by having and using the power of approval and by being the forum in which proposed policies are debated and finally settled. So despite their propensity

to accept committees' proposals, their role should not be underestimated. They challenge and probe committee reports. On local
government reform, for instance, the acquiescence of the Councils of
the former CCA and AMC could not be taken for granted. In the AMC
almost every proposal on reform, coming from the General Purposes
Committee between 1966-72, was challenged in council meetings.
Indeed, it took considerable skill on the part of the Chairman and
Secretary of that Association, as well as constant appeals for unity,
to avert defeat of proposals in the Council. A further important role
of the Council and Meeting is to provide a forum in which the now more
disciplined party groups on the Associations take part in political
debates.

The constitutional rules of the Associations, apart from stating that
a Secretary must be appointed, pay little attention to the role of
the secretariat. The practice of the Associations since 1945 has been
to appoint as Secretaries practising Town or County Clerks. This
practice was broken in 1976 when the AMA chose as their Secretary, Tom
Caulcott, an Under Secretary at the Department of the Environment. It
is difficult to assess the influence of Secretaries on Associations'
policies, not only because the secretaries are modest about the role
they play, but also because members of the Associations tend to stress
the constitutional rather than the actual position of the Secretaries
within the organisation. However, there is little doubt that the
Secretaries play crucial roles in the activities of their respective
Associations. Their influence is the result of a number of factors.

First, each Association undertakes a great deal of work each year,
while the representatives meet infrequently. These two factors mean
that much of the work of the Associations falls on the Secretary and
his staff. Second, the Secretary is the chief adviser to the whole
Association and to the various organs within it. When, for example,
the Association meets outside bodies and representatives of the
government departments, the Secretary or his deputies are present to
take full part in the discussions. Third, the tacit agreements which
allow committees to take decisions on behalf of the whole Association
extends to the Secretary. This discretion is reinforced by the close
proximity of the Secretaries to Westminster and Whitehall, while the
Chairmen of the Associations and chairmen of important committees might
reside in the provinces. Fourth, all official correspondence is
conducted through the Secretary's office. As a result he is able to
sense the mood of the members of the Association on any particular
matter. He also has a certain amount of discretion as to whether a
matter is brought to the attention of the Meeting or Council of the
Association. Fifth, the ground work for any major proposal is carried
out by the secretariat. In the submission of evidence to the Royal
Commission on Local Government in England in 1966 and in the response
of the Associations to the Commission's report, the part played by
Secretaries and their staff was crucial.

In relation to the amount of activity undertaken by the Associations,
the number of permanent staff serving each of them up to 1974 was
small.(17) The staff of the AMC and CCA in that year amounted in each
case to about thirty, including clerks and typists. The obvious
disadvantages of having so small a professional staff were reduced
by the practice of using the services of the professional staff of

44

member authorities to provide information and to prepare reports. With the advent of the ACC and AMA, concern has been expressed at this lack of permanent specialist advisers. It has been suggested, for instance, that the Associations cannot challenge government information and statistics, nor can they take the initiative in developing policies until they develop a stronger secretariat to provide the expertise necessary. In the last two years both the ACC and AMA have increased their professional as well as supporting staff. The AMA, for example, has increased its staff by twenty three of which eleven are professional officers and twelve clerks and typists.(18)

ACTIVITIES OF THE ASSOCIATIONS

In order to protect the interests of members, each Association engages in a number of activities, which fall into three main categories: activities involved with government departments and Parliament; the provision of information, advice and other aids to member authorities; and cooperation with other Associations.

Consultation between the Associations and departments takes place in a number of ways. First, meetings are frequently held between the Associations' members and officers and civil servants. If the issue to be discussed is of sufficient importance to the government or to the Associations these meetings will take place in the presence of the appropriate Ministers. Such meetings can be either bipartite, between representatives of the individual Association and the department to the exclusion of a third party or multipartite, in which representatives of more than one Association are present. Second, the Associations are usually asked to make detailed comments on official reports and inquiries which affect local government. Third, their views are conveyed to departments when they are asked to give evidence to investigatory bodies such as Royal Commissions. The preparation of such evidence involves a great deal of work. Usually evidence is drawn up by the officers of the Associations with help from local government officers of member authorities. Fourth, their views are solicited when departments issue consultative papers. Proposed legislation is divided into sections by the department concerned and the Associations are asked to comment on each section within a given time. For example, the Department of the Environment issued twenty five consultative documents to the Associations about the Conservative Government's White Paper and Bill on the reform of local government. In addition, many contacts between the Associations and government departments are made through letters and by telephone, for instance requests for information and clarification and the relaying of complaints.

The AMC and CCA were originally created to bring pressure to bear on legislation affecting members' interests. This objective is still of major importance. The Associations examine Bills for their effects on members and to propose changes. They maintain close links with Parliament. The AMA and ADC usually choose as their vice presidents Members of Parliament who they hope will support their views in the legislature. In their choice of vice presidents these two Associations seek representation in both Houses of Parliament and from the major political parties. Vice Presidents are not expected to support the Associations at all times, and do not act as a cohesive group on the

45

legislature. However, when a vice president is prepared to support an Association's policy the officers of the Association and the vice president work closely together.

The ACC, like its predecessor, chooses as vice presidents those who have given long and distinguished service to the Association, not all Parliamentarians. Nevertheless it has easy access to the legislature. It has a number of supporters in Parliament, the majority of whom come from the House of Lords, and many are members of county councils and of the Association.[19]

In the provision of direct services to their members the Associations provide a channel through which authorities can request changes in law, a review of local government practice, legal advice and aid in dealing with individual problems, and information about local government activities. In addition, the Associations undertake jointly activities which are designed to benefit local authorities as a whole, for example, the Local Government Training Board for fostering the training of local government staff, the Local Authority Management and Computer Committee, the Joint Advisory Committee on Local Authority Purchasing and the Local Authority Conditions of Service Advisory Board. In 1974 the newly formed ACC and AMA jointly set up the Central Council of Local Education Authorities to act as link between the education committees of both Associations.[20]

Since local authorities are intimately involved with such services as Education, Police and Fire, Social Services and Transportation, their Associations are represented on a large number of advisory bodies. In 1966 the AMC was represented on over 140 advisory bodies and committees on which it had over 200 places.[21] The choice of each Association's representatives on advisory bodies usually lies with its appropriate committee. The Social Services Committee of the AMC and ACC are responsible for the appointment of representatives to such bodies as the Central Council for Education and Training in Social Work, the Family Planning Association and the Advisory Council on Probation and After Care. In some cases the Associations make a financial contribution to these bodies.

The Associations are also involved in international activities. They are members of the International Union of Local Authorities (IULA), the Council of European Municipalities (CEM) and the European Conference of Local Authorities (ECLA). Whereas IULA and CEM may be regarded as private organisations set up and financed by local authorities, ECLA functions within the framework of the Council of Europe, an inter governmental organisation, financed and run by the governments of the seventeen member countries.[22] For the Associations, the importance of international bodies lies in ensuring that the claims and interests of local government 'are duly and adequately represented on the European scene'.[23] They argue that government action is increasingly being determined at the international and European levels and that local government must, if it is to protect its interests adequately, match this trend.

CHANNELS OF ACCESS

Local Authority Associations may be regarded as a unique type of
pressure group in Britain. This uniqueness springs mainly from the
constitutional position of the members they represent. Local
authorities are directly elected political units below the national
level of government. Each is a miniature of the national political
and administrative system. They possess characteristics such as
elections, employment of full time paid servants, political party
activities and quasi judicial, regulatory and executive
responsibilities. Although created by Parliament and subject at least
in law to a significant degree of central control, they are recognised
as having some claim to speak for the general public. Indeed, it has
often been argued that local authorities have a greater claim to speak
for the public than has Parliament because they are closer to the
electorate and represent its interests more directly. Another of their
characteristics, which could be considered unique, is that they have
come to be regarded as the most important consumer pressure group
existing in Britain. They seek to develop and expand communal services
at the local level. They aggregate and articulate demands for extra
resources for services such as education, housing and personal social
services.(24) These characteristics are reflected in the Local
Authority Associations. Indeed they become magnified when applied to
the AMA and ACC. These two Associations can boast that between them
they represent the whole of the population of England and Wales.

Local Authority Associations have the quality of being both
'protective' as well as 'promotional' groups. On the one hand they
represent members who pay subscriptions. These members expect their
interests to be the primary consideration of the Associations. On the
other hand, the ACC and AMA, as did their predecessors, often stress
the promotional aspect of serving the public and pursuing policies
which are in the best interests of local government. In their eyes,
there is no inherent conflict between the 'protective' and
'promotional' aspects of their work. To fight to keep member
authorities in being or to propose that the reform of local government
be based on the type of authority each has as members are tantamount to
protecting the public interest. Even in the provision of services for
members, as opposed to services for the public, the Associations argue
that the public interest is being served because such services
facilitate the efficient running of local government.(25)

ACCESS TO THE GOVERNMENT

The minutes of the Associations' committees show that they are in
constant touch with departmental officials and that they have frequent
meetings with ministers. The effectiveness of such consultations with
ministers and departments is debatable. One view is that their value
to the Associations is negligible because the mind of the government
is usually made up prior to the discussions. The same view suggests
that consultations are more useful to the departments whose ministers
can usually claim in the House of Commons to have consulted local
government interests. Another view suggests that, for the most part,
consultations with government are a genuine attempt on its part to
hear and assess the views of the Associations. Mr Robin McCall,

Secretary of the AMC from 1972-76, argues that although consultations
are a little ritualistic on many matters, such as on the reform of
local government, they are genuine.(26) Members of the Associations
who express this opinion do not suggest that they were always effective,
in the sense that they managed to change government policy. Effectiveness, in their case, is measured in terms of getting the views of the
Associations across to governments in the hope of influencing declared
policies or at least to 'prevent the Administration from perpetrating
nonsense'.(27)

An important innovation in the relationship between the Associations
and the government was the setting up of the Consultative Council on
Local Government Finance, which was announced in the budget speech of
April 1975. Its objective is to increase the part played by local
authorities in the overall planning of local government expenditure.
Chaired by the Secretary of State for the Environment, the Council is
composed of Ministers from those departments which have a major
interest in local government expenditure and members of the Local
Authority Associations.(28) The Council, which must meet at least four
times per year, in 1976 and 1977 met almost every month. For the
Associations the Council means a ready made and much more frequent
access to Ministers. The Chairman of the AMA in 1976, Sir Robert
Thomas, suggested that the Consultative Council has meant more
involvement of the Associations at the formulative stage of government
policy than was before possible.(29)

ACCESS TO PARLIAMENT

Studies of pressure groups in Britain usually find that group activity
is concentrated on the Executive and not on Parliament. Eckstein gives
two reasons for this concentration. First, the Cabinet system
supported by disciplined parties precludes groups from exerting
pressures through MPs. Second, contemporary social and economic
policies have shifted a considerable amount of work to the
bureaucracy.(30) Although the attraction of the Executive channel
cannot be denied, groups tend to use all channels available. The
preparatory stage of legislation is considered to be of major
importance by groups. It is at this stage they are most likely to
influence the course of events in consultation with the civil service.
However, once this stage is passed, groups proceed to the Parliamentary
stage, where, through contacts with MPs, they hope to influence a
Minister either to stand firm or to give way as their interests
dictate. While changes at this stage may be considered inconsequential
because they fail to change the principle of a Bill, such changes can
be of considerable importance to particular groups.

The most important of the Parliamentary stages for such groups is
deliberation in Standing Committees. S.A. Walkland argues that this
stage of a Bill usually provides the occasion for the introduction of
amendments on behalf of affected groups.(31) How effective this stage
is, as a means of influencing government policies, is open to doubt.
After a detailed examination of the impact of the Committee stage on
government policy in the parliamentary sessions 1967-68 - 1970-71,
J.A. Griffith concluded that governments are not often swayed from
their original intentions.(32) Changes are not ruled out. Griffith

suggests that within the rules of the game, governments do yield and are flexible, albeit on their terms.(33)

The Associations attempt to influence legislation going through Parliament in a number of ways. With the Local Government Bill of 1971-2 the AMC maintained close contact with its vice presidents throughout the Parliamentary stages and especially with those serving on the Standing Committee. All vice presidents were invited to a meeting with the representatives of the Association on the eve of publication of the Bill. Here they were acquainted with the Association's attitude toward the Conservative measures.(34) Vice presidents sympathetic to its cause were supplied with briefs, draft amendments and general information about the reform of local government.(35) On some occasions the AMC circulated information to all members of the Committee.

The CCA's attempt to influence the Parliamentary stages of the Local Government Bill varied little from that of the AMC. Although lacking the advantage of Parliamentarians as vice presidents, its views were heard in the legislature. All county clerks were asked to contact MPs in their constituencies to persuade them to support the CCA's cause. The clerks obliged, and as a result a number of MPs spoke on behalf of the Association.

Each Association can also make use of an individual local authority's desire to see that the local MP(s) support local and Association policies at Westminster. In February 1972, the Secretary of the AMC wrote to all member corporations impressing on them that the success of the efforts of the Association in Parliament (about reform) depended on the pressures that each authority could bring to bear on its MPs. Portsmouth wrote to all three of its MPs urging them to 'bring all possible pressure to bear on members of the Standing Committee to see that they vote the right way on all relevant matters'.(36)

The support that an MP can give to the Associations depends to a large extent on the nature of the subject being debated and the attitude of the government on the issue. On the Local Government Bill, the Conservative Government appeared to be unusually flexible in its consideration of changes in detail. Members who experienced conflicting loyalties between their parties and the Associations usually resolved the conflict by giving their verbal support to the Associations but their votes to their parties.

ACCESS TO POLITICAL PARTIES

Professor Robson observed that while the attitude of the Local Authority Associations may influence the policy of governments, opinions within the political party in office could, if strongly held, have a decisive effect.(37) In making such an observation Robson was acknowledging two important facts of British Parliamentary life. First, that important legislation usually emanates from governments and not Private Members. Second, that for proposed legislation to stand any chance of success it must normally have the support of the party in power at Westminster. A pressure group may hope therefore to influence government policy by influencing political parties.

The relationship between the national parties and the Associations has been changing. Between 1945 and 1960 there was little attempt to link the Associations' activities with those of the national parties, perhaps because up to 1960 both the AMC and CCA were Conservative dominated. The Conservatives saw no need for formal linkages while the Labour Party felt that Labour representatives on these bodies were hopelessly outnumbered. Mr J. Knight, speaking at the Annual Conference of the Labour Party in 1954, remarked: 'Labour members on the AMC were few in number and consequently when we attend various meetings we are invariably outnumbered by Tory representation'.(38)

In the 1960s the dominance of the Conservatives on the AMC was challenged.(39) The national party urged Conservatives on the AMC to organise themselves against the Socialists,(40) and advised that when Conservatives were in the majority on the AMC they should ensure that all important posts go to members of their own party.(41) The practice in the Association until 1968 was for the Chairman of the General Purposes Committee to serve until he retired. As a result there were only four Chairmen of this Committee between 1928 and 1966. In 1968, however, the then Chairman, Sir Mark Henig (Labour leader of Leicester City Council) was removed by the Conservative group on the Association and replaced by Sir Frank Marshall, a reflection of the new Conservative approach. The practice of the AMA now is that the Chairman comes from the majority party group on the Council.

At the present time the Associations have assumed a greater importance in the eyes of the national parties. It is now accepted that party groups on the ACC and AMA represent an important channel of communications between national and local politicians. As a result, the leaders of party groups on these Associations are automatically included on organisations of their national parties which deal with local government.

Access to national parties by the Associations takes many forms. There are formal organisations within the Labour and Conservative parties which bring together national and local party leaders. There is, on the Labour side, the Regional and Local Government Sub Committee of the NEC which has the functions of advising the national party on local government affairs, maintaining close liaison with Parliamentary leaders and providing information and advice for Labour groups on local councils. Its Conservative counterpart is the National Advisory Committee on Local Government. In each case the Committee consists of members from both national and local parties and the leaders of groups on the ACC, ADC and AMA. Both parties hold annual local government conferences of which one of their main values is the opportunity they provide for local politicians of similar party persuasion to meet each other as well as leaders of the national parties. Leading members of the Associations take active parts in these conferences.

Leading members of the Associations are usually leading members of the authority they represent and important members of their local parties. They are often courted by the national politicians. It is often the case too that they may be asked to serve on one or more organisations of their national parties. Thus contact, official and unofficial, is developed. Often the leaders of the Association, know leading Parliamentarians personally. Sir Mark Henig, former Chairman of the AMC, pointed out that in 1966-68 most of the Labour members of the General Purposes Committee of the AMC knew many of the Cabinet Ministers in a personal capacity and thus access to government and departments was fairly easy.(42)

The factors which make for ease of access by the Associations also allow parties to bring pressure to bear. It is generally believed that the national Conservative party brought great pressure to bear on the AMC and on its Chairman, Sir Frank Marshall, in an attempt to persuade the Association to accept the two tier principle proposed in the White Paper on local government reform (February 1971). It is thought that much of this pressure came through unofficial channels. On the other hand, some observers attributed the Conservative government's decision to institute a two tier system to the great pressure exerted, formally and informally, by Conservative members of the CCA and RDCA.(43)

BASES OF POWER

Samuel Beer has argued that the success of a 'protective' group usually depends on the bases of power. He suggests that in Britain the influence a group exerts over the administration springs from the dependence of the British government on these groups for advice, acquiescence and approval.(44) Beer writes that the 'most obvious instrumentality which producers command and which governments need is advice.'(45) It is claimed that the organisation, structure and functioning of British government is based on the assumption that groups can be relied on to provide information, specialist advice and criticism which are necessary for policy making and administration. To be in a bargaining position a group will usually have to possess an expertise which the government lacks.

For the second base, acquiescence, Beer argues that power tends to lie in the implementation of policies.(46) Sanction, whether it be non cooperation in refusing to give advice and information or actively to go on strike, is an important weapon in the armoury of any group. The government's task is made easier if groups in the relevant areas acquiesce in policies it puts forward. Thus a government has to solicit a group's help, laying itself open to making concessions.

For the third base, it is suggested, there are some groups whose approval of a particular policy is a substantial reason for public confidence in that policy, and conversely their disapproval is cause for public unease.

Finally, Eckstein has argued that, although groups may hold all other attributes necessary for success, the attitudes of some groups may limit their scope for action.(47) For example, a professional association may be inhibited from withdrawing its labour or taking action which smacks of trade unionism. Its chances of success are thereby diminished.

Applying this analysis to the Associations it is clear that central government is dependent on them to some extent. The Associations have expertise which central departments lack. Although they employ a relatively small staff they are able to obtain experts and expertise from member authorities. For example, when the AMC and CCA were

arguing their conflicting cases on the allocation of planning functions
in the Local Government Bill of 1971, they both called upon chief
planning officers from member authorities to provide statistics and
other information to support their arguments. Associations' members
have the practical knowledge of administering services which
governments need in order to develop or change policies.

Although the Associations appear to have expertise in particular
areas, they are conscious that more experts are needed if they are to
do more than react to central initiatives. As a result the new
Associations have been making attempts to remedy this defect. In
addition to extending its secretariat to include more specialist and
support staff, the AMA has also rationalised the advice and help given
to it by officers of member authorities. In 1976 two panels of
advisers were set up consisting of officers of all types of authority
in membership. There is a 'General Panel' of over thirty officers
designed to aid the Policy Committee and a 'Legal and Administrative
Panel' again of over thirty officers to advise the other
committees.[48] The intention is to provide a more permanent and
systematic method for the Association to obtain advice and information.
An innovation which aimed at benefitting all the Associations was the
setting up in 1974 of the Statistical Information Service under the
auspices of the Chartered Institute of Public Finance and Accountancy.
The Information Service was financed jointly by the ACC, ADC and AMC.
The functions of the Service were to provide basic information for
each group of services run by local authorities; technical support
in the form of general and financial statistics for all the
Associations; research studies on behalf of any of the Assciations and
an enquiry service for helping Associations to design, distribute and
analyse questionnaires.[49]

A number of Ministers have given the impression that the Associations
are in a position to bring sanctions to bear on the government in order
to protect their interests. In fact all Ministers of local government
between 1945 and 1965 publicly took the view that reform of local
government was not possible without the agreement of each of the
Associations.[50] Yet these bodies have never threatened to use
sanctions to further their interests: not even over the reform of local
government which threatened the very existence of their members.

Sanctions would be difficult to apply for a number of reasons. First
the attitudes of the Associations are conditioned by the constitutional
position in which they find themselves. They regard themselves as
constitutionally responsible bodies bound to use reasoned arguments to
fight their case.[51] Non-cooperation would compromise the aura of
legitimacy which they display. More importantly, such actions would
almost certainly be considered irresponsible by some members as well
as outsiders. This attitude does not prevent the Associations from
protesting against certain proposed actions, but persuasion through
reasoned argument appears to be as far as they will go.

Second the Associations are inhibited by their lack of cohesion.
Each Association represents members with varying interests and
different political persuasions. The unity of the ACC or AMA at any
given time depends to a large extent on the policies they are pursuing.
As a general rule, however, the policy of an Association is based on
broad compromises between interests within it. For sanctions to be

taken and to be made effective, policies would have to be more tightly
defined. There would have to be a unity of purpose which is usually
lacking on most matters coming before the Associations. It must also
be noted that decisions made by the ACC and AMA are not generally
considered to be binding on members and certainly do not preclude
individual authorities from making their own approaches to government
or Parliament or making other arrangements to advance their interests.
Thus the Central Policy Review Staff, commenting that in 1977 only the
AMA of the four Associations gave it any evidence in response to the
Layfield Committee Report, observed that this failure 'fits somewhat
oddly with the strong and well developed views expressed to us by
individual authorities.'(52) There is generally no official pressures
from the Associations on members to conform.

The third factor inhibiting the use of sanctions is the existence of
separate Associations and the built in conflict between them. It is
generally acknowledged that a pressure group will be most influential
if it speaks on behalf of all or most of the interests in the area in
which it operates. Conversely when several groups exist within that
area, the chances of influencing policy outcomes are considerably
reduced because any conflict between the groups can be exploited by
the government. Local Authority Associations often disagree on
important matters, such as reorganisation of local government and
'organic' change.

Whether the Associations possess the base of power Beer labels
'approval' is debatable. On the one hand various reports on local
government in the 1960s pointed to a lack of interest in and knowledge
of the subject. The work of the Associations is little known outside
local government circles.(53) It would appear, therefore, that
approval or lack of it by the Associations on any issue would have
little effect on public confidence. On the other hand, it is possible
for them to appeal to a rational professional ethic to criticise or
support a policy. The CCA appealed to this ethic in 1971-72 to
persuade the government to reverse its policy of splitting the plan
making functions of local authorities between counties and districts.
Their appeal was supported by the two most important professional
planning bodies - the Royal Town Planning Institute and the Town and
Country Planning Association.

INTER-ASSOCIATIONS' CONFLICT

The existence of separate Associations has been regarded by most
observers of local government as the principal weakness of the
Associations as well as of local government. W.A. Robson thought
that the most adverse feature of British local government was that
different authorities were allowed to set up separate associations.(54)
The Royal Commission on Local Government in England warned that it
would be a disaster for local government in the reformed system if
more than one Association were created.(55)

There are three major objections to separate Associations: First,
having more than one Association results in duplication of effort,
manpower and finance. If resources were pooled in one Association it
could develop expertise to challenge more effectively government

policies as well as initiate policies of its own. At the same time it would be able to provide better services for local authorities. Second, by being separate and involved in conflict between themselves, the position of the Associations is exploited by the central government for its own purposes. Third, separate Associations hinder speedy and effective communication between central and local government.(56)

The reorganisation of local government in 1972 presented the existing Associations with the opportunity to meet these criticisms. Between 1971 and 1973 they discussed three main possible structures:

(i)   one Association covering all types of authorities;
(ii)   a federation of separate Associations;
(iii) separate Associations which would between them jointly
       set up a central office to deal with common services
       and to put forward, where there was agreement between
       them, a common point of view to the government.

If the unitary authorities proposed by the Royal Commission had been adopted the one-Association idea would have stood a good chance of being accepted. The government's scheme of 1971, whereby four major types of local authorities (outside London) were to exist, rendered the chances of establishing one Association more remote. Nevertheless the existing Associations made a serious attempt to create one body to watch over the interests of all types of local authority. Their leaders were in favour of such a structure.(57)   On the AMC's side their chairman, Sir Frank Marshall, was a fervent supporter, arguing that without one Association the influence of local government would be severely curtailed.(58)

By the middle of 1972 the one-Association idea had died. Within the AMC the lead given by its chairman, Sir Frank Marshall, was not followed by several of the proposed metropolitan authorities. The West Midlands Joint Metropolitan District Committee (consisting of the seven proposed districts in that area) warned that the desire to speak with one voice should not prejudice the need for different types of authorities to put forward their own viewpoints.(59)   Sir Robert Thomas, leader of the Labour group on the AMC at this time, objected to the principle of a single voice speaking for local government and suggested that the objective should be a strong voice for urban areas.(60) Another factor which led to the abandonment of the concept was that the London Boroughs Association (LBA), unaffected by the reorganisation of local government, was reluctant to disband itself and join others.

In October 1972 the representatives of the four Associations and the LBA met to discuss a draft proposal for the creation of a federation of Local Authority Associations. The Associations' response to this proposal was favourable. By October 1973, however, the idea of a federation was also abandoned, and the new Associations were in the process of being formed. The reasons for its rejection were similar to those which led to death of the one-Association concept. Urban areas felt that their interests would take second place to those of the rural areas which would dominate a combined organisation.(61)

A major new factor affecting the position of the AMC was that elections for the new authorities resulted in a Labour majority on that Association. The leaders of the Associations who had been calling for some united voice in local government were all Conservatives. A Labour controlled AMC now changed its policy. It appeared inevitable to Labour members of the AMC that a federation would always be dominated by the Conservatives. As a result the AMC in 1973 decided that it would not be a party to the establishment of 'a federation or any similar policy making body superimposed above the Associations.'(62) The outcome of this turn around was that, from the very high hopes entertained in 1971 for one Association, by the end of 1973 there were three separate Associations, thus confirming the worst fears of those who had criticised the existence of four such bodies.

CONCLUSION

Judged by the criteria traditionally used to assess pressure group effectiveness, each Association has a number of strong features. Their constitutional position is important. It partly explains the apparent esteem in which the Associations are held by governments and Parliament. This esteem smooths the way for access to decision makers. Their contact with governments and departments is continuous and conducted at the highest levels. The setting up of the Consultative Council on Local Government Finance has added greatly to this already extensive contact. As a result, the government is well aware of their opinions and reactions to policies. The least that can be expected from such contacts is that they will 'moderate the worse excesses of a unilateral approach'.(63)

By being in close touch with Members of Parliament (through vice presidents and other MPs sympathetic to their cause) the Associations are assured of a hearing in the legislature. However, with most of the legislation relating to local government sponsored by the central government and 'with the whips on, it is not easy to secure amendments to Bills once they have been introduced'.(64)

On the other hand there are several factors which weaken the Associations. They admit that they have not the resources to challenge effectively the experts in government departments. Weakness springs also from their structures and organisation. None acts as a cohesive body since each has to represent members with different interests, especially the AMA and its predecessor the AMC. Further, partly as a result of this division, sanctions cannot be imposed on members to persuade them to follow agreed policy. In any case the separate Associations often oppose each other on important issues which makes it impossible for them to invoke sanctions against governments even if they wished to do so. They therefore lacked an important base of power.

However, if one is to test in a practical way the strength or weaknesses of the Associations, case studies of influence on particular government policies are required. On Local Government reform, it was suggested that they failed to influence, in any significant way, the final outcome.(65) It was a subject on which they were traditionally divided and it could be argued that this example is untypical. On the other hand the combined efforts of the Associations to keep responsibility for the reorganised health and water services in 1971-73 came to nothing. In fact the Associations do not appear to be an exception to the general rule which applies to pressure groups in Britain, namely that, once a policy has been decided on by a government, groups rarely change the basic principles although they sometimes affect changes in detail. The Associations harbour no illusions about their position. The AMC held the view that governments are unlikely to be deflected from their policy objectives by groups such as the Associations. What such groups could hope to do is to inform and warn governments of the possible results before a matter is finally settled. In this sense they 'are in effect "advice centres" for the government.'(66)

The Local Authority Associations constitute a most important channel of communication between the central government and local authorities. As the Central Policy Review Staff in 1977 noted they act as an efficient clearing house 'or post office midway between their members and central government.'(67) But many believe that their role should be much greater. It is suggested that they should be involved in the development of policies, and that at times they should give a lead rather than just react to government initiatives. Their critics suggest that until they and the local authorities create one body to represent them, their influence on policies will continue to be marginal. The ACC and ADC appear to share this view. Both have as one of their major objectives the establishment of one Association to represent local authorities.

Whether one Association would be any more influential than the existing three is open to doubt. Any one Association representing authorities in the present local government system would be representing members with widely differing interests. The more varied the interests are in a group, the less cohesive it is likely to be. The existence of just one Association would not necessarily ensure that local government speaks with one voice. In fact one Association could result in local authorities not speaking at all on vital issues where interests clash and no common viewpoint emerges, as happened with the AMC in 1945-72, when no clear policy on reform emerged because of the differences of interests between the county boroughs and the non county boroughs.

NOTES AND REFERENCES

(1)   There were three other Local Authority Associations. They were Association of Education Committees, the London Boroughs Association affiliated to the AMC and the National Association of Parish Councils.
(2)   The AMC also represented the London Boroughs as well as the Northern Ireland Boroughs. The Irish boroughs have played little or no part in the activities of the AMC.
(3)   The Inner London Education Authorities are for certain purposes treated as a separate Association, which is guaranteed one seat on the Policy Committee of the AMA.
(4)   G.W. Jones, 'The Regional Debate', Socialist Commentary, May 1965, p. 22.
(5)   J.A.G. Griffith, Central Departments and Local Authorities, Allen & Unwin, London, 1966, p. 33.

(6)   Royal Commission on Local Government in England (RCLGE), HMSO,
        London, Cmnd. 4040, Vol. 1, p. 32.
(7)   For example, Harry Eckstein, Pressure Group Politics, Allen &
        Unwin, London, 1960, pp. 15-39.
(8)   R.D. Coates, Teachers Unions and Interest Group Politics: a study
        in the behaviour of organised teachers in England and Wales,
        Cambridge University Press, London, 1972, pp. 112-129.
(9)   Laurence Welsh, The Royal Commission: Evidence in Brief, Charles
        Knight, London, 1969, p. 3.
(10)   Constitution of the Association of Metropolitan Authorities,
        Section 3.
(11)   Constitution of the Association of County Councils, Section 16.
(12)   Harry Eckstein, op. cit. p. 21.
(13)   The six county boroughs with the largest populations were
        automatically included on the Council.
(14)   Constitution of the Association of County Councils, Section 3.
(15)   C.A. Cross, The Association of Municipal Corporations: A study
        of Structure, (unpublished Masters thesis, University of
        Manchester, 1954, pp. 99-100).
(16)   Thus the ACC has the following committees, agriculture, consumer
        protection, education, fire, local government finance, national
        parks, planning and transportation, police, policy, recreation
        and social services.
(17)   The practice of the Associations is to appoint their professional
        staff officers from local authorities who have had experience
        in the area of work for which he/she has been appointed by the
        Assocations.
(18)   Municipal Review Supplement, November 1976, pp. 129-131.
(19)   Since reorganisation of local government the number of MPs who
        are also members of county councils has declined.
(20)   In the provision of information the Associations are aided by the
        publication of their monthly magazines - the Municipal Review of
        the AMC, the County Councils Gazette of the ACC, and the ADC
        produces the District Councils Review.
(21)   See Municipal Review Supplement, October 1966, pp. 282-286.
(22)   See C. Hull and R.A.W. Rhodes, Intergovernmental Relations in the
        European Community, Saxon House, London, 1977.
(23)   Municipal Review Supplement, January 1975, p. 14.
(24)   See L.J. Sharpe, 'Theories and Values of Local Government',
        Political Studies, 1970, pp. 153-184.
(25)   AMC, Aims-Activities-Results, A Survey of Work, 1973, p. 2.
(26)   Robin McCall, (Secretary of the AMC-AMA 1972-1976), Letter to
        the author dated 21 December 1976.
(27)   Sir Meredith Whittaker, Chairman of the CCA 1972-1974 and Chair-
        man of the ACC 1973-1976, Interview, 23 March 1977.
(28)   See the Institute for Operational Research, Communications
        Between Central and Local Government in the Management of Local
        Authority Expenditure, Tavistock Institute of Human Relations,
        London, 1977, pp. 59-63.
(29)   Municipal Review Supplement, November 1976, p. 129.
(30)   Harry Eckstein, op. cit., pp. 17-18.
(31)   S.A. Walkland, The Legislative Process in Great Britain, Allen &
        Unwin, London, 1974, p. 203.
(32)   J.A.G. Griffith, Parliamentary Scrutiny of Government Bills,
        Allen & Unwin, London, 1974, p. 203.
(33)   Ibid., p. 256.
(34)   Municipal Review Supplement, February 1972, p. 15.

(35) Mr. Arthur Jones, MP Chairman of the Local Government Advisory Committee of the Conservative Central Office, 1963-73, Interview, 28 January 1977.

(36) Letter from the Clerk of the Council, Portsmouth, to the Secretary of the AMC, March 1971.

(37) W.A. Robson, The Development of Local Government (3rd ed.), Allen & Unwin, London, 1954, p. 83.

(38) Report of the 53rd Annual Conference of the Labour Party, 1954, p. 192.

(39) The Conservatives with the help of the Independents had always dominated the CCA.

(40) Lord Brooke of Cumnor, Interview, 28 January 1977.

(41) The Report of the 87th Annual Conference of the Conservative and Unionist Party, Conservative Central Office, 1967, p. 97.

(42) Sir Mark Henig (Chairman of the AMC, 1966-68), Interview, 14 January 1977.

(43) See for example, Peter Hall, 'The County Fights Back and Wins', New Society, 17 September 1970, pp. 491-494.

(44) Samuel H. Beer, Modern British Politics, Faber and Faber, London, 1968, pp. 320-330.

(45) Ibid., p. 321.

(46) Ibid., p. 325.

(47) Harry Eckstein, op. cit., pp. 27-31.

(48) Municipal Review Supplement, February 1977, p. 15-16.

(49) County Councils Gazette Supplement, July 1974, pp. 203-205.

(50) Whether these views are genuinely held by Ministers or merely stated as an excuse for non-venturing in the field of local government reform for other reasons is a matter of debate.

(51) Robin McCall, Letter, op. cit.

(52) The Central Policy Review Staff, Relations Between Central Government and Local Authorities, HMSO, London, 1977, p. 37.

(53) See for example, Committee on Management of Local Government (Maud), Vol. 3, The Local Government Elector, HMSO, London, 1967.

(54) W.A. Robson, Local Government in Crisis, Allen & Unwin, London, 1966, p. 103.

(55) Royal Commission on Local Government in England, 1968-1969, Report Cmnd. 4040, HMSO, London, 1969, p. 32.

(56) AMC, 'The Future of the Associations', Municipal Review Supplement, November 1972, pp. 238-242.

(57) The RDCA favoured a federation of associations.

(58) Sir Frank Marshall (Chairman of the AMC 1968-73), Interview, 10 May 1977.

(59) Letter to the Secretary of the AMC, December 1971.

(60) Minutes of a Meeting of the AMC, 19 September 1972.

(61) See Municipal Review Supplement, February 1974, p. 346.

(62) Ibid.

(63) AMC, Aims-Activities-Results, op. cit., p. 4.

(64) AMC, The Association of Municipal Corporations, 1873-1973, (1972), p.10.

(65) K. Isaac-Henry, 'Local Authority Associations and Local Government Reform', Local Government Studies, No. 1, 1975, pp. 1-11.

(66) AMC, Aim-Activities-Results, op. cit., p. 2.

(67) Central Policy Review Staff, (cf. note 52)

6 Policy Planning Systems and Central-Local Relations

Bob Hinings

The theme of this essay is the ways in which the policies, aims and objectives of central government are related to the general policy planning processes within local authorities. This theme can be located within the framework of analysis adopted by the central-local panel of the SSRC in two senses.[1] First, the local authority can be seen as the focal organisation, with the various component parts of central government representing other organisational units acting upon, and involved with, the focal organisation. Second, it can be located within inter-organisational analysis through the concept of networks. In various areas of policy, local and central government are interdependent, and to handle that interdependence develop networks of reciprocal relationships. Of central importance are the ideas of interdependence and reciprocity; to understand the response of the local authority one would have to understand the impact it has on central government as well as vice versa. The move to a programmatic policy planning system in certain areas of central-local relations is one way of handling the interdependencies inherent in the system.

THE DEVELOPMENT OF POLICY PLANNING IN CENTRAL-LOCAL RELATIONS

The late 1960s and early 1970s saw a significant movement in British local government towards the adoption of more 'corporate' attempts to formulate and implement policy and coordinate policy making and budgetary procedures. New forms of policy making and organisational systems were developed. The emphasis was on policy planning systems: an attempt to be programmatic and future-oriented in policy making. The future orientation is the planning element of policy; the programmatic nature is the systematic element, leading to clear cycles of policy making together with built-in processes of review. Such policy planning systems have also been designed to be comprehensive, covering a wide range of activity. Indeed, the notion of the corporate plan in local government promised a set of formalised, integrated, systematic policies covering all activities.[2]

These movements were encouraged by a wide variety of select committee, central government and academic advice.[3] They were further consolidated in 1974, when the majority of the reorganised local authorities adopted management structures based on the Bains Report, and many also attempted to set up integrated systems of policy making and budgeting.[4]

That many local authorities are now attempting to operate within integrated policy making frameworks is something which, in itself, without any similar response from central government, one would expect to have implications for the nature of central-local relations.

However, there has been a not unrelated movement taking place in central government activity during this period, which has involved a proliferation of planning systems, developed by different central government departments (but predominantly within the Department of the Environment), for use at local government level. As within local government the emphasis has been on future orientation, with rolling programmes and a systematic and programmatic process. On the part of central government, this trend has accelerated since 1974, and has important implications for the organisational structures, policy planning systems and procedures of local authorities.

The rise of policy planning in both local and central government would seem to be a consequence of the increasing scope of government, financial pressures, beliefs in rational planning and attempts to control the subsequent complexity.

In a recent report published by the School for Advanced Urban Studies, twenty two planning systems were listed.(5) The ones that involve some form of relationship between local authorities and central government are PESC; Regional Reports (Scotland); Regional Strategic Plans; Financial Planning (Scotland); Transport Policies and Programmes; Structure Plans; Housing Plans (Scotland); Housing Investment Programmes; Community Land Programmes; Regional Recreation Strategies; Social Service Plans; Joint Care Planning; Police Service Planning. There are also Comprehensive Community Programmes and the Inner Area Partnerships and Programmes. All attempt to regularise the relationship between central and local government by means of some kind of policy and resource planning.

THE NATURE OF POLICY PLANNING SYSTEMS

There are many differences between these various initiatives. What they have in common is an attempt to formalise and to plan the relationship between the centre and the locality. One difference between them is in the level of specificity of the system. A Structure Plan is an attempt to deal with an interrelated set of problems and functional areas, as are Regional Strategies and Comprehensive Community Programmes. They are corporate in their nature, covering a wide range of activities and operating as a framework or set of guide-lines from which more specific and detailed policies can be developed. Other systems are more specific, dealing with a more discrete activity such as Social Service Plans and Police Service Planning. They are bounded departmentally at local authority level, thus organising the policy planning relationship between a central government department and a local authority department, rather than with the local authority as an entity. There are other systems which are intermediate between these two: they are not authority wide, but neither can they be seen in purely departmental terms. Examples are TPPs and Joint Care Planning.

A second difference in these systems is between those that are concerned with a substantive policy area and those which are primarily resource oriented. In the former category are TPPs, HIPs, Social Service Plans, while in the latter are PESC, Community Land, Financial Planning (Scotland). Again, it is possible that some systems are intermediate, formally involving both substantive policies and resource allocation, such as CCPs. In essence, this distinction deals with whether the main emphasis in the central-local relationship is control of policy or resources.

A third difference arises from the relative roles of central and local government agencies. In some cases the systems can be thought of as primarily helping central government with <u>its</u> planning, the local authority being either a base for information collection, or an agent for implementation of plans laid down at the centre. The PESC exercise would primarily fall into this category. Other planning systems have a joint purpose, the aim being to achieve better planning and policy coordination in both central and local government, such as TPPs, HIPs, Police Service Planning. A further category is where central government seeks to improve its policy effectiveness. Into this category would fall CCPs and Inner Area Partnerships and Programmes.

There are, then, a variety of policy planning systems linking central and local government. They differ in terms of:

   (i)   level of specificity.
  (ii)   service as against resource orientation.
 (iii)   the relative roles of central and local government.

Given such variety they provide an interesting and important area for the comparative study of central-local relations. What, then, are the questions raised?

AREAS FOR RESEARCH

The introduction of these new types of policy planning systems and instruments may prove difficult to integrate into the pattern of local authority operation, particularly in those authorities which have adopted a corporate structure and process. Certainly, it would seem likely that those authorities who attempt to integrate their various departmental activities will experience particular difficulties compared with those authorities in which the tradition of departmentalism is still strong. How, for example, are HIPs and TPPs to be integrated with a Structure Plan? How, in the Partnership Cities, are Inner City Programmes to be related to either HIPs or the relevant Metropolitan County Structure Plan?(6)

From the perspective of the local authority as a focal organisation a number of research strategies are possible. One is to compare local authorities having developed corporate systems with those that have a more departmental approach in their handling of a range of such policy planning systems. How do they actually handle their planning relationship with central government through these mechanisms? Are the links between the centre and the locality different as a result of the way in which the local authority is organised; in other words, does the organisational form of a local authority have an independent impact on the central-local relationship, through the various planning systems? Does the range of policy and financial planning systems make it more or less easy, or have no effect on the ability of the local authority to carry out its own planning?

A further possibility is to compare these new formalised systems with areas and functions where there is no apparent policy planning system as e.g. in education policy. Do the new planning procedures change the nature of the links between central government and the local authority? Does the existence of a systematic approach lead to more or less control of the relationship by either party? Do they represent attempts to 'de-politicise' the relationship, leading to less involvement in, and activity by, local politicians in the policy area concerned? Here the central question is does the existence of a policy planning system make any difference to the central-local relationship.

A third possibility concerns the inter-authority dimension. Some of the policy planning systems involve a more complicated set of relationships than just central government with a single local authority. The two tiers of local government have to consult with each other, and central government may find itself in the position of appeal court. Examples of planning systems where the tiers have to be involved together are Community Land and Structure Planning, although the relationships involved are likely to be very different.

The existence of some kind of formalised policy planning relationship is only a starting point for study. It is necessary to examine the actuality of any relationship. The comparisons mentioned above would be comparisons of practice, real relationships, actual patterns of dependence and influence. In order to operate a formal policy planning system a whole range of informal activity will develop. A central question would be the extent to which the planning systems are 'taken over' by pre-existing sets of relationships and activities, as against the possibility of developing in reality new relationships.

From the perspective of central-local relations, thought of as an interdependent system with a network of reciprocal relations, a set of somewhat different questions arises, largely centred on the flow of communication and influence in the network. Concentrating on the local authority as a focal organisation leads to a set of questions about the reactions of the local authority. In examining a network of relationships reciprocal influence and the machinery supporting it are crucial. New systems of policy planning are supposed to change the nature of the links, of the kinds of information flowing, of the relative influence of the parties involved and to create new arrangements which clarify both the structures and processes involved. Questions arise about how the various actors in the process (i.e. central government departments, local authorities and their departments, local authority associations, professional bodies) attempt to influence the thinking and action of each other, both at the stage of formulating machinery and procedures, and at the stage of determining specific policies and resource allocation. Again, there are a number of different possibilities for research.

One area is the problem of accountability in the network. It is not entirely clear whether all the various planning systems contain specific views of who is accountable for what in the relationships. A programmed system should in theory have a clearer specification of the various levels of accountability than in an informal, ad hoc system. But some of the initiatives, particularly in CCPs and Inner Area Partnerships, are attempting to introduce shared accountability while others have more clearly hierarchical notions. How do such differences affect the operation of influence, the direction of communications, the development of machinery, if at all?

A further possibility is to examine how far the structure and operation of the various networks differ from system to system. Are TPPs operated differently, in toto, from Community Land because of functional, professional and political differences? Does it matter that the time cycles for the various systems are different, with annual activities being handled differently from more long term exercises? There are a range of technical and political distinctions between the various policy planning systems which may have an impact on the ways in which the networks of relationships develop and are organised.

The argument so far is that there has been a proliferation of central government policy planning systems in the recent past which have to be handled by a local authority. In the relationship between the workings of these central government systems and the attempt by a local authority to deal with them inter-organisational relationships are developing, with the possibility of new networks linking the various agencies of government.

Essentially the questions are focused on whether such new systems:

  (i)   Change the nature of links from the pre-existing pattern between central and local government;
  (ii) Affect the process and substance of policies in areas covered by such systems compared with those not organised in this programmatic way;
  (iii) Alter relationships and networks compared with existing patterns of policy making.

A variety of comparisons become possible, namely:

  (i)   Between different kinds of policy planning system (specific/non-specific; service/resource; interventionist/ information).
  (ii) Between different kinds of local authorities (corporate/ non-corporate; metropolitan/non-metropolitan).
  (iii) Between different central government departments (those committed to policy planning systems/those lacking such systems).
  (iv) Between policy areas subject to programmed planning and those subject to different relations (Housing/education; transport/consumer protection).

In principle the introduction of such systems should change the nature of the central-local relationship. The research question is do they, and if so, in what ways and with what determinants? To help answer this question, it is necessary to suggest what concepts would be useful and applicable.

A FRAMEWORK FOR ANALYSIS

The emphasis must be on the development of actual practice in the operation of planning systems. The existence of some kind of formalised policy planning relationship is purely a starting point for analysis. It is then necessary to examine the 'problem' of implementation. But, neither can the formal system be ignored. One research question is whether the formal structure makes any difference to operation.

A distinction has already been made between studies of policy planning systems which concentrate on the local authority as the focal organisation and studies which start from the idea of such systems as an aspect of the central-local network of relationships. The emphasis here is on the latter. The focus is on central-local relations as an object of the study, not on the reactions of either the centre or the locality per se. The perspective is of central-local relations as an interdependent system with a network of reciprocal relations.

The starting point, then, is the existence of a programmatic, systematic policy making and/or resource allocation system which indicates the presence of a particular kind of linkage between the centre and the locality. Such a system represents a formalised, structured network. Conceptually, the formal properties of the system have to be described in order to test the proposition that the formal nature of the system will influence the actual processes of operation. These concepts are readily available from organisational analysis with its strong emphasis on structure. In particular, ideas of the way tasks are divided within the planning system (differentiation) and the formal handling of subsequent control (integration) are important. Through these ideas it will be possible to examine the extent of formal prescription of the system as well as the basic style.[8]

It is possible with this analytical base to examine possible similarities and differences between planning systems and unplanned relationships drawing on the extent and style of differentiation and integration of the networks. This starting point allows us to examine the proposition that central-local relationships which are on a programmed basis differ from those which are not programmed, i.e. does the formal structure of the relationship matter? It becomes necessary to extend the analytical description of the system to actual practice.

The formal framework of differentiation and integration systematically prescribes a scaffolding of roles, rules and authority relations. The extent to which this prescribed framework is realised depends upon the patterned regularities of interaction. A starting distinction would be between the form and content of interaction. Form centres on such things as the number of units involved, the structural location of these units, the frequency of interaction. Content is the necessary additive so that the analyst has knowledge of the aims of interaction; thus his concern is with the kinds of issues dealt with, the nature of the information being passed. The description of framework and interaction provides the initial description of the properties of the planning system (and also of non-programmed relationships). In order to develop further we have to examine the 'action' properties of the system, and place it in context.

To understand why a planning system has the features it does and how
it actually works questions have to be asked about the resources being
used and distributed, the assumptive worlds of the actors and the power
relations and strategies at work.[9] This approach allows a focus upon
the orientation of the actors, the aims, purposes and intentions which
they bring to a situation in order to exert control. There will not be
one order of meaning but many, the centrepiece becoming the interaction
of individuals and groups, and the inevitable struggle and conflict as
groups attempt to impose their framework of meaning at the expense of
others and achieve the kind of control they desire.

Any system of relationships, such as a planning system linking central
and local government, has a variety of purposes built into it because of
the variety of actors involved. There will be civil servants and
politicians from different departments; officers and members from
different authorites and different departments within those authorities;
professional associations; local authority associations. These actors
bring their own assumptive worlds to bear; that is, they have values,
beliefs, opinions which are 'operationalised' within the context of the
network of relationships. To understand how a particular system works
and develops it is necessary to analyse the values of the various
actors. Immediately a distinction can be made between values which
are primarily concerned with ends and those concerned with means. Not
only do actors in central and local government have ends which they are
pursuing, e.g. 'better allocation of resources in housing', they also
have ideas about the proper ways in which the relationships should be
organised, e.g. 'partnership'. Both of these kinds of values are
important.

While all actions can be seen as purposeful, it does not follow that
all purposes are based on values as defined here. Concepts are needed
to take account of 'sectional interests' and 'interested parties' who
are striving to maintain or enhance their position. The actors have a
variety of resources at their disposal, such as those outlined by
Rhodes,[10] which are used to justify courses of action and, in the
context of scarce resources, things to be worked for as well as with.
That is, as well as having value type ends to pursue (and to use),
actors also have more material ends in the sense of resources to pursue
(and to use). Any set of central-local relationships involves a
network of interests and one of the critical aspects of a planned,
programmed relationship is that it attempts formally to involve certain
interests but not others. In a looser arrangement it may be easier to
accommodate a range of values and interests. Once a system is
formalised it is possible to see who is legitimately in, and who is
excluded.

Concepts of values and interests allow us to indicate what is at
stake in a set of relationships, what the extent of conflict and
consensus is; they do not allow us to say what the outcomes will be.
Values and resources act as the purposes or springs of action; for
successful action to ensue, power is necessary and strategies of action
have to be pursued. Within any system of relationships power will be
differentially distributed. Those with and without such power will
pursue different strategies of coalition formation, bargaining, open
conflict, and behind the scenes consensus. Again, a formalised
planning system is supposed to bring such aspects into a known set of

authority relations. It is meant to be different from an unformalised set of relationships. In principle it should be more difficult for behind the scenes power to operate because of the underlying rational, programmatic basis of the relationship. It should be more difficult for some of the more frowned upon strategies to be brought to bear.

Therefore, to describe and understand a planned, programmatic network of central-local relations we have to utilise six conceptual categories, namely, <u>structure</u>, <u>interactions</u>, <u>values</u>, <u>interests</u>, <u>power</u>, and <u>strategies</u>. Suggestions have been made about further definition and breakdown of these concepts, but there is a further area which needs elaboration, that of context or constraints.

There is an inherent danger with an action perspective of greatly over estimating the autonomy of actors and groups within organised relationships to construct their world in accordance with their own wishes. If the actor, imposing his values upon the situation in proportion to the power he possesses, is an integral part of any adequate conceptual framework, it is equally clear that he does not exist in a vacuum. There are constraints, a context, which provides the milieu, the problems and obstacles, within which social life carries on. A great deal has been written within the study of organisations about external constraints.(11) The important point is that any planning system has certain characteristics of its own, and is surrounded by other characteristics which impose limitations upon the behaviour of the actors and the nature of the relationships that can be developed. They are aspects of the situation to which actors have to respond.

Examples of characteristics of the system itself would include the number of relationships formally prescribed, e.g. HIPs involving approximately 400 local authorities and TPPs involving not many more than 50 (officially). There is the functional and technological basis of the activity. There are differences in the predictability and possible routinisation of some tasks as against others. Also some aspects are more politically sensitive than others at particular times. The actors involved in the system have only limited control over these features; in this sense they are constraints.

Requiring further conceptual exploration is the idea of a particular planning system having an external or environmental set of constraints, for instance the operation of other such systems. It is likely that the development of one will influence another through learning and imitation. Similarly, there will be an environment of ideas about planning, strong at one time in regard to certain functions, weaker at others. Central-local relations operate within an ideological environment.

Our framework, then, essentially has six categories, all of them highlighting aspects of the planning system that have to be dealt with in any research on central-local relations using an inter-organisational perspective. They are:

    (i)   structural characteristics of the system.
    (ii)   patterns of interaction.
   (iii)   the purposes of actors; values and interests.

(iv)   power distributions and strategies.
 (v)   constraining system characteristics.
(vi)   constraining characteristics external to the system.

DIRECTIONS FOR RESEARCH

In principle, the six conceptual categories could be used to suggest
areas of difference to explore within a comparative study. Planning
systems could be chosen which emphasised differences in structural
characteristics, or value patterns, or power or system characteristics
or externalities. Some of these categories are not open to knowledge
prior to investigation. However, both structural characteristics of
the system and the constraining system characteristics are likely to
be. In terms of both academic and practical interest these would seem
to be the appropriate starting points, because planning systems through
their structural characteristics are supposed to change the nature of
links between central and local government. Also, there is inherent
interest in the impact of function, in particular, on the possibility
of organising relationships in a planned, programmatic way.

On this basis two possible distinctions can be made, although any
particular study could cover both kinds of distinction. The first
distinction is between different kinds of policy planning system, e.g.
specific/non-specific; service/resource. Essentially this approach
starts from the system characteristics emphasising functional
differences. The second distinction is between policy areas subject
to programmed planning and those which are not. This distinction
centres on differences in the formal structural characteristics
linking the centre and the locality.

It would seem to be particularly important to cover the second type
of distinction as one can assume that programmed systems are expected
to introduce a different kind of central-local relationship. Important
to the whole approach both academically and practically is the question
of whether a programmed system changes the nature of central-local
relations. Are values, resources and power mobilised in a different
way; does the environment have different expectations? The central
question is: do the new planning systems alter relationships and
networks compared with existing patterns of policy making?

NOTES AND REFERENCES

(1)   This inter-organisational framework is outlined in the paper by
       R.A.W. Rhodes, Research into Central-Local Relations in Britain:
       A Framework for Analysis, in, Central-Local Government
       Relationships, SSRC, London, 1979.
(2)   For examples of these developments see R. Greenwood and J.D.
       Stewart (eds.), Corporate Planning in Local Government, Charles
       Knight, London, 1975.
(3)   See, for example, J.D. Stewart, The Responsive Local Authority,
       Charles Knight, London, 1973; Committee on Management in Local
       Government, Volume 1 (Maud Report), HMSO, London, 1967;
       Committee on the Staffing of Local Government (Mallaby Report),
       HMSO, London, 1967; The Reorganisation of Central Government

(Cmnd. 4506), HMSO, London, 1970; Sir Richard Clarke, New Trends in Government, Civil Service College Studies, 1971.

(4)   The New Local Authorities: Management and Structure (The Bains Report), HMSO, London, 1972. For Scotland see, The New Scottish Local Authorities: Organisation and Management Structures (The Paterson Report), Scottish Office, Edinburgh, 1973.

(5)   Planning Systems Research Project, Final Report, SAUS, 1977. Also see, M. Stewart, 'Some of the Issues in Planning Systems Development' and J. Earwicker, 'Service Plans as Corporate Hazards', both in Corporate Planning Journal, Vol. 4, No. 3, March 1978.

(6)   These observations derive from research currently being carried out at the Institute of Local Government Studies into management systems, area management experiments and comprehensive community programmes.

(7)   The framework draws on the ideas put forward in Stewart Ranson, Bob Hinings, and Royston Greenwood, 'The Structuring of Organisation Structures', Administrative Science Quarterly, December 1979.

(8)   The ideas of differentiation and integration derive from the work of P. Lawrence and J. Lorsch, Organisation and Environment, Harvard University Press, Cambridge, Mass., 1967. They have been applied in the local authority context in R. Greenwood, C.R. Hinings and S. Ranson, 'Contingency Theory and the Organisation of Local Authorities: Part 1', 'Differentiation and Integration', Public Administration, Spring 1975.

(9)   For the analysis of central-local relations these concepts are also dealt with by Rhodes, op. cit., and by K. Young, 'Values in the Policy Process', Policy and Politics, June 1977.

(10)   Rhodes, op. cit.

(11)   For an overview see F.R. Kast and J.E. Rosenzweig (eds.), Contingency Views of Organisation and Management, Science Research Associates, New York, 1973.

7 Implementation, Central-Local Relations and the Personal Social Services

Adrian Webb and Gerald Wistow

INTRODUCTION

The personal social services, namely the one hundred and sixteen local
authority social services departments in England and Wales and the
related work of countless voluntary organisations, provide an
interesting context in which to explore issues of central-local
relations and the implementation of national policies. Local authority
social services departments were created only in 1970/71, primarily by
merging the previously separate childcare and welfare functions of
local authorities. In the eight or nine years of their existence they
have faced, in extreme form, the burdens of exaggerated expectations,
rapid growth followed by a period of abrupt retrenchment (since the
first substantial 'cuts' of December 1973),(1) and an initial lack of
cohesion combined with limited public support for the key group of
professionals, social workers. The succession of 'battered baby
scandals' is the most consistent illustration, but reactions to the
social workers strike of 1978/79 revealed some particular intense
criticisms. The development and articulation of clear national policy
and guidance is especially pertinent in these circumstances, albeit
from a central department previously characterised as rather non-
directive. The forms such guidance might be expected to take can best
be illustrated by noting key features of these services.

   The personal social services are not readily identified with a single
'task' or skill; the work varies from an essentially interventionist
and change oriented approach of the kind adopted over juvenile
delinquency, through supportive or interventionist strategies with
the families of children 'at risk', to the rehabilitation and basic
care of the elderly, disabled and mentally disordered. Field social
workers, although the 'dominant profession', account for about only
ten percent of the work force; only two thirds of them are fully
trained; and they are divided over appropriate goals and methods of
work. The single most characteristic 'objective' of these services
has been to develop the range and quality of community based services
needed to effect a fundamental shift of responsibility for the care of
elderly, chronically sick, disabled and handicapped people from the
health to local authority services and from institutions to 'the
community'. This central 'objective' arises from the needs of the
health service and from cost-conscious management as well as from the
presumed preferences of clients.(2)

   Given the nature of the problems, national policies might be expected
to include guidance on:

professional and service objectives;

current theories and knowledge about social problems;

the implications of such theories for the choice of service
outputs and professional practice;

professional standards;

the reconciliation of resource scarcity with the exercise of
public accountability (primarily through enquiries into
mistakes and disasters);

priorities between client groups (not least because of the
demographic pressure from the elderly population);

priorities between types of service provision and intervention;

the local compatibility of personal social services with health
service planning (over which the DHSS has direct control,
nominally at least);

the compatibility with other statutory services (e.g. housing
and education) and with voluntary and informal provision.

Whether national policies and guidelines of such a comprehensive kind
would be readily accepted by local authorities is a moot point, but the
Secretary of State's overall responsibility for the services, combined
with the history of reorganisation, uncertainty over goals and
priorities, and increasing interdependence of social services could
justify such an approach.

The remainder of the essay concentrates on two questions: what do we
mean by implementation; and what processes and issues have characterised
central-local relations in the personal social services? We end by
considering whether the system of central-local articulation meets the
requirements of effective implementation of those national policies
which have been developed and advocated.

CENTRAL-LOCAL RELATIONS: THE PRINCIPAL CHANNELS OF ARTICULATION

The governance of the personal social services represents an
essentially traditional picture of channels and processes, though with
one or two unusual features. Four arenas of central-local articulation
may be identified, each of which may be characterised by several
specific processes and channels of communication and all of which may
be indistinguishable in practice: the policy, resource control,
professional, and political arenas.[3]

Articulation through policy

The first refers to what we shall call 'service policies':[4] decisions
about the scope of services; the problems to be tackled; the service
provisions and methods to be used; and the priorities to be pursued
with scarcity of resources. The DHSS is basically organised in client
divisions, each of which embraces the full range of health and social

service professional staffs working with a core of 'administrative' civil servants. Service policies are developed within these client divisions and are expressed in legislation, orders, circulars, and other forms of advice and guidance to 'field units', either health or local authorities. However, since the first concerted moves were made in the early sixties towards a 'community care' policy which spanned health and social services, recurrent attempts have also been made to develop detailed forward planning of a complementary kind in both services.

The ten year forward plans of the sixties(5) firmly reflected a 'laissez-faire' approach towards local authorities.(6) Each local authority was asked to outline its own thinking on its future development without guidance on likely resource trends or on preferred patterns of service provision. The idea of ten year planning was revived in 1972, but a growth rate of ten percent per annum was specified and service provision guidelines were issued.(7) The latter could be interpreted in two ways. The recommended level of residential places and home helps per thousand of the elderly population, for example, could be seen as a general indication of the overall coverage to be achieved as a minimum, with authorities free to substitute more home helps for fewer residential places. Alternatively, it could be assumed that DHSS had calculated a precise and optimum mix of services. These alternative perceptions go right to the heart of central-local relations. The second perception would favour a comparatively 'mechanical' implementation at local level of a policy which was spelled out in terms of detailed service inputs. The implications of the former perception are less apparent. If the guidelines were not to be taken too literally, what did they mean? Did they enshrine policy in any meaningful way? At best they could be seen as indicating the approximate balance between types of service and client group favoured at DHSS; or a statement of minima. Even this last interpretation would raise problems. No indication was given of how a local authority was to discount home helps against residential places if it favoured the former. Nor was any indication given of how these or other resources were to be used.

Most local authorities interpreted guidelines as a means of assessing how they were progressing without taking them too literally as a precise target. Nevertheless, some local health authorities took guidelines far more seriously as targets which local authorities should meet, without varying the 'mix'. Some local authority members viewed them either as targets to be chased or as maxima not to be exceeded in times of resource constraint. Consequently, guidelines raise central questions: what does policy mean; how is it interpreted by DHSS in relation to the 'field units' with which it has such different relationships; how do these different types of decentralised authority view the same communication; how are, or should, policies best be given expression; how best does a central authority achieve compatible implementation from different types of field unit; and what in practice, rather than constitutionally, are the limits of DHSS and central government influence generally on local social services departments? For the present we can simply note that service policies must, at minimum, arise from and through a complex interplay of service division guidance on general, or specifically 'professional', matters and the more quantitative, resource input juggling involved in forward planning.

The need to reconcile these 'philosphy' and 'inputs' strands of planning is acknowledged in two ways by DHSS. First, there is a structural device, the Local Authority Social Service Division, which exists to coordinate forward planning and the work of the client divisions and reflects that local authorities are not decentralised units of the DHSS. More recently (since 1977) a three year forward planning cycle has been introduced,[8] the more ambitious ten year cycle having collapsed almost before it began because of the 'resource shock' of 1973/4. This three year cycle is also based on statistical returns of resource input trends, and guidelines are updated as a basis for the exercise, but local authorities are now requested to include a 'narrative statement' which explains their broad strategy. Whether DHSS has reciprocated and provided a broad statement of philosophy and of currently perceived problems is arguable. In 1976 a comprehensive statement of priorities was issued which cut across the health and personal social services.[9] It was a broadly quantitative response to the needs of NHS planning and to the squeeze on public expenditure, indicating the priorities between client groups, health and local authority services, and types of service provision on which the DHSS intended to proceed. However, it still could not be interpreted as a carefully analytical expression of optimum service 'mixes', or as a declaration of policy on how home helps, residential homes, hostels, or meals on wheels were to be used to produce particular kinds of outcomes. The various facets of service policy had not been completely integrated.

Articulation through resource control

By comparison, the resource control arena may seem far more clearly dominated by a single and well integrated process of public expenditure control. The DHSS contribution includes a programmed budgeting approach,[10] operating through client groups and therefore spanning health and personal social services, as has already been seen in the approach to forward planning and priorities. But much of the expenditure control process involves central government departments other than DHSS, and the link is with the local authority associations and central committees and departments of local authorities rather than social services departments. The lack of direct DHSS influence over local authorities' use of rate support grant monies is highlighted by the rate support grant process. For example, the need to support the elderly and to develop effective child care services is reflected in negotiations and in the 'needs elements' of the formula, but expenditure on these items cannot be enforced or guaranteed.

The major form of direct DHSS integration of service and resource policies has traditionally been the administration of key sector loan sanctions,[11] which has operated through the regionally based 'professional inspectorate' namely the Social Work Service. However, the opportunity to impose central priorities by granting or withholding loan sanctions declined with the decentralisation of control over local capital programme priorities to the local authorities in 1975. In effect, service policy decisions have been pre-empted since that time by the need to protect the revenue account as a first priority; capital spending has been decimated.

The distinction between 'service' and 'resource' policies may seem arbitrary; it would seem sensible to agree with the Treasury and see policy as the confluence of decision about what is to be done and what is to be spent on what. Nevertheless, service and resource decisions are structurally differentiated and operate within different constraints and 'rules of the game'. However much they may seek to influence, DHSS divisions have limited control over the scale and distribution of personal social services expenditure planned for by central government but spent by local authorities. The constraints can be seen to have differed significantly in recent years when the service policy need has been for simultaneous expansion of capital and revenue budgets and projects, but the revenue consequences of past capital expenditure have dictated the dramatic squeeze on the capital side. Similarly, the long term goal of shifting the burden of care from the health service to the personal social services has been undermined by the determination to bring high spending local authorities under closer control. The problems of integrating the components of .service policies, and of service and resource policies, cast doubt on any simple approach to the problem of 'implementing' central government 'policies'; it casts doubt on the very notion of 'policies' being readily identifiable, let alone being the core influence on how services develop at the local level.

Nevertheless, one innovative feature involves, belatedly, a high degree of coordination between resource and service policies. In 1976 a pool of 'joint financing' monies was earmarked within the health service budget,(12) and was to be spent in collaboration with local authorities. This arrangement introduced a direct incentive to area health and local authorities to plan their services jointly, as had been required of them in the 1974 reorganisation. It also introduced a mechanism for directly transferring resources from health to personal social services to match the long term 'transfer' of responsibilities. The sums remain miniscule as a proportion of the health service budget, but joint financing projects already constitute a large proportion of new developments for many local authority social service departments. The attempt to coordinate the services through a central system of forward planning has arguably been given a local counterpart. If the DHSS can effectively influence planning in both services at the local level, the final effect on service provision may be greater than the sum of the parts.

By comparison with public expenditure control, manpower planning is a small, though growing, feature of central-local relations. However, it too contains both service and resource policy elements, with the planning of future manpower needs and the exploration of manpower substitutability a much longer term task than the resource control features of local manpower budgeting and the 'manpower watch'.

Articulation through professional and political channels

The professional and political arenas must be relatively neglected here despite their undoubted importance, because far too little is known about them. However, if the transfer of child care responsibilities from the Home Office to DHSS resulted in a more 'interventionist' approach to forward planning than that adopted in the old Ministry of Health, it seems to have had the opposite effect on the professional front in transforming the Home Office child care inspectorate into a less overtly interventionist professional corps. The language and style of 'inspection' has been carefully played down in the Social Work Service and advice and consultation have been emphasised. But the involvement of the Service in capital planning has given social work professionals a direct entry to policy and planning processes and has strengthened their role in multi-disciplinary client group teams.

IMPLEMENTATION: A BASIC MODEL

Implementation concerns the processes intervening between the expression of broad policy intentions and policy impact: the achievement, or otherwise, of these intentions. Policy implementation encompasses at least three major tasks: the explication of policy intentions and the communication of policy intentions or sub-goals to relevant 'actors' (individuals, organisational sub units or entire organisations); obtaining the compliance of these actors; and securing an environment conducive to implementation (e.g. ensuring that actors have appropriate material resources and authority to act and that different actors are related one to another by appropriate organisational structures and processes). This essay concentrates on explication and compliance.

Explication

Explication means spelling out in some detail what a policy means and implies. In practice, a policy may be presented in a number of different ways, each of which may be appropriate for different groups of actors involved in implementing the policy. Each form of expli-cation can usually be communicated through a variety of channels: government circulars; professional inspectorates; the party political system (issues of communication are not discussed here). For example, a policy may be delineated by identifying:

  inputs, the resources to be devoted to it (e.g. x number of home helps per 1,000 of the elderly population);

  intermediate outputs, the services to be made available to the public (e.g. y number of hours of work of a specified kind by home helps per 1,000 of the elderly population);

  final outputs, the impact to be achieved on a target population or community (e.g. a reduction of z percent in the number of old people dependent on residential care); or

  guiding philosophies, the broad objectives, ideologies and values which are the hallmark of the policy (e.g. preserving the dignity of old people by enabling them to remain in their own homes to the greatest extent possible while maximizing the cost-effectiveness of all local authority services - all public services? - for this client group).

While these different approaches to explaining and identifying the nature of a policy may be obvious, it is far from clear that the implications are well understood or well addressed in practice.

Compliance

The classical identification of compliance strategies by Etzioni
remains pertinent. He noted three approaches: the application of
sanctions for non-compliance; the offering of incentives; and the
moulding of the normative structure within which people operate.(13)
Each of these can be applied to individual actors within an
organisation, or to the interaction of organisations, of which central-
local relations are one aspect.

The overt use of sanctions is limited in central-local government
relations, though it is by no means irrelevant. One form of sanction
by opprobrium, the publication of 'performance leagues', is strongly
resisted by local authorities, and crude inter-authority comparisons
are discouraged though not entirely successfully. Performance leagues
are a double-edged weapon. Unless public expenditure is growing
rapidly, economy-minded members are perhaps as likely to pressurise
officers in the high-achieving authorities as are officers to urge
increased expenditure in low-achieving authorities. The internal
dynamics of 'leader' and 'laggard' authorities are not well understood
but are central to one dimension of implementation.(14) The
development of unambiguous service provision minima, backed by
sanctions, has been urged without effect in the personal social
services. As with planning guidelines service minima could introduce
real problems of rigidity into policy implementation, but would
provide a clear basis for applying sanctions to laggard authorities.

The use of incentives is greatly limited by the principle of 'block
grant', rather than 'specific grant', funding of local authorities.
Nevertheless, the urban programmes have in effect offered incentives
for particular types of projects; key sector capital loan sanctions
have in the past been used to favour (and thereby to discriminate
against) particular lines of development; and the recent move towards
a system of 'joint financing' is a powerful incentive to local
authorities to collaborate with health authorities. Less directly,
the regional offices of the professional inspectorate, the Social
Work Service, can offer a range of supportive and advisory services in
addition to their role in capital programming. Whether, and to what
effect, they use these limited opportunities to shape local authority
services is not known. Similarly, there is little empirical research
into the extent of bargaining behaviour between local authorities
social services departments and regional and central divisions of
government departments. But the variation in local perceptions of the
'rules of the game' of central-local relations has been illustrated
by Judge in his work on capital programming.(15)

To ensure compliance by 'normative control' is both a more attractive
and a more uncertain option than those noted above. If a central
authority can even partially shape the 'assumptive world'(16) of local
policy makers, it can hope to influence choices in a desired direction
even in a period of turbulent change. The assumptive world of actors,
either individuals or groups of individuals acting as a collectivity,
must comprise many diverse values and perceptions of the world, but it
is worth selecting a few which are crucial: theories of problems;
theories of solutions; priorities; and ideologies about 'market
expansion' or 'market compression'.(17)

By theories of problems we mean understandings of what constitutes a social problem, the conceptualisation and the measurement of the scale of specific problems, and explicit or implicit theories of the causes of these problems. Logically, theories of solutions, which comprise ideas about effective and acceptable responses, would flow naturally from theories of problems. In practice it cannot be assumed that there is a progression from problem to solution; solutions can attain a degree of 'autonomy'.(18) They may acquire such a status within political and professional philosophies that problems are defined to be compatible with a favoured solution (or incompatible with an unacceptable solution). The relationship between identifying problems and solutions is therefore far from simple and may be further complicated if the theory of a problem logically implies a solution which lacks legitimacy or is not seen as feasible. An example was the radical redefinition in the sixties of juvenile criminality as essentially a product of structural defects in the social system. The rethinking of solutions resulted in changes in juvenile justice and in a move away from 'punishment' and from the use of institutions. However, the logic of reducing structural inequalities was not pursued rigorously and could not have been prosecuted merely within the personal social services. In the event, even the less radical rethinking of solutions proved difficult to implement, because of resource shortages and the doubts of the magistracy. The normative approach was of limited value outside the social work profession.

The remaining dimensions of the assumptive world of actors enlarges the scope of normative control. Theories of problems and solutions are a limited basis for action because they influence assumptions about what needs to be done, but not what most needs to be done or what can be done. The setting of priorities and the trade-off of pressures for market expansion and contraction determine the wider context. Biases in favour of particular client groups and types of intervention have been a consistent and increasingly coherent feature of the DHSS attempt to influence local priorities. The shift from a 'need' to a 'resource' bias has been less specifically but even more pervasively reflected in the language, conceptual base, analytical tools, and processes of forward planning and resource control. Normative control need not be affected only through the more obvious means of policy explication, professional training and party political channels. The development of a standardised system of planning and of analytical techniques, which has been attempted in the health service but not in the personal social services, can itself predispose local staffs towards a more uniform set of planning assumptions. The more explicitly normative approach of explaining and persuading is primarily the role of the client group divisions of the DHSS and of the Social Work Service.(19)

The major problem of normative control is its diffuseness. In the absence of strong unions, the ability to offer incentives or impose sanctions rests primarily with central authorities, but the ability to influence assumptive worlds is more widely dispersed. Incentives and sanctions can themselves exert a strong effect on assumptive worlds, but reference groups outside the governmental system are also crucial: national and local professional associations; political parties; staff colleges and other training institutions; and promotional pressure groups. Precisely because the assumptive worlds of the 'implementing' agencies and staffs are shaped by a variety of sources,

the impact of central authorities is unpredictable. We currently
possess no concerted explanations of how, for example, professional
social work thinking, campaign groups, and central government processes
and pronouncements interact to influence the assumptive worlds of
different groups of staff in different types of local authorities. We
certainly do not have any detailed 'maps' of ideologies, expectations
or perceptions of the duties and obligations which arise from tenure of
a particular post or membership of a social service profession.
Consequently, we cannot begin to understand how these factors, inter-
acting with specific incentives and sanctions, shape local decisions
and actions.

The best which we can do at present is to add another pair of factors
to our conceptual model of 'implementation'. These are: salience; and
congruence.(20) The first means the perceived relevance of a
particular statement of policy, guideline or command. The problem with
any one attempt to influence action is that its salience can vary
widely among groups or individuals all of which are equally crucial to
implementation. For example, the need to incorporate a range of social
criteria in assessing the appropriate point at which to discharge a
hospitalised old person is self evidently relevant to social workers
but may be excluded from consideration by a hospital doctor dominated
by thoughts of 'through-put' and bed occupancy. Even assuming that the
doctor considers social criteria to be relevant in principle, however,
the idea that social isolation may contribute to senile dementia may
be dismissed because it is not congruent with a medical view of
dementia as a degenerative disorder. Salience is primarily determined
by definitions of role and perceptions of what are the primary
objectives appropriate to that role; congruence refers to the
compatibility of a proposed action with the theories of problems and
solutions, and therefore the political and professional ideologies,
to which the actor subscribes.

Using these concepts, we can more fully comprehend the task
confronting a central authority which needs to secure the compliance of
actors with diverse roles and orientations. At least three strategies
could be adopted:

the entire policy could be presented in such a manner as to
appear equally salient and congruent to all actors;

the assumptive worlds of the different actors could be
modified, wherever possible, to make them equally receptive
to the policy;

or the policy could be segmented so as to present the pertinent
aspects of the policy to each actor or group in a way which
would accord with their assumptive worlds.

In practice the first is rarely possible, especially when the
relevant actors range from chief officers, financial administrators,
service planners and field professional staff, to domestic staffs
(as, for example, in policies affecting residential care).(21) The
more usual approach is the third, the segmentation of policy, combined
with some attempt at the second, the modification of assumptive worlds.
However, to segment a policy without losing its essential coherence
requires the careful integration of the component parts at each level

of implementation and to do this requires what can be called intermediate levels of theory.[22] Such theories are needed, for example, to specify the appropriate relationship between types of care, such as day, domiciliary or residential in the context of the overall policy. Each component of a policy has in turn to be given a degree of coherence in light of the assumptive worlds of its implementors without losing the coherence of the whole. This step is perhaps one of the most critical and undervalued in policy implementation.

Intermediate theories are a prime determinant of what actually happens at the operational levels, but they often remain implicit. Our concern is with explicit intermediate theories, which range from the input models developed by planners (which specify a desired mix of, say, home helps, meals on wheels, and long or short stay beds for the elderly), to guidelines for the role of home helps in the long-term support of a disabled old person compared with their role in the short-term rehabilitation of a mentally ill housewife. The first type may be described as intermediate theories of service production and the second as intermediate theories of professional practice. There seems at present to be a significant imbalance between them in the personal social services. The less professionalised care services (residential care, home help, meals on wheels) are being quite heavily subjected to intermediate theorising of the first kind with the subsitutability of different inputs being examined in cost-effectiveness terms, but with much more limited discussion on how in practice to use home helps, volunteers, para-professional staff, meals on wheels. On the other hand, professional social work has a long history of this latter kind of intermediate theory combined with a resistance to the more resource conscious approach.

One of the most significant problems of policy implementation in the personal social services, therefore, appears to be that of developing adequate intermediate theories of both kinds, of integrating the resource and professional practice types of theory, and determining where such theories can best be developed and how best they can be communicated (by central government departments, by national and local professional advisory services, by professional associations or professional training institutions). But the first task seems more prosaically to be that of discovering what currently happens and how service outputs are presently shaped.

The basic framework for understanding the implementation task is that implementation entails a set of processes: policy explication and communication; the creation of an appropriate context within which implementors can operate effectively; and the securing of their compliance. Two substantially different, but overlapping, strategies of implementation have been noted: the direct approach of specifying appropriate actions; and the more indirect approach of influencing the assumptive worlds of the implementors. Both the explication of policy and the securing of compliance take different forms within these strategies. The specification of inputs and intermediate outputs and the application of sanctions and incentives are to be expected in the first; the elaboration of desired final outputs and the use of normative controls will be more typical of the second. But in both cases policy needs to be presented in such a way as to maximise its salience and congruence for implementors. The development of intermediate levels of theory which segment but retain the coherence of the policy is a crucial feature of this task.

Although the framework for discussing policy implementation began with a rather 'traditional' view of organisations, namely that central authorities seek to implement coherent and explicit policies, it has subsequently emphasised the alternative assumption that 'organisation' conceals a variety of actors and groups motivated by different interests, values and ideologies. The argument is that a central authority which wishes to implement a given policy has to develop a coherent implementation strategy capable of meeting the problems that have been outlined. An alternative is to devise policies with the problems of implementation in mind, for example, to 'go halfway' by considering the interests, needs and assumptive worlds of the implementors.[23]

CENTRAL-LOCAL RELATIONS: AN APPROPRIATE VEHICLE FOR IMPLEMENTATION?

The previous discussion of central-local processes of articulation within the personal social services revealed a mismatch between the dominant implementation strategy employed by the DHSS and the control capabilities of the Department. Its emphasis on the service policy side has been predominantly towards a direct strategy of specifying in some detail desired service inputs. This approach is fraught with serious difficulties.

The DHSS is singularly ill-equipped to secure the adherence of local authorities to detailed guidelines and priorities. Social Service Departments (unlike Area Health Authorities) are not the agents of central government. They cannot be expected simply to work towards targets determined in Whitehall. If a local authority chooses to ignore the guidelines, the limited range of sanctions and incentives available to the Department provide few additional opportunities for influencing local authority expenditure decisions or social service department planning. In particular, the block grant system prevents the DHSS from tying resource allocations to specific service planning objectives.

Thus, key features of the relationship between central and local government have important consequences for the DHSS in its search for more effective policy implementation. As long as the existing situation holds, an indirect implementation strategy, which attempts to maximise normative controls, may therefore have the greater likelihood of success. This approach would involve the strengthening of the 'philosophy' strand of the planning process and the weakening of the input strand. The suggestion is that a more fruitful relationship between the DHSS and social service departments is likely to arise from a greater emphasis being given to the discussion and formulation both of social policy objectives and of intermediate theories of service production and practice appropriate to the local planning task.

This conclusion is reinforced by a second set of difficulties arising from the direct approach to implementation. Whereas the first problem was that of non-compliant authorities, the second is that of the 'over-compliant'. There is a tendency among some local authorities to accept planning guidelines as a dirigiste substitute for local analysis and responsiveness. They allow guidelines to dominate their planning processes irrespective of local circumstances. Considerable variations in existing stocks of resources and levels of provision exist, not only between social service departments but also in the total balance of services provided in any one locality by matching AHAs and by the voluntary sector. Consequently, a slavish adherence to national guidelines and priorities, whether interpreted as maxima, minima or as statements of the optimal service 'mix', could only rarely, if at all, constitute an appropriate response to local conditions.

The implication, once again, is that the DHSS needs to develop a stronger indirect strategy, particularly in joint planning. Health Authorities may well expect social service departments to adhere mechanically to central planning guidelines, but their hopes will be frustrated unless both types of authority are encouraged to develop service objectives and intermediate theories based upon shared appreciations of local circumstances. The 'Balance of Care Model', which was sponsored by the DHSS and is now being developed in a number of localities, ought to have this effect.(24) Certainly, its employment in exploring the different service mixes possible given varying levels of local resource inputs renders centrally determined guidelines irrelevant. Because there cannot be one best model of resource input mix applicable to varying local circumstances, there cannot be a single best approach to professional practice. The need to develop and test experimentally intermediate theories of both resource use and professional practice is therefore crucial. If this indirect approach to implementation were to be more fully adopted, a key vehicle for its deployment might be the regionally based, but strengthened, Social Work Service.

The dominance of the direct approach to implementation also has important consequences for the earlier distinction made between service and resource policies. The indirect strategy of influencing implementor's decision premises has been only weakly developed. The policy instruments most fully developed by central government have been those associated with a direct implementation strategy, such as RSG settlements, cash limits and input guidelines. But such instruments are particularly appropriate to the quantitative and input orientations of resource control and, therefore, of resource policies. Consequently, it is not only easier for central government to secure the implementation of resource policies (at least in total volume terms), but there is also a greater possibility that service policies will be subordinated to resource policies and that the development of intermediate theory will be neglected.

This position is radically different from the traditional view which tends to see service policy as real policy and, therefore, treats resources as merely a key element in the creation of a favourable climate for implementation. The inadequacy of this view is highlighted by two factors already discussed: the relative autonomy of social service departments vis a vis the DHSS and the block grant system which prevents the Department from securing a relationship between resource allocations and service objectives at local level. The argument suggests, therefore, a reversal of the relationship between 'policy' and resources, as traditionally expressed. That is, the autonomous nature of the authorities involved and of the processes through which

resource and service policies are expressed permits the treatment of
service policies as part of the environment for the implementation of
resource policies. At a time of severe constraint upon public
expenditure, therefore, the modification of service policies becomes a
requirement for successful economising. The suggestion by local
authority associations that statutory service obligations may have to
be removed to allow the implementation of current 'cuts' is a direct
example of this process.

The power of Self's observation that public authorities are
characterised by market compression is that a tension exists between
resource and service objectives and the processes and modes through
which they are expressed. There is no simple unanimity of purpose
between them. Also, public social services tend to oscillate between
the dominance of market expansion, when resource considerations can be
seen as largely subservient to service policy planning, and the
dominance of market compression, when resource objectives can
completely undermine service policy. These considerations expose a
critical question rarely faced in public sector management: in what
circumstances is a service policy no longer viable? When should the
pretence of implementing it cease in the face of resource shortages?
As with many of the questions raised here, the essay makes no attempt
at an answer. There is a need for further conceptual and empirical
work.

NOTES AND REFERENCES

(1)   For a more detailed discussion see A.L. Webb, 'Priorities in the
      Personal Social Services', in H. Glennerster, (ed.), Labour's
      Social Priorities, Fabian, London, 1976; and 'An Absence of
      Concern for Equality in the Personal Social Services?', in
      N. Bosanquet and P. Townsend, (eds.), Labour and Equality,
      Fabian, London, forthcoming.
(2)   The development of this objective may be followed in, for
      example, 'Health and Welfare: the Development of Community
      Care', Cmnd. 1973, HMSO, London, 1963; DHSS, 'Priorities for
      Health and Personal Social Services', HMSO, London, 1976;
      DHSS, 'The Way Forward', HMSO, London, 1977.
(3)   The characterisation of interactions between central and local
      government as a system of 'articulation' was developed by
      L.J. Sharpe, and has been applied to the particular case of
      the personal social services in A.L. Webb, 'Central-Local
      Relations in the Planning of Personal Social Services',
      publication pending.
(4)   A further discussion of the distinction between 'service' and
      'resource' policies is to be found in A.L. Webb, 'Decision
      Making in Social Services Departments', in T. Booth, (ed.),
      Policy-making and Planning in the Social Services, Blackwell,
      Oxford, forthcoming.
(5)   Cmnd. 1973, op. cit. (reference 3).
(6)   The characterisation of the Old Ministry of Health in these terms
      was made in Griffith's classic study of central-local relations
      in the early 1960s: J.A.G. Griffith, Central Departments and
      Local Authorities, Allen and Unwin, London, 1966.

(7)   The ten year planning cycle was initiated by DHSS Circular
        35/72. See: A.L. Webb and N. Falk, 'Planning the Social
        Services', Policy and Politics, Vol. 3, No. 2, December
        1974; and C. McCreadie, 'Ten Year Averages', New Society,
        2 May 1974.
(8)   The 'LAPS' cycle was initiated by the DHSS in 1977 under the
        terms of LASSL(77)13, 'Forward Planning of Local Authority
        Social Services', DHSS, London, June 1977.
(9)   DHSS, 1976, op. cit. (reference 3).
(10)   On the development of programme budgeting in the DHSS, see,
        J.D. Pole, 'Programmes, Priorities and Budgets', British
        Journal of Preventive Social Medicine, Vol. 28, 1974; and
        also H. Glennerster, Social Service Budgets and Social
        Policy, Allen & Unwin, London, 1975.
(11)   See K. Judge, Rationing Social Services, Heinemann, London,
        1978.
(12)   The arrangements for joint financing were first detailed in DHSS
        circular HC(76)18 (March 1976) and later modified in HC(77)17
        (May 1977). Both circulars were entitled: Joint Care Planning:
        Health and Local Authorities, DHSS, London 1976 and 1977.
(13)   A. Etzioni,A Comparative Analysis of Complex Organisations, Free
        Press, New York, 1961. Etzioni's discussion of compliance was
        also used by Van Meter and Van Horn as part of their framework
        for the study of implementation. This was an important
        starting point for our own conceptual work on this subject.
        See, D.S. Van Meter and E.C. Van Horn, 'The Policy Implement-
        ation Process: A Conceptual Framework', Administration and
        Society, Beverley Hills, 1975, Vol. 6, pp. 445-488.
(14)   The Davies triology on territorial justice represents the most
        specific application to the personal social services of
        aggregate data studies of local authority expenditures and
        performance: B. Davies, Social Needs and Resources in Local
        Services, Michael Joseph, London, 1968; B. Davies et al.,
        Variations in Services for the Aged, Bell, London, 1971;
        B. Davies, et al., Variations in Children's Services, Bell,
        London, 1972.
(15)   K. Judge, 1978, op. cit. (reference 11).
(16)   Ken Young employed this term to denote 'the several strands that
        co-exist in policy makers' subjective understandings of their
        environments', K. Young, 'Values in the Policy Process',
        Policy and Politics, Vol. 5, June 1977, p. 3.
(17)   P. Self, Administrative Theories and Politics, Allen & Unwin,
        London, 1972.
(18)   This point is discussed in P. Hall, H. Land, R. Parker and
        A. Webb, Change, Choice and Conflict in Social Policy,
        Heinemann, London, 1975.
(19)   For a more detailed discussion of the SWS, see: B. Utting, 'The
        Role of the Social Work Service of the DHSS', Social Work
        Service No. 16, July 1978.
(20)   See, A. Webb and G. Wistow, 'Policy Implementation in the Personal
        Social Services', paper to the SWS, 1978 (publication forth-
        coming).
(21)   See, A. Hall, The Point of Entry, Allen & Unwin, London, 1974.
(22)   An early discussion of intermediate theory may be found in G.
        Wistow, 'The Policy-Action Gap', paper to SSRG Annual
        Conference, March 1978. The concept is developed more fully
        in A. Webb and G. Wistow, 1978, op. cit., (reference 20).

(23) See 'Implementation and the Central-Local Relationship',
      Appendix II of Report of the Panel on Central-Local Government
      Relationships, SSRC, London, 1979.
(24) For a description of the local application of this model see
      R. Carwin, 'Balance of Care in Devon', Health and Social
      Services Journal, 18 August, 1978, pp. c. 17-c. 20.

8 Why Should Central-Local Relations in Scotland be Different from Those in England?

Edward Page

The Scottish pattern of central-local relations is said to have characteristics that could 'usefully be applied further south',(1) yet there have been few studies of this topic. While one may point to literature concerned mainly with England, or England and Wales,(2) and assume that the insights of these works apply to central-local relations north of the border, the extent of the similarities and differences remains to be explored. This essay examines some of the evidence for believing the pattern of central-local relations in Scotland to be different from the pattern in England.

It is useful to distinguish between differences in structure, process and output. Structure refers to the statutory and non-statutory arrangements which shape the nature of central and local government and the interaction between them. Process refers to the relationship itself, and output refers to the effects of the relationship between central and local government on the provision of services by local government.

The importance of structure is twofold. First, structures may be seen as 'codifications' or 'crystallisations' of pre-existing practices.(3) Thus, differences in structures may be indicative of different forms of relationships. Second, the structures tell us who talks to whom about what, and thus pose constraints upon the process of central-local relations. However, structures alone cannot describe the process.(4) Unfortunately, little research has been conducted into the process of central-local relations in Scotland. Thus an examination of output has an added importance; as well as describing the outcome of the process of central-local relations, a statistical analysis of output will be used to throw light upon the process itself. Because such statistical inferences can never be a satisfactory substitute for an examination of the process, the results of the analysis of output can only be suggestive.

STRUCTURE

The structure of local government in Scotland was reformed in May 1975, one year after the reforms in England and Wales. The pre-existing structure consisted of four counties of cities, 21 large burghs, 197 small burghs, 33 counties and 196 district councils. The distribution of functions between these authorities was complicated. For example, the function of a county varied from area to area depending on whether the area was covered by a town council for a small or a large burgh.(5)

The 1975 reorganisation, embodied in the Local Government (Scotland) Act 1973, was based upon the recommendations of the Royal Commission on Local Government in Scotland (the Wheatley Commission). The Act created nine regional authorities, fifty three district councils and three all purpose island authorities. The regions were given responsibility for education, police, water and sewerage, social work, roads, fire and consumer protection services, whereas major district functions were housing, refuse collection, libraries and museums, environmental health and licensing. Some powers, including the maintenance of parks and museums, are held concurrently, and planning is shared. In three regions, namely Borders, Dumfries and Galloway and Highland, planning, libraries and museums, building control and parks and recreation are regional functions in contrast to elsewhere in Scotland.[6] In addition the 1973 Act made provision for Community Councils (of which there are at present approximately 1,100)[7] which have no statutory powers and no guaranteed independent finance.

One major difference between the structure of local government in England and Scotland derives from the extreme imbalance in population, area and penny rate product among Scottish local authorities.[8] The most extreme imbalance is that one region, Strathclyde, contains over 47 percent of the Scottish population. One district, Glasgow, contains 17 percent of the population of Scotland and more people than all other regional and island authorities except Strathclyde. Perhaps the obvious English parallel is the position of London. However, there are two major differences. First there is a difference of scale: London contains only 15 percent of the English population. Second, the difference between London and the remainder of England is explicitly acknowledged in the structure of English local government. No such explicit provisions are made for Strathclyde and Glasgow.

The Wheatley Commission recommended that local authorities should be represented by only one association as opposed to the position before reorganisation in Scotland and to the current position in England. Wheatley commented that 'with local government as a whole there will always be more common ground than disputed ground and a single association would undoubtedly be better placed to represent this to the outside world than two associations would be'.[9] On the basis of this recommendation the Convention of Scottish Local Authorities (COSLA) was set up in 1975.

There is also a distinctive set of Scottish professional associations. Some, such as the Society of Local Authority Chief Executives (SOLACE), are United Kingdom organisations with a separate Scottish Branch having its own constitution. Others, such as the Society of Directors of Administration in Scotland (SODAS), are purely Scottish organisations. The significance of these associations is that some of them are consulted by central government directly over legislative proposals or interpretations of legislation; they prepare reports for COSLA committees and are invited to nominate members to act as officer advisers in COSLA.

The organ of central government in Scotland for local government is the Scottish Office. It consists of Central Services, comprising divisions such as the Scottish Information Office and the Finance Division, and five major departments: the Scottish Development

Department (SDD), the Scottish Home and Health Department (SHHD), the
Scottish Economic Planning Department (SEPD), the Scottish Education
Department (SED), and the Department of Agriculture and Fisheries for
Scotland (DAFS). Each is formally responsible to the Secretary of
State for Scotland, although the Minister of State and the three
Parliamentary Under Secretaries have defined areas of responsibility.
These are grouped as follows: agriculture, fisheries and the Highlands
and Islands; industry, oil development and education; health and social
work and home affairs and environment. The identification of junior
ministers with specific policy areas was strengthened in 1979 when the
Conservative Government included a definition of their responsibilities
in their titles.

The SDD, created in 1962, is charged with general responsibilities
for local government, along the lines of the Department of the
Environment in England. The SDD, in conjunction with the Finance
Division of Central Services, administers the Rate Support Grant and
specific grants, monitors local authority capital borrowing, and
'guides, encourages and coordinates the work of agencies and
authorities in providing local services and in exercising their
statutory responsibilities'.(10) It has specific responsibility for
planning, housing, roads and transport, new towns and environmental
services. The SED carries out the functions in Scotland exercised by
the Department of Education and Science in England and Wales, with the
major exception that some of the functions associated with the DHSS
are exercised by the Social Work Services Group in the SED. The SED is
also directly responsible for the maintenance of teacher training
colleges, other further education colleges ('central institutions')
and the distribution of further education awards. The SHHD has
responsibility for certain DHSS and Home Office functions such as the
National Health Service, public health and fire and police services.
The SEPD was set up in 1975 to coordinate economic planning. One
major point of contact between the SEPD and local authorities is through
the Scottish Development Agency (set up in December 1975) which acts
under guidelines drafted by the Secretary of State through the SEPD
and cooperates with local authorities in the provision of advance
factories and environmental improvement schemes. Another point of
contact is through the administration of the EEC Regional Development
Fund grants to local authorities. The major points of contact between
the DAFS and local authorities are in animal and plant disease control,
the regulation of slaughterhouses and planning affecting agricultural
land.

The structure of financial provision to local authorities in Scotland
displays significant differences from the practice in England. The
Rate Support Grant contains the same three elements: needs, resources
and domestic. However, differences occur in the negotiation of the
amount of relevant expenditure to be financed by the Rate Support Grant
and in the distribution of the needs element. The total relevant
expenditure to be financed by RSG is built up on the basis of
negotiations between COSLA and the Scottish Office about the level of
growth in expenditure in individual local services. Once the total
relevant expenditure and the aggregate grant to local authorities
(apart from housing subsidies) are determined and the resources and
domestic elements of the RSG fixed, the needs element of the RSG is
distributed in a three stage process based on a weighted population

86

measure.(11) It is distributed first between islands and regions, then
between regions and finally between regional and district councils
within the region.

There are differences in the allocation of capital finance to
Scottish local government. First, there is no division of capital
expenditure into key sector, intermediate sector and locally determined
sector as in England and Wales. Second, the controls exercised by the
Secretary of State are exercised over items of expenditure and not over
capital borrowing as in England and Wales.(12) Thus the Secretary of
State for Scotland has a more direct control of the capital expenditure
of local authorities than his counterparts in England. However, since
1977-8 Scottish local authorities have had block allocations of capital
spending. This system may be perceived as allowing greater individual
freedom to local authorities to determine priorities in capital
spending.(13) Since the system is relatively new, it is rather
difficult to assess its full impact, although initially local
authorities felt that allocations were too small to allow for an
element of real choice.

V.D. Lipman wrote in 1949:

> 'In the way in which English and Scottish local authorities
> come into existence and obtain their powers, in their method
> of finance and in their relationship to their respective
> central authorities they resemble one another so much as to
> be indistinguishable when contrasted with the outside world'.(14)

While recent changes in the structure of Scottish central and local
government require this conclusion to be modified, it raises the
difficult question of the type of criteria to be employed in the
comparison of the two systems. Despite the differences in size, the
distribution of functions, the number of local authority associations
and the structure of central government, to what extent are the
similarities greater than the differences? The effect of structural
differences can only be assessed when they are examined in conjunction
with the differences in the process and output of central-local
relations in Scotland. Similarities in these respects may outweigh the
differences.

PROCESS

One argument postulates that the scale of the relationship between
central and local government makes for differences in central-local
relations. Because there are only 65 local authorities as opposed to
411 in England (excluding London) there are more likely to be 'close'
relations between representatives of Scottish local government and
representatives of the Scottish Office, allowing each side to have a
greater understanding of the needs and problems of the other. This
difference is the most common perceived between English and Scottish
central-local relations. In oral evidence to the Select Committee on
Scottish Affairs, a member of the Association of County Councils in
Scotland stated ".... when I attend meetings in the south ... I realise
that we have less formality with our Scottish set-up in all the fields
of administration in local government'.(15) This view was also

expressed in the Wheatley Commission's Report, the Report of the Layfield Committee and the Scottish Office's Green Paper on local government finance.(16)

However, the importance which should be attached to this aspect of central-local relations is not clear. While it may be easier to remember the Christian names of a smaller group of people, it does not necessarily follow that the substance of the relationship will be different. Indeed, instead of drawing the conclusion that the smaller number of local authorities leads to 'mutual understanding', one could say the reverse, that the close relationship leads to <u>closer central control</u>:

> 'The Scottish Office has a more detailed knowledge of local strategies, circumstances and resources. This knowledge has enabled them to go a stage further than in England and Wales and to suggest, during 1975-6, appropriate spending levels for each authority.(17)

A related argument is that the Scottish Office departments, because they are located in the same buildings and under the responsibility of the same Secretary of State, are able to take an 'overall' or 'corporate' view of the activities of local government. While the various Whitehall departments give conflicting advice to local authorities the Scottish Office acts in a more 'corporate' fashion. The Royal Commission on Scottish Affairs commented in 1954:

> 'There is one major difference between the relationship of Scottish and English local authorities respectively with the central government in which to our mind Scotland has the advantage. In England Ministerial responsibility for the domestic functions affecting local authorities is distributed among a number of Ministers, and English local authorities are obliged to undertake consultations with several Ministers. In Scotland, however, one Minister, the Secretary of State exercises responsibility for the great majority of matters with which local authorities are concerned.(18)

This view was shared by the Central Policy Review Staff and is further reinforced by the role of the Finance Division in the Scottish Office. It coordinates those communications with local authorities which involve finance, thus avoiding the 'push-pull' effect of contradictory advice from the centre.(19)

However, statements about the corporateness of the Scottish Office are far more numerous than analyses. While the common responsibility of the Secretary of State is probably important in coordinating the approaches of the five departments, undue importance must not be placed on the role of the Secretary of State as a focus for a corporate approach by the Scottish Office. He is in London four days a week, and in view of the wide range of his activities it cannot be assumed that he exercises a strong coordinating role over the activities of the Scottish Office departments. Complaints about the 'push-pull' effect of uncoordinated central departments by local authorities are by no means absent in Scotland. For example, the

Association of County Councils in Scotland complained about the
'.... variations of approach which occur between central departments
with economic responsibility and those involved in expending
services'.(20)   In addition, there are reasons to doubt the success of
the Finance Division in coordinating the relationship between central
departments and local authorities. According to the Scottish Office's
evidence to Layfield, departments 'sometimes forget that every
exhortation to spend should be cleared by the Finance Division'.(21)

There are other mechanisms for fostering a coordinated approach.
Regional Reports are viewed as being a medium for cooperation between
central and local government in Scotland. They are seen as corporately
produced documents requiring a corporate response. As a result, some
observers have argued that Scotland has a lesson to teach England and
Wales. Required under 1973 Local Government (Scotland) Act, the first
Regional Reports were submitted in 1976. This innovation had two
consequences. First, in drafting the Reports, there was close
cooperation between central government and regional and island
authorities. The Scottish Office sent representatives to local
authorities to discuss the process of drawing up the Reports and issued
planning notes to help them in this task. 'All regions had worked
through drafts which had been seen by the Scottish Development
Department and so the final versions contained no great surprises for
central government'.(22) Second, the Regional Reports provide,
potentially, a means of communication between central and local
government which went beyond a focus on land use planning. J.D. Stewart
sees the Reports as

> '... new procedure (which) could reverse the strange
> imbalance of a system which provided a channel of
> communication about details of architectural design
> for a particular school, but not for discussion of the
> overall allocation of resources between programmes'.(23)

They provided a corporate rather than a service by service or
'functional' means of communication between central and local
government.

However, despite claims made for Regional Reports, there is, as yet,
no substantial evidence to show what impact they have had. The hopes
of J.D. Stewart may be balanced by the doubts raised by local
authorities about the '... value of striving towards a corporately
produced document when serious doubts exist about the ability of the
Scottish Office to respond corporately'.(24) The precise differences
made by the Regional Reports to the system of central-local relations
in Scotland depends on how this medium of communication is developed
by both sides. At present, it may be argued, the Scottish Office is
coming to regard Structure and Local Plans as more appropriate methods
of corporate planning.(25)

Since students of central-local relations in England place emphasis
upon the arrangements for the finance of local government, it may be
expected that differences in the grants system should result in
differences between England and Scotland. There are three major
reasons for suggesting that differences in the financial provisions
will cause different patterns of central-local relations. First, local

government receives a greater proportion of its total expenditure from central government funds than in England and Wales. The Layfield Committee commented:

> 'In Scotland, the drift towards centralisation has been even
> more marked. Local government services expanded rapidly
> during the 1960s and, as in England and Wales, this expansion
> was not only generated from the centre but also substantially
> financed from national taxation. The proportion of current
> expenditure financed from central grants grows even faster,
> and is now even greater, than in England and Wales'.(26)

Second, the Layfield Committee commented that the manner in which the level of the needs element of the Rate Support Grant is determined and the manner in which it is distributed 'provided greater opportunities for Ministers to influence local authorities than the formula based system of allocation in England'.(27) Third, the level of capital expenditure in Scotland is higher, and since it is subject to more stringent controls than current expenditure throughout the United Kingdom, the extent of central control in Scotland is greater.

While the level of central finance is frequently cited as a reason for the increase in central control over local authorities, caution is needed before inferring that local authorities in Scotland are more subject to central control simply because a greater proportion of their current expenditure is provided by central grants. Davey argues that independence of revenues can lead to increased autonomy only through the intervening variable of the centre relaxing administrative controls.(28) This view is reflected in the oral evidence to Layfield from the Association of County Councils in Scotland: 'If the will is there, local authorities will be given autonomy to deal with matters as they wish. If the will is not there it does not matter very much whether the grant is 70-75-80 percent or whatever.'(29)

However, the level of central finance does have an impact on the overall growth of local authority expenditure. Since the proportion of expenditure financed by central grants is higher in Scotland than in England and Wales, the decision to expand expenditure over and above the level provided for by central government grants will involve a proportionately higher increase in the rate burden. The Association of District Councils in Scotland submitted:

> 'While it is possible for individual authorities to develop
> single services at a rate in excess of the level provided
> for in the grants settlement, any authority developing at
> a faster rate over all the services distorts the grants/rates
> ratio and leads to increased rate burdens'.(30)

This statement relates to Layfield's second point: that the distribution of the needs element leads to an increased possibility of central control over specific services. There is no prima facie reason for believing this argument. The distribution of the grant by a weighted indicator may be cruder than the regression model applied to England and Wales, but there is no cause to assume that it leads to increased central control. The manner in which the RSG is built up, by bargaining about the growth of services within each functional area, may offer greater potential control except that the bargaining around these individual services does not impose a binding constraint upon local authority expenditure in that service area. Rather, it provides the local authority with an amount of central financial support which it can reallocate as it chooses. In the Rate Support Grant White Paper the purpose of financial control is described as follows:

'The Secretary of State is primarily concerned with the determination of grant related to the aggregate of local expenditure, so that estimates in the following paragraphs do not encroach upon the responsibility of individual local authorities for financial allocations to particular services in accordance with priorities determined by them'.[31]

This view of central finance is supported by the Association of County Councils in Scotland in reply to a question posed by the Layfield Committee:

'Q.   You don't make much pretence of having been given a Rate Support Grant and then it is your own to spend as you wish.

A.   Yes, we accept that. This is only a method of building up what we consider to be a realistic total of expenditure which the Rate Support Grant is going to support'.[32]

Thus the conclusion is that the provision of the Rate Support Grant, while it is different from that of England and Wales, does not necessarily lead to a greater potential for central control. It is still a block grant with no effective close ties to specific service areas.

The structural imbalance of the population sizes of local authorities in Scotland leads to two potential differences in the process of central-local relations. First, there is a difference in the 'logic of collective action'.[33] The activities of one region (i.e. Strathclyde) are more likely to have an effect on the overall system of local government in Scotland than is the case with local authorities in England and Wales. For example, in 1975-6, it was announced that overspending by local authorities would result in a corresponding reduction in the total RSG allocation in the following year. Hammersmith Borough Council could afford to pay less attention to this threat than Strathclyde. In Hammersmith, a reduction in the RSG for England and Wales would be imperceptible.[34] In Strathclyde, on the other hand, the effects of overspending would be more directly reflected in cuts in future grant income. Strathclyde's decisions affect half of the population of Scotland: no one local authority in England and Wales has such a direct stake in the system of local government.

The second potential difference revolves around the political 'clout' of the larger authorities. There is little evidence that the larger authorities such as Strathclyde have 'special relationships' with the Scottish Office, but conclusive evidence on such a relationship will

be difficult to find. The Scottish Office may try to anticipate the
reactions of Strathclyde Region to its proposals and tailor them
accordingly: smaller authorities may not benefit from such
consideration. Such problems to one side, it is clear that smaller
authorities are apprehensive about the role of the larger authorities.
In the passage of the 1973 reform legislation smaller local authorities,
especially those within Strathclyde, expressed fears about the
dominance of Strathclyde and Glasgow in the new local government
system.(35)   More recently, concern about the 'apparent influence of
the political big guns of the central belt'(36) led the smaller rural
authorities to campaign for amendments in COSLA's representative
structure, above all to reduce Strathclyde's representation on COSLA
committees. These amendments were narrowly accepted in July 1978.
Whether this change will mean that Strathclyde will be forced to leave
COSLA, making it impossible for the Convention to claim to represent
local government in Scotland, or whether the amendments will be
reversed, is still uncertain. However, this split within COSLA may
also reflect a concern among the smaller authorities about the role of
larger authorities in the pattern of central-local relations in
Scotland.

Any organisation which represents such a diverse group as Scottish
local authorities must expect some tension between its members.   In
addition to the cleavage between the 'big guns' of the central belt and
the smaller local authorities, two other tensions have appeared in
COSLA's ranks. First, there is a partisan cleavage: either between
Labour and Conservative controlled councils, or between Independent
controlled councils and councils controlled by one of the major parties
(perceived by the Independents as a 'political' versus 'non political'
cleavage). Second, there is a region-district cleavage, especially in
matters where powers are held concurrently or where legislation
requires a high degree of cooperation between region and district.
Usually conflicts within COSLA are the result of at least two of these
cleavages 'overlapping'. For example, recent complaints about the
excess influence of the 'political big guns' manifests a large
authorities-small authorities and a partisan ('political' versus non
political') cleavage. The controversy over the Housing (Homeless
Persons) legislation(37), where COSLA submitted two sets of comments
upon the proposed legislation, reflected a district-regional cleavage
superimposed on a partisan (Labour versus Conservative) cleavage.

The future of COSLA remains to be decided. However, at present there
is one local authority association representing local government in
Scotland as a whole. This arrangement is certainly at variance with
English practice, yet the substantive differences in central-local
relations which result are difficult to determine. As with the 'close
relationship' argument, the effect of the existence of one local
authority association is potentially double-edged. On the one hand a
single association may, as Wheatley proposed, present a united front in
its dealings with central departments, but on the other hand a single
local authority association may be more susceptible to central control,
since it may be argued with equal justification that it is easier to
persuade one group of people to do something than four.

The final important difference between English and Scottish central-
local relations derives from the existence of the Scottish Office.

Since the Scottish Office has a specific geographical or territorial
focus (compared with the functional focus of most Whitehall departments)
and has responsibility for most local government functions, it may have
a harmony of interests with local government in Scotland to gain
benefits from the centre in London. The argument is analogous to the
studies of French territorial administration where the prefect depends
upon the mayor to 'get things done' in his department, and the mayor's
success as a 'leader of the local community' depends upon the prefect's
ability to gain benefits from the centre for his commune. Both have a
common interest in securing the maximum benefits for their respective
regions from Paris and support each other in this common pursuit.
While there are few studies of the role of the Secretary of State for
Scotland 'getting the goods for Scotland' within the Cabinet(38), the
extent to which there is such a harmony of interests between the
Scottish Office and Scottish local authorities remains to be explored.
The higher aggregate local authority expenditure per head, as well as
the higher attributable public expenditure per capita, in Scotland than
in England is consistent with this hypothesis. In addition, Keating
has examined the role of the Scottish Office in securing benefits for
Scotland from Whitehall and, citing the evidence given by Haddow to the
Select Committee on Scottish Affairs in 1969, argues that Scotland has
had two major advantages over English regions. First, the Scottish
Office has secured a recognition in Whitehall that Scottish needs
required a higher level of public expenditure per head of population.
Second, excess funds could be claimed from Whitehall for specific
services, which could then be allocated to other services, thus
maximising public expenditure in Scotland:

Mackintosh: ... it would be possible for you to go and say
               we do not want to spend so much on, let us say,
               housing in Scotland, but this has not got to
               slip back into housing in England: it must come
               to roads or bridges or something in the Scottish
               total. I got you quite correct on that?

Haddow: Yes.(39)

Thus, to a certain extent, functional allocations from Whitehall are
transferred by the Scottish Office to other functional areas. This
aspect may be part of a 'game' between central and local government
along the lines of the 'games' articulated in the French studies.(40)
One would expect that reallocation across functional areas by the
Scottish Office would arouse opposition from local authorities,
complaining they were not receiving the amount of money for specific
services they 'should be getting'. However, they may be seen to
benefit not only because in absolute terms Scottish local authorities
get more money from central government but also because they are free
to reallocate within the total limit centrally allocated funds
negotiated for specific services.

There are, then, a number of potential differences between the process
of central-local relations in England and Scotland, which derive
largely from the structure of central and local government.
Unfortunately the evidence used to support the exposition of the
differences consists of more or less isolated statements thinly spread
about the sparse literature on Scottish government. There have been

no studies of the process of central-local relations in Scotland. Consequently, to examine the validity of statements about Scottish distinctiveness examination is required of the output of the relationship between central and local government.

OUTPUT

The output of central-local relations in Scotland is examined from the point of view of the nature and the impact of central finance upon local authorities' own expenditure decisions. The empirical analysis is in three parts. The first gives aggregate details of the level of central finance of Scottish local government. The second examines some of the hypotheses about the effects of central finance raised by Boaden.[41] The third attempts to measure more directly the influence of 'central pressures' upon local authorities in the light of requests by the Scottish Office to reduce the level of growth in local authority expenditure over the period 1976-7 to 1977-8.

In the year 1979-80, 61 percent of relevant expenditure in England and Wales was financed by central government grant, while the figure for Scotland was 68.5 percent. If one accepts the argument that the method of determining and allocating the needs element of the Rate Support Grant offers the Scottish Office a greater potential for control, then its control is further strengthened because the needs element forms a larger part of the exchequer grant to relevant expenditure than is the case in England and Wales. In 1979-80, the needs element made up 52 percent of the total exchequer grant in England and Wales and 72 percent in Scotland. There is, however, a difference between regional and district councils in Scotland. In 1978-9 regional councils, which spent 84 percent of total local authority relevant expenditure or 68 percent of expenditure including the housing revenue account, received over 67 percent of their relevant income from central grants, whereas for the districts the figure was 50 percent. Furthermore, the needs element of the Rate Support Grant made up 78 percent of the total exchequer grant for relevant expenditure in the regions whereas in the districts only 42 percent.

Layfield's comments about the level of capital expenditure being higher than in England and Wales and thus more subject to central control are less than well founded. The per capita level of capital expenditure is indeed higher in Scotland (around 15 percent), yet according to Layfield's own figures for 1973-4 the proportion of the total budget which is formed by capital expenditure was only 0.8 percent higher than the figure for England.[42]

The major conclusion to be drawn from the aggregate pattern of central finance is that Scottish local authorities gain more money from central government than is the case with their English counterparts. Local authorities have, therefore, been able to spend more per head of population than in England and Wales. Since 1972-3 Scottish local authorities' per capita expenditure has been between 10 and 14 percent higher than in England and Wales. How far is this apparent advantage balanced by a higher degree of central control over local expenditure?

Boaden examines the hypothesis that central pressures will make for uniformity in the provision of local services,[43] which he measures by per capita expenditure over a number of services. He concludes that because there is such a wide diversity in the expenditure patterns of authorities in England and Wales the 'agent' model of local authority relationships with central government is seriously challenged. If this test is accepted, then the case for central control in Scotland is probably weaker than in England and Wales. Taking the coefficient of variability, the standard deviation divided by the mean, of per capita expenditure on services in England and Wales and comparing them with the Scottish figures (although no direct comparison is possible in a number of services), we may conclude that if the English and Welsh figures are sufficient to reject the 'agent hypothesis', the Scottish figures are even more so: the coefficient of variability of per capita expenditure is on average much higher in Scotland (see Table 1).

Table 1: Coefficients of Variation in Per Capita Expenditure on Selected Services 1976-7 in Scotland and 1964-5 in England and Wales

Scotland Regional Services (N=12)		Scotland District Services (N=56)		England and Wales	
Education	0.17	Cleansing	0.29	Education	0.08
Roads and		*Libraries and		Libraries	0.22
Lights	0.58	Museums	0.41	Welfare	0.25
Social Work	0.24	*Planning	0.80	Children's	
		Leisure and		Services	0.28
		Recreation	0.41	Health	0.17
		Housing	0.36		
Mean = 0.32		Mean = 0.45		Mean = 0.20	

*N = 40

This approach may be criticised on the grounds that central government is not interested in securing uniformity in service provision, and still less in per capita expenditure on individual local services. Another approach was adopted by the members of the Layfield Committee. They felt that Scottish local authorities were 'closer to the government's wish' than their English counterparts since expenditure growth deviated only slightly from Scottish Office projections.[45] Indeed, in 1977-8 local authorities were praised by the Secretary of State for keeping within £2 million of government projections. However, soon after this praise had been given came reprimands for likely overspending by £30 million in 1978-9. Whether the 1978-9 figures are a minor lapse in the normally obedient behaviour of local authorities in Scotland or falsify the assumption that local authorities are more obedient is difficult to determine. To point to compliance in aggregate terms not only hides variability between authorities, but also tells us nothing of the mechanisms by which 'obedience' is secured.

To try to overcome some of these problems in analysing the output of the relationship between central and local government in Scotland, an examination was conducted of the reaction of individual authorities to a specific attempt by the Scottish Office to influence the behaviour of Scottish local authorities. A series of circulars issued in 1976 set out the government's wish to see local authority expenditure growth in 1977–78 kept to a minimum.(46) By focussing upon the extent to which local budgets grew over this period and the correlates of the level of growth some conclusions may be reached about the mechanisms of control at the disposal of the Scottish Office and the degree of discretion left to local authorities in decisions affecting expenditure growth.(47)

The level of central finance was found to have a negligible effect upon decisions to expand local authority expenditure. This conclusion calls into question the statement by the Layfield Committee that higher levels of grant in Scotland, and particularly the level of the needs element of the Rate Support Grant, permit greater control over local authorities by the Scottish Office. The political complexion of the local authorities also had little effect on the level of expenditure growth. Although the calls for stringency came from a Labour government, Labour authorities were no more likely to reduce expenditure growth than non-Labour councils. Neither were they less likely to do so, even though it could be argued that Labour philosophy is more strongly opposed to reductions in the level of growth than that of Conservatives, Nationalists and Independents.

The factors which exerted a greater influence upon expenditure decisions were beyond the direct control of the Scottish Office. Authorities which had to support expenditure in the previous year by heavy use of balances were likely to undertake high levels of growth in the year 1977–78. Authorities with high rate poundages were less inclined to expand services at a fast rate in 1977–78 and thus raise the rates to an even higher level in the following (election) year. Finally, the level of additional resources available to the authority, primarily through grant increases (although this cannot be interpreted as central control through the medium of grant levels),(48) had an influence on expenditure growth: the greater the increase in financial resources the higher the level of expenditure growth.

Similar analyses were conducted for other district services,(49) and similar conclusions were reached: the level of central grant and the needs element of the Rate Support Grant do not provide the Scottish Office with a means of pressurising local authorities to comply with the wishes of central government. In addition the analyses examined the hypothesis that districts within Strathclyde, and Glasgow District in particular, enjoy a special relationship with the Scottish Office. No statistically significant differences were found in the levels of expenditure growth of these specific authorities. However, the thesis that the size of Strathclyde and Glasgow has an effect on central-local relations in Scotland cannot be rejected for three reasons: first the analysis was confined to district expenditure only; second, the effects of this relationship may not be directly measurable as financial outputs; and finally, the other, albeit fragmentary, evidence for asserting that the imbalance in population sizes affects the process of central-local relations is strong.

CONCLUSION

This essay set out to show that there are a number of dimensions to the differences between central-local relations in Scotland and the remainder of Britain. These dimensions and undoubtedly a number of others still remain to be explored.(50) The examination of these differences has largely been suggestive, yet the positive conclusion is that the differences cannot be reduced to one dimension. The differences in structure, scale, the logic of collective action and the possibilities for a relationship with Whitehall which is not found in England, and possibly not even Wales, through the nature of the Scottish Office, and the differences in the provision of central finance, mean that a characterisation of central-local relations in Scotland as essentially the same as those in England and Wales is misleading.

To reduce the differences to one dimension, such as asserting that central government has 'greater control' over local authorities in Scotland, is equally misleading. First, the available evidence does not offer unambiguous support for this hypotheses. Second, to adopt the terminology of French students of central-local relations, the pattern of interactions between central and local government is a 'game'. Both sides are competing for advantage within a set of acknowledged rules. In the Scottish game there are not only different people, but different structures, strategies, playing fields and rewards. If further analysis were to show that local government in Scotland is 'closer to the government's wishes' than English and Welsh authorities, and this essay has shown that such a simple assumption cannot be made without further research, the results of any 'compliance' are likely to be different in the Scottish context. 'Even passiveness is always the result of a choice'.(51) In Scotland it is possible that the benefits from 'compliance' are different from those in England and Wales. In France the mayor's compliance with the prefect is a strategy to gain greater benefits for the commune from Paris, and the existence of the Scottish Office may give rise to a similar harmony of interests. In addition, 'compliance' may be more easily acknowledged in the smaller network of central-local relations in Scotland.

That there is a degree of satisfaction with the present rules of the game is demonstrated by the reaction of Scottish local authorities to suggestions to a change in these rules. In its evidence to the Layfield Committee the Association of County Councils in Scotland made it clear that it did not want a fundamental reform in the system of local government finance or in the pattern of central-local relations, but rather more money, or more specifically, a higher Rate Support Grant.(52) Similarly, the Convention of Scottish Local Authorities displayed a high degree of attachment to the present system in its reaction to the proposals to establish a devolved Scottish Assembly.(53) The fears of Scottish local authorities stemmed from uncertainty over three vital areas in central-local relations: first, over whether devolution would involve a further reorganisation of local government in Scotland; second, over whether the Assembly would seek to expand its powers by closer control of individual local services; finally, there was uncertainty over whether the benefits of the 'close and harmonious' relationship would be lost when Scottish local authorities had to negotiate with an elected assembly which may have had a different conception of its relationship to local authorities.

Since a restructuring of the local government system was identified by many as an early priority for the proposed Assembly,(54) the repeal of the Scotland Act meant that the future of the present structure of local government and central-local relations in Scotland were less uncertain. Although one commentator has referred to 'central-local government relationships in an uncertain future'(55) even after the repeal of the Scotland Act, the structure of the system is likely to remain essentially intact. The Conservative government has declared its intention of setting up a committee to review the functioning of local government in Scotland. However, the Secretary of State does not envisage any major structural changes resulting from this inquiry; the committee is likely to recommend minor boundary changes and alterations in the allocation of responsibilities such as planning among regions and districts. Perhaps the most important issues facing central-local relations in Scotland at present are identical in nature, if not in extent, to those in England and Wales: the calls for reductions in local expenditure and the sale of council houses. It remains to be seen whether, despite the apparent differences in the rules of the game, the results will be the same.

NOTES AND REFERENCES

(1) See for example Central Policy Review Staff, Relations Between Central Government and Local Authorities, HMSO, London, 1977.
(2) For a detailed review of the literature see R.A.W. Rhodes, Central-Local Relations in Britain: A review of the literature and a framework for analysis, SSRC, London, May 1978.
(3) See M. Crozier and E. Friedberg, L'Acteur et le Système, Le Seuil, Paris, 1977.
(4) See for example P. Gremion, 'Introduction a une étude du système politico-administratif local', Sociologie du Travail, 1/1970, 50-73; and J.P. Worms, 'Le préfet et ses notables', Sociologie du Travail, 3/1966, 276-295.
(5) For a full description see Royal Commission on Local Government Scotland, Report, Cmnd. 4150, HMSO, Edinburgh, 1969, pp. 25-38.
(6) For a comparison of local government functions in England and Scotland see: Committee of Inquiry into Local Government Finance, Report, Cmnd. 6433, HMSO, London, 1976, pp. 371-375.
(7) See 'Community Councils Research Projects', Scottish Office Central Research Unit Papers, Edinburgh, September 1978.
(8) Layfield Report, p. 378. (See note 6).
(9) Royal Commission on Local Government in Scotland, Report, p. 241.
(10) Commission on the Constitution, Written Evidence Vol. 2 (Evidence by the Scottish Office), HMSO, London, 1973, p. 16.
(11) For a description of the distribution of the grant see The Rate Support Grant (Scotland) Order 1978, No. 1871 (S. 165), HMSO, London, 1978.
(12) Local Government (Scotland) Act 1973, (Chapter 65), HMSO, London, 1973, section 94.
(13) See A.F. Midwinter, 'The Scottish Office and Local Authority Financial Planning: A Study of Change in Central-Local Relationships', Studies in Public Policy, University of Strathclyde, Glasgow, forthcoming.
(14) V.D. Lipman, 'Some Contrasts Between English and Scottish Local Government', Public Administration, Vol. 27, Autumn 1949, p. 168.
(15) Select Committee on Scottish Affairs (Session 1969-70), Minutes

of Evidence, HC 267-I, HMSO, London 1970, p. 61.

(16) Scottish Office, Green Paper on Local Government Finance, Cmnd. 6811, HMSO, Edinburgh, 1976, p. 5.

(17) Layfield Report, p. 87.

(18) Royal Commission on Scottish Affairs 1952-4, Report, Cmnd. 9212, HMSO, Edinburgh, 1954, p. 78.

(19) See: Relations Between Central Government and Local Authorities, p. 41 and Layfield Report, Appendix 10 (Evidence by the Scottish Office), p. 25.

(20) Layfield Report, Appendix 2, p. 81.

(21) Layfield Report, Appendix 10, pp. 27-8.

(22) S.T. MacDonald, 'The Regional Reports in Scotland', Town Planning Review, Vol. 49, No. 3, 1977, p. 233.

(23) J.D. Stewart, 'Have the Scots a Lesson to Teach?', Municipal Journal, 19 January 1977.

(24) B. Howat, 'Policy Planning and the First Regional Reports in Scotland', Occasional Paper No. 2, The Planning Exchange, Glasgow, 1976, p. 5.

(25) For an examination of Regional Reports in Scotland see: J. Friend, G. Lind and S. MacDonald, 'Future Regional Reports. A Study of Form and Content', Scottish Development Department, Edinburgh, November 1978.

(26) Layfield Report, p. 87.

(27) Layfield Report, p. 87.

(28) K. J. Davey, 'Local Autonomy and Independent Revenue', Public Administration, Vol. 49, Spring 1971, 45-50.

(29) Layfield Report, Appendix 10, p. 19.

(30) Layfield Report, Appendix 2, p. 91.

(31) The Rate Support Grant (Scotland) Order 1978, HC 40, HMSO, London, 1978, p. 5.

(32) Layfield Report, Appendix 10, p. 15.

(33) M. Olson, The Logic of Collective Action, Harvard University Press, Cambridge, Mass., 1969.

(34) See J.P. Mackintosh and B. Lapping, Inside British Politics, Granada Television, Manchester, 1977, pp. 62-66.

(35) M. Keating, 'The Scottish Local Government Bill', Local Government Studies, New Series Vol. 1, No. 1, 1975, pp. 55-6 and pp. 58-60.

(36) Municipal and Public Services Journal, 26 May 1978.

(37) Municipal and Public Services Journal, 17 June 1977.

(38) See for example M. Keating, 'Administrative Devolution in Practice: The Secretary of State for Scotland and the Scottish Office', Public Administration, Vol. 54, Summer 1976, pp. 133-145.

(39) Quoted in Keating, 'Administrative Devolution in Practice', p. 138.

(40) The interpretation of central-local relations in France drawn upon in this section is taken from Crozier and Friedberg, L'Acteur et le Système. See also: M. Crozier and J-C. Thoenig, 'The regulation of Complex Organised Systems', Administrative Science Quarterly, (21), 1976, 547-70; J-C. Thoenig, 'State Bureaucracies and Local Government in France' in K. Hanf and F.W. Scharpf (eds.), Interorganisational Policy Making, Sage, London, 1978.

(41) N. Boaden, Urban Policy Making, Cambridge University Press, London, 1970.

(42) Layfield Report, p. 380.
(43) Boaden, Urban Policy Making, pp. 11-20.
(44) Figures derived from Boaden, Urban Policy Making, p. 14. All
      figures about individual local authority expenditure in this
      paper are derived from Chartered Institute of Public Finance
      and Accountancy, Rating Review, CIPFA, Glasgow, annual.
(45) Layfield Report, Appendix 10 (Oral evidence from the Association
      of County Councils in Scotland), p. 11.
(46) See especially Scottish Office Finance Division circulars 27/76
      and 46/76.
(47) For more detailed discussion of this analysis see earlier versions
      of this paper which appeared in Studies in Public Policy 21,
      Centre for the Study of Public Policy, University of
      Strathclyde, Glasgow 1978 and Public Administration Bulletin,
      No. 28, December 1978, pp. 51-72.
(48) See E. Page, Public Administration Bulletin, op. cit.
(49) The services examined were cleansing and leisure and recreation
      services.
(50) Other differences include arrangements for auditing local
      authority accounts in Scotland, the possibility of closer links
      between local and national politicians through local parties
      and informal networks, and the argument that a large number of
      local authorities in Scotland are unable to employ personnel
      with a sufficient degree of specialised knowledge to deal with
      the complex set of arrangements which regulate central-local
      relations in Scotland.
(51) Crozier and Friedberg, L'Acteur et le Système, p. 47.
(52) Layfield Report, Appendix 2, pp. 80-1.
(53) See Convention of Scottish Local Authorities, 'Memorandum of
      Observations on the Government White Paper 'Our Changing
      Democracy', Edinburgh, 1975.
(54) For an examination of the campaign, results and consequences
      of the 1979 Devolution Referendum see D. Balsom and I.
      McAllister, 'Constitutional Change by Popular Choice: The
      Scottish and Welsh Devolution Referendums', Parliamentary
      Affairs, No. 3, 1979, pp. 394-409.
(55) L. Gunn, 'Central-Local Government Relationships in an Uncertain
      Future', Paper presented to the Convention of Scottish Local
      Authorities, St. Andrew's, Fife, March 1979.

An earlier version of this chapter appeared in Public Administration
Bulletin, December 1978.

9 The Network of Consultative Government in Wales

P.J. Madgwick and Mari James

INTRODUCTION

The relations of central and local government in Wales differ from
those in England because of the existence of the Welsh Office. Broadly
the Welsh Office acts as an intermediary in a centralised system,
presenting Welsh interests to the centre and, within limits, modifying
and adapting central policies in Wales. In particular, the Welsh
Office works through a network of consultation with local government in
Wales. The character of the system is in consequence central control
modified by continuous fragmented consultation. This network is a
subtle and elusive complex of relationships, and its nature is not
amenable to neat classification, except in confused or contradictory
terms: neither sharply hierarchical, nor profoundly devolutionary;
pluralist in some sense, but also tightly controlled. In a phrase
first applied to the government of medieval England, government in
contemporary Wales might be described as 'self-government at the
Queen's command': local self-government as an aspect of central control.

   Such an ambivalent conclusion might or might not be a matter for
rejoicing, depending on taste and political circumstance. However,
the area of independent action for any government is severely
restricted by external and economic constraints, the massive forces of
inertia and the growing militancy of workers and consumers.
Governments at any level can rarely soar into the blue sky of policy
innovation or variation. Hence judgments of the distribution of power
are concerned with modest incremental change, not with the remaking of
the Welsh economy and society. In sporting terms contemporary
government is a percentage game, but at the end of the season there are
few victories to record, only a shift of a point or two in the table of
averages, although political values may have been enhanced by the
struggle to achieve such shifts.

THE WELSH OFFICE

Since its establishment in 1964, the Welsh Office has developed into a
substantial, if relatively minor, department of state. It began with
two ministers and an establishment of 225; there are now three ministers
and a staff of over 2,500. Its vote in 1965-66 was £26 million, in
1974-5 £241 million. Initially the Welsh Office took over the functions
of the Ministry of Housing and Local Government and responsibility for
roads, together with a shadowy 'oversight' function on behalf of the
departments of Agriculture, Education, Health, Labour, Trade and
Transport and largely advisory functions arising out of its links with
the Welsh Planning Board and Economic Council. By 1978 it had acquired

responsibility for agriculture, economic planning and education
(except for universities); health and social services; manpower and
selective assistance to industry; sport, tourism and forestry.
Altogether it is responsible for over £1.1 billion of public spending.
'Responsibility' is used here as a term of British constitutional art,
which ranges in meaning from power with very little accountability to
accountability with very little power.

The growth in the scope and formal power of the Welsh Office was on
balance encouraged by the political changes of the sixties and
seventies. Devolution was fashionable and figured in arguments about
good government, as well as in peripheral and national protest.
British accession to the EEC weakened the claim for the integrity of
Westminster sovereignty. Participation was identified as a neglected
value in government and a remedy for alleged alienation and indubitable
militancy. Some tendencies which favoured the development of the
Welsh Office were not part of the devolutionary tide, such as the need
to set a limit to local government expenditure, the deflection of the
importunities of the pressure groups and the wrath of the media, and
the pacification of centrifugal elements in the centralist Labour
Party. Thus, the Welsh Office is a creation of the art of politics as
well as the science of public administration.

It is difficult to be precise about the influence of the Welsh
Office. The distribution of power might be seen to lie within a
matrix relating to the dual relationship of the Welsh Office towards
central government and towards local government, as in the figure
below.

		Welsh Office/Central Government Relations	
		Agency centre = London	Autonomy centre = Welsh Office
Local Government/ Welsh Office Relations	Agency	centralist	devolved centralist
	Autonomy	centre-local division of power	devolved pluralist. Centre (Welsh Office) - local division of power

It is unlikely that the Welsh Office can be permanently and firmly
placed in one of the four boxes in the matrix. Its position is likely
to shift according to the policy and the political context. Thus, on
the issue of official recognition of the Welsh language, the Welsh
Office could be expected to have a considerable degree of autonomy from
central government. Hence on this issue one of the two right-hand boxes
would be appropriate. If the particular aspect of Welsh language
policy in question is bilingual education, over which local authorities
have a considerable amount of discretion, then the 'devolved pluralist'
box would be the most appropriate. If, on the other hand, the issue
was bilingual road signs on trunk roads, which come under the
jurisdiction of the Welsh Office transport division, then 'devolved
centralist' would be more appropriate.

In practice it can be difficult to fit the relationships tidily into
one category. The strongest pressures, no doubt, are towards the first
(centralist) category, but there are some countervailing pulls towards

the fourth (pluralist). In the Welsh Office's relations with London, some elements in British government press it towards the agency category. Amongst these are the conventions of the constitution; the assumptions and organisation of the major parties; the structure and traditions of the civil service; functional and jurisdictional jealousies; the relative homogeneity of British society and the commitment to equality in public services.

Other factors are ambivalent and may push towards autonomy. First, the Welsh Office may develop (may have developed) a departmental culture favourable to independence. It is young, comparatively small and consciously Welsh in its staffing. It passed its first decade in an atmosphere of peripheral assertion and nationalist sentiment, when the promotion of a particular Welsh interest was no longer universally condemned as parochial aberration. Some differences in outlook show up in the Welsh and Scottish evidence to the Commission on the Constitution. It is not entirely fanciful to detect a departmental culture which maintains a pressure towards administrative independence in the Welsh Office. Such a tendency is favoured by departmental loyalties (of which it is a special case), but strongly discouraged by the centralist tradition of the British Civil Service.

Second, the Secretary of State gains from his ministerial status a protected position in the bureaucratic warfare of Whitehall. A guiding rule of the civil service is 'don't make trouble for the Minister' which means that the Secretary of State for Wales can expect that his interests will be defended and promoted in interdepartmental relations: he has a team entered in the game. This advantage may be as significant in the long run as the place of the Welsh Secretary in the Cabinet. In the British system a Cabinet minister has influence, but much depends on his seniority and political standing, his place in Cabinet committees and the acceptability of the departmental interests he represents. Viewed from London, the weighting of Welsh interests is an aspect of the government's regional policy. The persistent advocacy of a country interest may run against UK and English regional interests and may not often fit departmental and functional perspectives. Nor will it make for the expedition of decision.

Third, the Welsh Office has a special standing with the centre because of its own proximate relationship to local government. Meeting councillors 'over the table' is not an unknown experience in Whitehall, but most of the exchange there is with representatives at one remove, through the local authority associations. The Welsh Office can claim to speak with the special force of people with first hand knowledge.

These points arise from a general interpretation of the system and are difficult to validate. But the judgment is about modest relativities. The question is not whether the Welsh Office is or is not autonomous, but whether it should be regarded as lying a few points along from the agency end of the measure. Judging by impression again, it is clear that for a good deal of its work the Welsh Office is not an initiator but an agent for the London departments: not a 'front' or 'facade', for there is no deception, but an outlying office. What is then at issue is whether at the same time it has some scope for independent action, or effective pressure, in furtherance of independent views.

The function of the Welsh Office is intermediary. It is at once a
headquarters and a regional office, understanding the local authorities
and briefing ministers. It is always more than a regional office,
since its minister takes part in the crucial processes of Cabinet,
Public Expenditure Survey and, for local government, the Consultative
Council on Local Government Finance. Hence the centre-local relationships of Wales differ from those of England, in substance as well as
form.

Within this intermediary role, the Welsh Office has four functions:
executive; oversight; consultation; spokesman.

Executive

This function applies where the Welsh Office acts in the place of a
London department. It may be executing a different policy from that
of the appropriate London department or, more usually, just adding a
Welsh Office stamp and a Welsh language translation to the Whitehall
documents.

Oversight of government in Wales

This function is primarily exercised over local government in Wales and
involves the implementation of centrally determined policies by local
government. Also relevant here is oversight of non-elected bodies with
powers in Welsh government, such as the Welsh Development Agency, the
Development Board for Rural Wales and the Area Health Authorities.

Consultation

On the formal level this function is almost entirely with local
government through the local authority associations and their
committees. Most important here are the Joint Consultative Committees
of Welsh Office and local authority associations.

Spokesman in central government

This function represents the other face of the Welsh Office Janus. In
exercising the first function of 'Executive', the Welsh Office is acting
as the voice of London in Wales; in this fourth function the Welsh
Office is the voice of Wales in London. The most obvious and visible
manifestation of this function is the Secretary of State's seat in the
Cabinet.

Judged by decision and policies, the influence of the Welsh Office
has been modest though not, in relation to its size and all reasonable
expectations, negligible. In a whole range of matters of concern to
Wales the will of the centre has plainly prevailed. Limits on public
expenditure, the reform of local government, the abolition of REP, the
bias of funding towards the metro-cities and the rundown of the steel
industry are all examples.

The will of the centre applies just as sharply in the English regions.
The question is not whether the (more or less) even-handed centralism of
British government applies to Wales, but whether Wales has some special
claims to make its case, receive deferential treatment, and even
occasionally decide for itself.

In some other matters the Welsh Office seems to have had some influence on central government decisions; for example, closures in the steel industry have been at least delayed; Wales benefited from the adjustment of rate relief in 1974-5 (though the English cities have benefited more consistently from this kind of adjustment). There is no scale by which such influence can be measured: it amounts to adaptation and adjustment, but is not without significance.

In some other matters, where central interests were not at risk, the Welsh Office has more positive achievements to its credit. Thus it appears to have had the major influence in the establishment of the Wales Tourist Board, the enactment of Leasehold Reform, the preservation of some railway lines, a vigorous policy for derelict land, the priority given to the M4 motorway and action (or some would say inaction) on the one indubitably special problem of Wales, the Welsh langugage.

By contrast the influence of the Welsh Office with local government is substantial. The Office is the source or channel for central government power, especially in financial provision. The devolving of power from London to Wales has no necessary 'knock-on' effect in the devolving of power from the Welsh Office to local government. In its relations with local government the Welsh Office works through a network of consultation which softens the impact of power and may enhance the level of consent, without maximising it consistently.

THE WELSH OFFICE AND LOCAL GOVERNMENT: THE NETWORK OF OVERSIGHT AND CONSULTATION

There exists a complex network of consultation between the Welsh Office and local government, fitted on to the network of Welsh Office relations with the centre. The term 'network' implies a multiplicity of linkages, uneven in pattern and density, but with a significant nodal point in the Welsh Office. The quality of the flow is also uneven, ranging from regulation through information to consultation and negotiation. Command is generally too strong as a description. The characteristic mode is consultation rather than negotiation, with regulation or control as the objective.

The multiplicity of the system of consultation may be indicated by the following examples of bodies in regular consultative relationship with the Welsh Office:-

All local authorities individually at official level, and occasionally through councillors; the local authority associations including, Association of County Councils, Association of District Councils, Welsh Counties Committee, Council for the Principality (Welsh District Councils); territorial groups of local authorities, e.g. the three Glamorgans and Gwent, the Heads of the Valley district councils; professional associations concerned with local government, e.g. surveyors, teachers, social workers; the nominated all-Wales bodies, e.g. Welsh Council, Welsh Development Agency, Development Board for Rural Wales, Welsh Tourist Board; special government consultative bodies, the Consultative Council on Finance (Wales), the Consultative Council on Housing (Wales). A full list would be so long that it may seem the balance between taking action and talking about taking action favours talk rather than action.

Most of these consultative bodies are similar to those existing
elsewhere in the United Kingdom, but some are part of the special
Welsh network which centres on the Welsh Office.

The Welsh Local Authority Associations

The Welsh Counties Committee is formally a committee of the
Association of County Councils and thus tied into the England and Wales
network. Its members are the county representatives to the ACC, plus
one additional member. The honorary secretary (at present the chief
executive of Mid-Glamorgan) is a policy adviser to the ACC. The
Committee meets several times a year, but works also through panels of
advisers (usually chief officers). The Welsh Office consults
frequently with WCC on specially Welsh matters, but ACC remains the
major body for government consultation with local authorities.

The WCC might seem a rather shadowy organisation. It has no staff
or headquarters; its honorary secretary is likely to deal with the
Welsh Office in at least three other significant roles (on behalf of
ACC and as a chief executive for his own county, and in concert with
the three other southern counties). Some influential figures from the
old counties have departed (notably Lord Heycock). The WCC is probably
less significant in itself than as an additional expression of the
relative cohesiveness of the Welsh counties.

The Council for the Principality is the association of district
councils, established following the reorganisation of 1974. Its title
may properly suggest a certain commitment to a Welsh perspective and,
implicated in that, some sense of apartness from the counties. Like
the WCC, the CFP is linked to the England and Wales body, the
Association of District Councils, and again is partly shadowed or
paralleled by its Welsh Committee. It has no staff and is administered
by an honorary secretary, at present the chief executive for Merthyr
Tydfil. It has a small grant from ADC for office expenses, and an ADC
assistant secretary provides administrative services for its meetings.

The Council for the Principality has ready access to the Welsh
Office. But, as with the Welsh Counties Committee, there is little
which it does that might not be done as well by the councils themselves or the senior or parent Association of District Councils.
Judged by its output, the CFP has modest achievements to its credit.
It negotiated with the Minister for consolidated fees for land
transactions under the Community Land Act and it secured appropriate
commission for direct billing on behalf of water authorities. It has
successfully urged that applications for second improvement grants
should no longer be called in to the Welsh Office. It has helped to
promote regional groups to deal with the problem of industrial waste
(in Wales District Councils are responsible for disposal).

This kind of problem is more than the small change of local government, and not to be despised. However, the major impact of the CFP
probably lies in the furtherance of communication between the Welsh
authorities and with the counties and the Welsh Office. There has
been close consultation with the counties on finance, with 'pre-

meetings' to consider strategy; and on unemployment and on some
planning matters, notably out-of-town shopping facilities (there is
now a Joint Planning Conference). With the Welsh Office the CFP has
been concerned in the establishment of the Welsh Housing Consultative
Committee which initially was concerned with underspending on housing.

Rather more than the Welsh Counties Committee, it looks like a body
with some political vitality. There is a Labour majority, and the
Labour Secretary of State for Wales happily supported it, in
preference to the Conservative controlled ADC (1978). It is organised
on party lines; its focus on Wales expresses nationalist (and Welsh
Labour Party) aspirations; and the parties out of power, Plaid Cymru
and until 1979 the Conservatives, use it as a forum. Its members
tend to be of high calibre. They are all agreed on the extension of
district powers, and advocate further reorganisation of Wales into
unitary authorities (based on the districts) and working to an
Assembly. This political edge occasionally sharpens the blander
exchanges of consultation. But in the end its lack of staff,
including specialists in the major fields, weakens it, in comparison
with the ADC and the councils themselves.

Thus it seems that the prime function of the local authority
associations is to provide a forum for the exchange of views by
practitioners at particular levels of local government. But an
equally important function is to enable the authorities to make more
effective representations to central government in the form of the
Welsh Office. These representations take two forms; they are either on
a specific issue, subject or problem of implementation and as such can
take the form of an appeal for clarification, for separate Welsh
treatment or even for an extension of a closing date. The more regular
form of consultation is through the formal consultative committees.
The Welsh Office as well as the Welsh Counties Committee and the
Council for the Principality are represented on the two principal
committees, that on Housing in Wales and on Local Government Finance.
The latter has so far largely devoted its time to a pilot negotiation
for a separate Welsh Rate Support Grant. The existence of these
committees is an official manifestation of the need for continuous
contact and consultation between the Welsh Office and local government.

The network of consultation so far described lies within a political
system in which parties and pressure groups have a continuing and
occasionally substantial role. The influence of parties shows up in
the relations of councillors and the Welsh Office Ministers. Under a
Labour government and a Labour dominated Council for the Principality,
the party system acted as a strong reinforcement to the normal channels
of communication. It was a major factor in the decision by the Welsh
Office to recognise the Council for the Principality in preference to
the Association of District Councils for official negotiations, and it
served to minimise, although not altogether prevent, any problems of
disagreement between that level of local government and the Welsh
Office. It also helped to put what might otherwise have been rather
formal relations onto an informal and friendly footing. Intervention
by Welsh Office Ministers (which always has an impact on decisions)
may also arise from party and constituency pressures.

Among pressure groups, it is known that bodies like the CBI and the
Welsh TUC, NFU and FUW make continuing representations to the Welsh

Office. Local and <u>ad hoc</u> protest groups attract considerable
publicity and plainly exert pressure on the Welsh Office. Spokesmen
may blush or bluster; sometimes decisions are modified. There are
recent examples of the Welsh Office 'standing firm' and 'backing down'.
More exact assessment is not possible yet, but at least it may be
concluded that the Welsh Office is not always insensitive to public
outcry.

Sensitivity might not imply concessions, actions to redress
grievances and the modification of policy. One view of the Welsh
Office function is that it deflects and defuses dissatisfaction and
criticism. It is the whipping boy or 'Aunt Sally' of the system. Its
job is to blush, to say 'ouch!', making its critics feel better, while
holding the central government's policy line.

THE NETWORK OF CONSULTATION

This complex network of consultation for control might be seen as two
interlinked channels. The distinction is purely analytical: the
analogy is with stereo signals, one riding 'piggy-back' on the other.
One channel is concerned with control and draws its power from the
statutory basis of the whole system, reinforced by Treasury's concern
for macro economic planning, and utilising the regulatory instruments
of grants and cost yardsticks, national standards, audit; and backed
by the final sanction of new legislation for control. But the channel
does not work smoothly: the signal to noise ratio is unsatisfactory.
The intention was never rigid control, and the instruments are not
entirely adequate to such a purpose. There may be more destructive
interference from party, interest groups and popular politics.

Hence there is a second channel, concerned with consent. It is
softer and fuzzier, essentially a noisy channel, and not always in
phase with the control channel. Sometimes the control channel
overrides the consent channel, mostly the latter softens, diffuses and
confuses control. When the two channels interlock, the music is indeed
sweet, and the full harmonies of consultation are heard. This is 'self-
government at the Queen's command'. But even when there is disharmony,
there is still scope for dissent within the ambiguities of the message.

The Welsh Office communicates vigorously on both channels, helping to
integrate the network and join the process of control to the process of
consent. 'Crosstalk', interference by one channel with the other, is
a necessary function in the political system.

This analogy fits some recent interpretations of centre-local
relations. The objective of governments since 1945 has been to
encourage local choice within an overall framework of control, or
control in outline set by the centre. The Layfield Report quotes the
White Papers of 1957, 1970 and 1971 in illustration, and argues that
the intentions have not been met and that the system has diminished
local discretion. Nevertheless, governments struggle to temper control
with consent through local choice (pp. 68-70). Rhodes, in his paper
for the Layfield Committee, argues that centre-local relations form
'a system of complex interactions ... the basis is negotiation and
bargaining ... control appears to be a completely inappropriate
description of the relationship' (pp. 190-191). These terms,

negotiation and bargaining, may in fact overrate the strength of local government in the relationship. But local authorities are not entirely without a negotiating position, for their dependence on central funding is balanced by the centre's dependence on the local government's continuing to deliver services at a standard and cost which will not reflect adversely on the centre.

Ashford concluded that

close examination of the patterns of expenditures for the local government system of Britain, and I suspect for most other industrial countries as well, suggests that the term 'control' is hardly relevant. The only local expenditure where the British government was able to establish something deserving the label 'control' was education ... [1]

The catch for central government here is that it often takes the blame for the failings of local government, and this distortion of democratic responsibility perversely enhances the cause of local democracy. Both Ashford and Rhodes emphasise another factor in the centre-local relationship, inertia. 'The forces of inertia (which) central direction has to overcome are phenomenal'.[2]

Now inertia may or may not represent local choice, but it certainly does not indicate rigid central control. Rather it suggests either that central and local government are both sunk in happy consensual immobility, or that the centre has a hard time trying to promote any kind of action in the locality. For this stimulative function, it needs to alert, persuade and excite as well as press, influence and command: in short it needs the dual control/consent process of consultation.

Thus it appears that the consultative process as described here fits some general understandings of the nature of centre-local relations. The process fits too into the bureaucratic culture. There is first a fraternity or community of official policy makers, whose relations are governed by the conventions of civilised intercourse: courtesy; a reluctance to disturb, still less to break up the group; occasional weariness. First names are used, but the relationship is still comparatively formal, friendly but not matey. Civil servants are not professionally gregarious: they want to get on with their work. Nevertheless, the process of consultation is more than merely courteous and gains a momentum from personal relationships. Consult and the world consults with you; command, and life can be altogether lonelier

Consultation again suits the bureaucratic convention that efficiency must be softened by democracy; that, while good government is undoubtedly the objective, that target itself includes an element of representativeness and consent. The civil service view of local government is not without ambivalence. Consider this extract from a work of fiction

'With the vicar, Mrs. Poulteney felt herself with two people. One was her social inferior, and an inferior who depended on her for many of the pleasures of his table, for a substantial fraction of the running costs of his church and also for the happy performance of his non-liturgical duties among the poor;

and the other was the representative of God, before whom she had metaphorically to kneel'.[3]

There is perhaps an analogy here for the centre's view of local government. Admittedly the first part is more appropriate than the second. Awe of divinity may be too strong as a characterisation of the good civil servant's view of the democratic value inherent in local government. Rather he has a firm respect for constitutional propriety, and some sensitivity to the occasional political salience of local government issues. In practice the reconciliation of efficiency and democracy is accomplished (so it is believed) by the general strategy of local choice within central outline control; specifically by local formulation and central allocation; and through non-specific and formula grants.

Finally the process of consultation fits the ambiguities of the system, which if not intended are now established. Some of the ambivalence arises in Wales from the very proximity of the centre to the local authorities; for proximity may promote both sensitivity in responsiveness and particularity in control. There is a confusion of responsibility, in the sense of a shifting or avoidance of initiative and answerability. The special qualities of consultation for control and consent thrive in the gaps and hesitations of this system.

This interpretation does not fit the persistent and well-supported arguments of the local authorities for emancipation from restriction and restraints. Each new device in the central-local relationship, it is claimed, has been designed for and sold as providing local choice within a centrally determined framework. Yet the experience of local authorities has been that the Housing Investment Programme, housing cost yardsticks, Transport Supplementary Grant, have all turned into processes of tight and detailed central control. While conceding the force of these complaints it may be countered that recent governments have acquired an understandable terror of excessive public expenditure, and that local authorities have contributed heavily and without much central restraint, indeed with central encouragement, to that expenditure. Some local complaints are admittedly concerned with comparatively trivial interference, and delays. The Welsh Office's resistance to specific grants is a continuing indication that its conscious objective is not unmitigated central control.

The pattern of centre-local relations indicated here is not easy to evaluate. It is not 'centralist' in the pejorative sense, nor is it highly diffused and participatory. It does not move in a highly directed way, nor much at all. But the term 'directionless consensus' applied by Rose to British central government (under Wilson) could not catch the ceaseless activity in the networks of control, persuade, check, dissuade. That network to consultation is the nerve-system of central-local relations, and in Wales of the relations of Welsh Office and local government.

THE NETWORK AT WORK

The central function of the Welsh Office is financial. It colours all other relationships and indicates and marks off (or even fixes and defines) the intermediate area in which the Office moves. The Office

takes part in the processes of the Public Expenditure Survey, and
negotiates the 'global' allocations of funds to Wales including capital
and current expenditure, loan sanctions and Rate Support Grant. The
PESC process involves lengthy official study and negotiation, with final
decisions by the Cabinet. The RSG process involves formal consultation
with local authorities through the Consultative Council on Local
Government Finance (for England and Wales) and its Welsh counterpart
(for purely Welsh concerns).

Negotiations with central government tend to be dominated by the
Treasury, which has abandoned its traditional obsession with candle
ends for a concern for macro economic planning. The history of public
spending in Britain since 1945 shows that the Treasury never won the
war to control public spending until it introduced the brutal
instrument of cash limits. The Rate Support Grant is intended to be a
sensitive form of control, but is obscure and uncertain, and tends to
confuse responsibility. The Consultative Councils also diffuse
responsibility. These are in fact characteristic devices in the
system of consultation for control. According to one view, the
Consultative Councils were intended to appease the Treasury's demand
for tighter control: that is, they were devices for control not
participation. If so, this example is a classic illustration of the
nature of consultative management.

The Welsh Office fights for global funds for Wales, arguing for a
particular pattern of allocation. Once the settlement is made there
remains a modest discretion in actual distribution. A Welsh Office
official, in evidence to the Layfield Committee, said 'it is true to
say that we in one sense have more opportunity than Whitehall
departments for virement'. He went on to give as an example the use of
part of the roads allocation for derelict land reclamation. But the
central departments had the advantage of much bigger allocations. For
example, in the case of derelict land, Wales had four times more than
its proportionate share of five per cent of UK funds, but England,
concentrating its expenditure on two regions comparable with Wales,
was able to spend well over twice as much as Wales on each.

The official concluded his remarks on financial discretion by
minimising its significance:

'... it is rarely used, because the fact is that we are anxious
that all our programmes should be successful ones. We want to
have good roads, good hospitals, good schools, all at least as
good as they are in England. It is sometimes said in certain
quarters that the Welsh are lucky, that they can choose between
having good roads or good hospitals, but I have found, having
been principal finance office of the Welsh Office for the last
two years, that by and large it is an unreal power.'(4)

Even limited financial discretion requires that the Welsh Office must
first win the money from the centre, and, second, control its expending
in the localities. This concern raises new difficulties where the
spending is within the jurisdiction of local authorities and the grant
is not specific. Further the local authorities may and do appeal
directly to the centre, thus nicely pointing up the occasional
ambivalence, not to say vacuousness, of the Welsh Office's position.

Notwithstanding these limitations, the local authorities depend on central finance, and the Welsh Office is the channel through which it flows. Thus, finance is the key to the influence of the Welsh Office, and is at the heart of its engagement in the network of consultative government.

The Welsh Office is responsible for trunk roads, but the counties act as agents and are deeply involved in the planning of trunk road schemes. For other roads, the local authorities have discretion in making up a programme, but the Welsh Office negotiates for funds for county roads, and allocates to the authorities. Thus the Office has the power of final choice over a major area of public goods (amounting to £123 million in 1975-6). Many of the criteria of choice are open to quantification or to technical argument, and the consultative network is largely in the hands of professionals.

Given the problems of resource allocation, tension inevitably arises, and officials mentioned the occasional difficulties in securing information, and coordination. However, the priorities set by the Welsh Office for the building of trunk roads probably reflect the sum of pressures. These are in the order: M4 (E-W link in the South); A55 and to a lesser extent A5 (E-W link in the North); A470 (North-South road). The last appeals to those who want a Welsh road system, rather than a system which ties Wales into the major English routes. The priority given to the M4 motorway reflects the overriding objective to revitalise the Welsh economy. Its building is the most positive act of government towards that end, and recent development in the motor industry in South Wales could be regarded as a first indication of its success. Almost everybody in the consultative network is eager to claim responsibility for the priority given to the M4. In the nature of this kind of decision making, all such claims have some validity. However, it does seem that the Secretary of State gave a vital push to a cause which reflected a good deal of political pressure and the best advice and most advanced preparations of his professional advisers.

The construction of roads, more than any other policy in the field of the Welsh Office, is subject to formal procedures for public participation. Here the network extends to the people themselves, through the procedures of public inquiry. Some of the Welsh Office's endeavours to present the choices by means of exhibitions, publications and public meetings are impressive, and do not look at all like the work of 'bureaucratic tyranny' and the 'centralist enemy.' Nevertheless conflicts over the route of highways, and over the allocation of resources, are sensitive politically. They are subject to inter-governmental tension and complaint ('the Welsh Office as a whipping-boy'), and to occasional 'political' intervention by Ministers.

With housing the Welsh Office carries out in Wales the functions of the Department of the Environment, mainly involving the negotiation of a global sum for housing expenditure in Wales, and its allocation according to needs as perceived by the Welsh Office after consultation with the local authorities. This brute power is largely negative. The Welsh Office can approve and encourage but not compel; it does not build houses. Further the Welsh Office has regulatory powers over building standards and cost yardsticks (it has recently ruled that solid oak staircases were, in the official phrase, 'over yardstick'). It has some quasi-judicial functions, for example, the confirmation of demolition and compulsory purchase orders; and it spends considerable time offering advice, for example, on dealing with the Housing Corporation and Housing Associations, and on the better care of housing stock, which was circulated at the express wish of the Housing Consultative Committee.

The Welsh Housing Consultative Committee was established in 1977, mainly as a response to the revelation of substantial underspending on housing. It includes councillors and officials from the districts and officials from the Welsh Office with an official chairman. It has worked in two groups, on needs and rehabilitation.

Housing looks to be one of Wales' less tractable problems, and the consultative network seems to have done little more so far than enable councils to express their frustration, and the Welsh Office to demonstrate its patience in face of (what it sees as) unjustified criticism. Some critical participants in this consultative system believe that it allows, indeed encourages, the blurring or shuffling off of responsibility ('it's not our fault') and the discouragement of initiative ('we can't do much ourselves').

Following the reorganisation of the health service in 1974, the functions of the old Welsh Board of Health were taken over by the Welsh Office (except for the Welsh Health Technical Services Organisation). The Health and Social Work Department of the Welsh Office comprises three groups, two headed by Under Secretaries and one by a Chief Medical Officer (assisted by other medical officers, a Chief Dental Officer, a Scientific Adviser and a Pharmaceutical Adviser). The Department is responsible for (deals with, oversees) the eight Area Health Authorities of Wales.

Its major responsibility is again the allocation to the areas of funds allotted after due consultation by DHSS. It is assisted in the process of allocation by an official Steering Committee on Health Service Resource Allocation. The reorganised health service, like reorganised local government, was equipped with a new 'management philosophy' as well as a new structure. While local government was more consciously managerial in style and concerned with corporate management, the new health service was born with a commitment to consultation. This process was intended to include the consumers of the service, as well as the medical professionals; and might be thought to compensate for the reduction in the number of elected representatives involved in the management of the health service.

The problem of the health service is not simply 'a centralist pull from the height of the civil service hierarchy in London to the outer extremity of the machine in Wales'.(5) Given the enormous cost of the service, there is no escape from central control of funding. Nor is there any way within the present system by which local people can choose between spending on their own area and a neighbouring one. In practice the system of administration has been characterised by central allocation and local agitation. The processes of consultation seem to have failed to secure consent for what is fairly tight central control. Popular attachment to local hospitals sometimes seems peculiarly irrational; though equally it may be a perfectly valid judgement of consumer interests. In Wales both ministers and members of parliament have interested themselves in local discontents, the former with more power to affect the outcome. There has been a distinct danger of the growth of a kind of pork-barrel politics, in which localities compete with each other for public goods which ought to be allocated by criteria of comparative need.

CONCLUSIONS

This review of particular policy areas shows that finance is the central function of the Welsh Office, and determines in general the shape and direction of the relationships, of the Welsh Office with both the London and local governments. But the nature, the texture of the relationships is characteristically consultative management, which ranges from direction and formal regulation, to informal advice and friendly suggestion. Different policy areas and different times attract different styles of management, within the general character of consultation.

The terms 'network' and 'consultation' are central to this account of government in Wales. While the term network implies a complex but comparatively free flow of communication, exact measures of political network have still to be developed. These tests would include some assessment of density, pattern (peaks and nodal points), stability, flow (free or inhibited), evenness and quality. The term consultation is here rather heavily loaded to imply a form of management employing consultative processes to achieve control and consent.

The process of consultation has to operate in conditions and in a climate hostile to consensual government, in which a government under severe financial constraints faces militant workers and consumers in a contest disrupted from time to time by the incursions of local and group oriented politicians. However, these conditions enhance the political value of the consultation process; indeed they make it necessary. The consultative process softens the hierarchical ordering of authority and supplements the constitutional procedures of responsibility; it assists accommodation (the achievement of control and consent) in a system otherwise characterised by adversary relation-ships; and improves the articulation of politics.

Consultation is not intended to be a disguise for central control. Rather the objective is the achievement of the public good as seen by the central government through courteous and intelligent discussion. The management philosophy strongly favours local autonomy (consider the elaborate devices to avoid specific grants to local authorities) though management practice is affected by the paternalism associated with any profession which sells its expertise for what it sees to be the benefit of others.

In the end the system cannot be characterised simply as either centralist or pluralist. It is essentially a centralised funding system operating through a pluralist network of execution and implementation, confused and even disoriented by size, complexity, inefficiency, as well as more or less legitimate pressures. It is a 'democratic' system within the British tradition.

NOTES AND REFERENCES

(1)   D. Ashford, 'The Effects of Central Finance on the British Local
        Government System', British Journal of Political Science,
        Vol. 4, 1974, p. 320.
(2)   R.A.W. Rhodes, 'Centre-Local Relations', p. 190. in a Report of
        Committee on Local Government Finance, Appendix 6, HMSO,
        London, 1976.
(3)   John Fowles, The French Lieutenant's Woman, Panther, London, 1969,
        p. 24.
(4)   Committee of Inquiry into Local Government Finance, notes of a
        meeting, Cardiff, 10 February 1975, p. 6.
(5)   J. Osmond, The Centralist Enemy, Christopher Davies, Ammanford,
        Dyfed, 1974, p. 86.

10   Social and Political Theory and the Issues in Central-Local Relations

Patrick Dunleavy

This essay(1) reviews four major theoretical approaches to the analysis of the state with a view to setting out the different conceptions of the major issues or problems in central local relations which they suggest. The main aim is to show both that these issues or problems cannot be defined or identified in any theory-independent way, contrary to the premises of much administrative or management orientated work in this field, and that many of the most substantively interesting questions in central-local relations have been conspicuously ignored in the existing literature. The four theories are pluralist analysis; elite theory; neo-pluralist approaches and Marxist analyses.

PLURALIST ANALYSIS

Work in a pluralist perspective has been the predominant theoretical approach adopted by political scientists in North America and (less self-consciously) in Britain since 1945. Essentially pluralist theory posits the existence of a state apparatus which is highly autonomous and at least potentially neutral, capable of adjudicating fairly the struggles of conflicting social interests.(2)

  Pluralist accounts of national and local politics see governmental institutions as made responsive to the wishes of citizens by the mechanisms of representative government, such as electoral competition, an extensive interest group process, and the safeguards built into the recruitment and socialisation of political leaders ensuring deference to the public interest. Political power in this view is concentrated in the hands of elected officials, who themselves operate in legally defined contexts.(3) The close contacts between decision makers and a large number of separate elites are recognised, but decision makers are presented as extensively constrained by the existence of an open political process and by rigorous public and media scrutiny.(4) The individual citizen, interested minority groups and 'public opinion' are all seen as potentially important political influences.(5) Their effectiveness is sustained by a participatory political culture stressing the ability of ordinary citizens to organise themselves in groups, to procure administrative redress through their elected representatives or judicial procedures, and to exert a fundamental measure of control over the development of their society.(6) Pluralist theory has thus been overwhelmingly input orientated.

  This input orientation, and the consequent uneven development of empirical research, have had detrimental consequences for pluralist theory's application to problems of central-local relations. Since attention has fastened on the relations between citizens and representative government, there has been a tendency for interrelations between tiers of government, within the state apparatus, to disappear from view. The problems of assessing the extent of representative institutions' control over the remainder of the state apparatus and over state policy have been the subject of little systematic inquiry, although there has been no shortage of polemics against the rise of an 'administrative state'.(7) In the absence of well developed approaches to the analysis of policy formulation and of policy outcomes, intra-state relations seem to have been treated as unproblematic or 'non political' in the sense of being concerned with problems capable of rational technical solution.

Only when central-local relations are more intrinsically involved with aspects of democratic legitimacy and with the input mechanisms of representative government have problems of central-local relations been viewed as more important. The two basic justifications of local government in pluralist theory draw on first, J.S. Mill's argument that the existence of local institutions strengthens and enhances democracy by affording wider opportunities for participation in government and for the training and involvement of citizens in politics;(8) and second, the argument from differential preference intensities, according to which the strong local preferences of minorities should be focused within local political institutions where legitimate local interests (i.e. those not interfering with the basic methods of societal control and direction through majority rule) can be identified.(9) Central-local relations could raise serious issues for pluralist theory in a number of circumstances. First, they would become problematic where levels of participation in local government are less than those in national politics. Where levels of local participation are less than might realistically be expected, and this lack of involvement can be shown to be causally linked to the extent of central control over local government, then obviously Mill's justification of local government is called into question. Second, where national and local polities are separately constituted and elected then central-local conflicts can pose problems of democratic legitimacy; two or more 'electoral chains of command' are set up, linked to different sets of citizens and representatives, and capable of producing different or contradictory results. Third, central-local relations could become problematic where there are marked differences in the 'democratic quality' of government between the two tiers, i.e. where the democratic legitimacy of the two tiers is unequal.

Although these three issues are apparently contradictory each of them has been raised by different groups of researchers as relevant to the British context.

First, British local government presents a classic instance of low levels of participation in local politics coinciding with apparently high levels of central government influence over local policy formation, and numerous commentators have unhesitatingly identified a causal link between the two.(10) Most recently the Layfield report has argued that low levels of citizen involvement in local government can be directly explained in terms of the shrinking financial autonomy of local authorities vis a vis the central departments. Layfield argued that unless a decisive attempt to reverse this position is made, the justification of local government will become so attenuated that it would be more rational for some key local functions (such as education) to revert totally to the central state.(11) The problem with this view

is that no satisfactory evidence of the causal mechanisms involved
seems to have been produced. The account given is plausible enough:
basically it argues that people do not vote in local elections or
participate in local politics (even though there is a numerically
greater probability of an individual's vote or participation making a
difference to policy decisions at this level), because the scope of
such decisions is so narrowly circumscribed in advance that the
potential benefits do not exceed the costs of involvement.[12] But for
this argument to be accepted as relevant to central-local relations in
Britain it is necessary to show that political behaviour approximates
the rational interest model which underlies so much representative
theory.[13] In fact, it is easy to demonstrate that this condition is
not met. There is very little evidence that people's political
behaviour is governed by the considerations cited by Layfield. In
French rural communes, turnout at elections is around eighty per cent
(over twice the top levels in British local government); but not only
do French rural communes have very little administrative or financial
autonomy, the elections where such turnouts are recorded are frequently
both overtly non-partisan and contested only by a single 'list' of
candidates.[14] Just as political behaviour here clearly has little
to do with the extent of local autonomy, so Layfield failed to cite a
single piece of scientific evidence that turnout at British local
elections ever has been or ever will be affected by changes in local
government's autonomy or powers. The available evidence on patterns of
political behaviour in Britain suggests that such considerations have
very little influence.[15] Certainly one can be reasonably confident
that Layfield's suggested reforms would have next to no impact on the
existing entrenched patterns of electoral participation.

The second problem of central-local relations highlighted by
pluralist theory, the existence of potentially conflicting lines of
democratic or electoral legitimacy, presents considerable difficulties
in Britain because of the lack of any formal constitutional entrench-
ment for local or sub-national political institutions.[16] This lack
of a distinctive legal underpinning for the scope of operations of
local government places the existence of a decentralised government
tier as a policy issue on a par with other policy issues. Thus a
clear set of institutional issues cannot be separated from substantive
debate over policy. Historically this consideration has tended both
to undermine the theoretical justification of local government in terms
of spatially based differential preference intensities, and to impart
a pronounced normative/ideological slant to pluralist discussions of
central-local relations. The so-called 'agency' and 'partnership'
views of the central-local relationship are good examples of this
tendency.[17] Underlying much of the rhetorical debate which these
views crystallise, however, there are serious scientific questions.
These concern the origins, structural form and social distribution of
pro-decentralisation values; the ways in which attitudes to decentralisation are maintained and changed; and the social and political
interests involved in change. For example, many pluralist writers
have linked the diminishing 'autonomy' of local government to the
growth of 'redistributive politics' under the 'welfare state'; but the
extent to which the two trends are linked has never been systematically
researched.[18]

The third problem highlighted by pluralist theory, the possibility of
variations in the levels of democracy between different tiers of the

state, raises particularly serious issues in the British context. The only account of representative government which provides a clear mechanism by which political elites can be made responsive to a mass electorate is the Schumpeterian model of electoral competition and its later rational choice variants.[19] Such accounts play a key role in British pluralist analyses. But whatever their application at the national level, they are basically inappropriate at a local level, because turnout and partisan swing at local elections seem to be predominantly influenced by movements of opinion for or against the national government, and to be very little influenced by local considerations. Newton concluded: 'No more than ten per cent of the variance in Birmingham election results (in the period 1945-65) may be attributable to local factors.'[20] If more comprehensive analyses show the determination of local election results by national factors to be as extensive as Newton suggests, an insurmountable problem would be posed for Schumpeterian accounts. Instead of competitive party elections at the local level constituting the Pareto-optimal mode of social choice posited by some rational-choice theorists, they would serve only as a means of randomly destabilising incumbent local elites, irrespective of their responsiveness to local opinion. If local decision makers remain ignorant of (or refuse to accept the importance of) national factors, and thus continue to subscribe to local democracy myths and adjust their policies in the light of local election results, then local elections could only function to introduce irrationality into policy, by leading to policy changes in response to electoral 'signals' with which local policies are almost wholly unconnected.[21] Finally, this problem of the absence of local mechanisms for producing responsiveness to public opinion is further magnified by the extent of continuous one party control of local government. In a recent analysis the 1973 local election results have been used as an index of maximum Labour gains and the 1976-8 results as an index of maximum Conservative gains since both are good years for the parties in national opinion swings. The results suggest that at the most important governmental tier (i.e. at the London borough, metropolitan district and non-metropolitan county levels), up to seventy five per cent of the population live in areas where variations in party control of the council will not occur.[22] Taken together both these points raise a serious issue for pluralist analysis, since the democratic content of central decision making is likely to be very much greater than that of local authority decision making (using the criteria for ascribing democratic legitimacy to policy which are accorded key importance by pluralist theory itself).

ELITE THEORY

For much of the early post war period elite theory defined the principal alternative to pluralism within North American political science and political sociology. Essentially elite theory approaches posit the existence of a cohesive ruling elite in which power is concentrated over a wide variety of issues and whose commitments can be seen as fundamental in interpreting social policy.[23] Decision making in this view is not confined to elected officials, but is extended beyond governmental institutions by a number of mechanisms, which include interlocking organisational ties, informal influence groupings, friendship and socialisation networks, and close continuities of values and social position between elite members in the state

apparatus and those in other institutions.(24) Elite theory is
fundamentally individualistic in approach, placing elite actors at the
centre of its explanation. The links between elite members are viewed
almost entirely as personal relations and interactions, and individual
level value formation.(25) Although no contemporary elite theorists
have postulated anything approaching a conscious elite 'conspiracy',
most elite theories depend heavily on a model of individual action
motivated by personal values and shaped primarily by personal
interaction for their explanations of how values and attitudes come
to be transmitted, to affect policy and to produce a cohesive elite
operating largely independently of non-elites, who are seen as 'passive
observers or at best sporadic participants but never directing
agents.'(26)

   In describing the political process at a national level all elite
theory approaches pose a clear alternative to pluralist analysis,
emphasising the insulation of the state apparatus from any sustained,
effective or broad ranging political inputs from non-elites, and the
selective openness of state decision makers to informal influence from
other elite groupings. In contrast to pluralist analyses, elite theory
stresses the peripherality of electoral politics and inputs to the
process of policy change, the limited area of state activity controlled
by representative institutions or accessible to influence by elected
politicians, and the growth of bureaucratic allocation and control in
association with an elite-dominated interest group process.(27)
Primacy in determining the pace and direction of state policy is
normally ascribed to social and economic elites, particularly to the
owners and managers of large private corporations. Following Michels,
elite theory organisation analyses stress the growth of entrenched and
powerful oligarchies within voluntary associations, political parties
and the trade union movement, and the convergence of interests between
those in positions of institutional power whatever the interests of
their organisational bases.(28) 'Corporatist theory' takes this theme
furthest in a sophisticated Weberian argument, centering on the
incorporation of organised labour and business into the definition and
realisation of state policy, and the primacy of a bureaucratic
rationality of 'the national interest' imposed on social development
by the worsening world economic situation of advanced industrial
societies.(29)

   But when elite theory has tackled the problems of intra-state
relations there has been a fairly basic divergence in the accounts of
local and sub-national governments. One strand of elite analysis,
deriving from sociological accounts of national elites, views local
government as essentially of peripheral significance. Local government
is seen as a residual legacy of pre-industrial or early industrial
society, of declining relevance and importance in the contemporary
period. Much conventional elite theory simply points to the loss of
functions by local government to higher levels of the state apparatus
as indicative of a linear centralisation of power in liberal
democracies.(30) A more sophisticated position, enunciated in
C. Wright Mills' 'power elite' thesis, points to the concentration of
'history making' decisions in the hands of top level groups in key
institutions: in the USA, the corporate rich, an administrative elite
in the federal government and top military commanders. For Mills this
elite rules because of the strategic importance of its decisions, not
because of the pervasiveness of its presence.(31) Thus Mills was

prepared to concede both the existence and the genuine decisional influence of some representative input mechanisms, interest group processes and legislative bargaining, particularly in the operation of Congress and in many state and city governments. But, he argued, this pluralism is confined to the 'middle levels of power', to the level of intermediate and non-fundamental decision making where it serves to disguise and to distract attention from the ruling capacity of the power elite.[32] The power elite is not seen as functionally dependent on particular power configurations at the middle levels of power, nor as very directly concerned with intervention aimed at or regulation of non-elites.[33]

A second strand of elite theory analysis associated with the community power debate coined a very different view. Writers such as Floyd Hunter devoted their primary efforts to showing that elites ruled at the community level, and that even in the most apparently favourable context, a pluralist picture of the political process was inaccurate. Elite theory community power studies argued that, at the level of government most accessible to ordinary citizens, power is still concentrated in the hands of economic and social elites, democratic procedures are by-passed by informal influence networks, and policy is made in the interests of the most powerful sections of the community.[34] Hunter, and later Domhoff, extended this argument by developing a view of local and regional elites as functionally integrated into a coherent sub-structure supporting a single national-level elite.[35] For them the structure of national elite rule depends on the maintenance of pervasive elite control of localities. Local and regional elites both control social and political life in ways favourable to the perpetuation of the national elite's position, and serve to define this elite through political recruitment and the interchange of personnel between tiers of government.

The differences between the Mills and Hunter's views define two radically opposed views of central-local relations (Figure 1).

Applying elite theory in a British context to central-local relations presents problems because of the weaknesses of elite studies at a national level and their virtual absence at a local level. Nationally elite studies have never yet superceded a rather primitive state in which the paradigm of elite research has been a social background analysis of traditionally (often anachronistically) defined elite groups. Bishops, army officers, professors, the landed aristocracy, top civil servants, MPs, and businessmen have been well covered.[36] But the key groups involved in the welfare state, such as middle level administrators, the professions and local government as a whole, have been left virtually unstudied. Local elite studies are very sparse and in many ways are direct local level replications of national studies.[37] A number of virtually unstudied areas of central-local relations nonetheless clearly pose opportunities for elite studies to shed light on important issues.

First, the extent of personnel interchanges between central and local government may be important for two reasons. The first is the extent of 'non-executant' central government, pointed out by Sharpe and Mackintosh, which implies the retention of operational expertise at a local level, and hence a necessary recruitment of central staff at least partly from local authorities.[38] The second is the existence

Figure 1

Alternative Elite Theory Views of Central-Local Relations

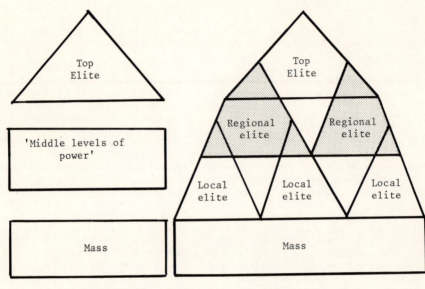

Mills' view   Hunter's view

of professions which interpenetrate both tiers of government over most
areas covered by central-local relations.(39) Clearly the links formed
by such occupational communities help to establish a strong basis for
personnel interchange. Central government planners, architects,
engineers or school inspectors all spend much of their time supervising
the work of their professional colleagues in local government.(40)

Second, there are virtually no existing accounts of the patterns of
personal and political relations involved in central-local relations,
either in political parties and patronage, or in administrative or
professional dealings. A few scattered studies of 'local government in
Parliament' are the only British counterparts to the extensive research
pioneered by Kesselman in France.(41) According to pluralist treat-
ments this neglect is because inter-governmental relations operate in
technical and uncontentious contexts, with decisions reached on public
interest grounds with no significant bargaining or lobbying worth
sustained description.(42) This argument is implausible, and a new
generation of policy studies present a very different picture of a
closed elite process, operating in secret and removed from public
scrutiny.(43)

Third, the interdependence of national and local elites in a broader
social context has remained almost completely unstudied in Britain. In
the pluralist orthodoxy there are no 'community power structures' in
Britain, and the only serious question raised by local elite

involvement in community politics is why it is so low profile or
exceptional.(44) Thus, the study of national-local elite relations is
dependent on the production of some serious local elite studies, such
as Saunders' singular study of Croydon, so far the only serious
community power study carried out in Britain.(45) The main areas of
inter-elite relations which suggest themselves include obvious
candidates, such as party politics, patronage networks and the role of
local 'burgher communities' in implementing central government
functions.(46) But they also include less obvious concerns, such as
relations between national corporations and local elites, between local
business and national corporations, between local and national levels
of voluntary associations, pressure groups and trade unions. Each of
these areas seems to have considerable implications for central-local
administrative or political relations on particular issues.(47)

   Finally, there has been no British parallel to the US 'Great Society'
programmes which 'circumvented city governments in order to make sure
that benefits reached ghetto voters when city governments ... had
become recalcitrant, obstructing the flow of services to the black
voters massing in the ghettoes'.(48) But there have been scattered
attempts by central government agencies to set up intermediaries to
represent clients to local government (e.g. housing aid centres).(49)
The presence or absence of such attempts may be an important area in
which to study the integration of local elites (however they may be
defined) into the achievement of national elite objectives.

NEO-PLURALIST THEORY

Neo-pluralism denotes a body of work which has successfully
incorporated the central points of Mills' elitist critique into a
distinctively pluralist position, while simultaneously jettisoning the
considerable elements of classical or early pluralist theory which are
anachronistic in advanced industrial societies. Representative neo-
pluralist writers are Bell, Galbraith, Etzioni and Sartori.(50) Their
writings offer what is in effect an account of 'elite pluralism'
standing in the same relation to the classical pluralism of Bentley or
Key as revisionist accounts of 'elite democracy' stand in relation to
classical democratic theory.(51)

   Neo-pluralists accept Mills' point that the traditional representative
polity is a dwindling core in an expanding state sector and that its
activities relate increasingly only to the 'middle levels of power'.
They acknowledge the growing importance of planning as a social process
and of the management of technical and social change to societal
development.(52) The distinctive form of organisation associated with
this rise in the importance of knowledge based occupations is the
profession. The success of professionalism and the extent of professionalisation are attributed, however, not just to the growth of
technical knowledge (which could be organised in other ways), but also
to the organisation of professions around a conception of the 'public
interest'.(53) The typical 'professional ethic' places responsibility
to clients and service to the public at the centre of its ideology,
socialisation, training and self-regulation. Thus neo-pluralists see
the diffusion of political/administrative power away from the
representative institutions as non-threatening because control over

the extended state increasingly rests with professional groups. Their
form of occupational organisation is seen as providing strong
alternative safeguards to representative mechanisms, safeguarding
citizens against the abuse of state power.(54)

A second reason why neo-pluralists feel able to acknowledge a
downgrading of representative politics from its central position in
classical pluralism concerns the organisational development of the
extended state apparatus, which they characterise as broadly
decentralist, pointing out that the core representative institutions of
liberal democracies are intrinsically limited in their capacity to
handle a growing volume of political issues; legislatures, for example,
cannot continuously expand their organisational capabilities in the
manner arguably open to bureaucracies.(55) So the extended state has
typically developed by devolving functions where highly 'political'
issues are not involved onto a range of non-departmental national
institutions, including public corporations, QUAGOs and QUANGOs,
'third sector' or not-for-profit companies,(56) and by assigning more
functions to sub-national administrations, especially to democratically
elected local authorities. The extension of the state apparatus as
decentralised administrative networks is thus seen as fragmenting the
augmentation of power associated with increased intervention. The
resulting power concentrations have only narrow fields of influence,
covering issue ranges relevant to their expertise, and located in a
complex, pluralist organisational and administrative context.(57)

Professionalism and decentralisation in the context of an open and
participatory political culture, supplemented by an increasing
organisational capacity among ordinary citizens to articulate and
defend their interests,(58) are seen as producing a situation where
power is exercised within a framework of rational administration and
debate and towards ends defined as communal objectives. The most
substantively democratic element of neo-pluralism is its commitment to
the view that, despite the attentuation of representative interest
processes, the advanced industrial state is the most efficient means
of meeting the needs of ordinary citizens and is overwhelmingly
orientated to those needs. A certain insulation of the administrative
process from destabilising or non-rational political mechanisms, such
as interest politics and its concomitant log rolling, coalition
formation, deals and compromises, is on this view functional in
preventing sectional interests producing a 'rationality deficit' in
public policy.(59) And if fragmented elite rule is a requirement for
effectively meeting citizens' needs then it should be accepted. For
example, Sartori argues:

'Micro democracies can still be conceived in input, that is, as
a demo-power. But macro democracies are best conceived and
furthered in output, that is in terms of demo-distribution. What
can still be mightily improved is not the power end of the problem -
more power to the people - but its end-result; more equal benefits
or less unequal privations to the people ... It can hardly be
denied that for the public at large popular rule means the fulfilment
of popular wants and needs'.(60)

In Britain central-local relations clearly involve both decentralisation and professionalism, the twin themes of much neo-pluralist work.

Decentralisation itself is an ambiguous concept. Neo-pluralist writers typically use the term to denote organisational decentralisation, that is the diffusion of responsibilities and functions to a broader range of agency types. But spatial decentralisation, namely the relative growth of sub-national or local agencies vis a vis central agencies, is also of major importance. The existing central-local relations debate in Britain fails to distinguish these processes in its anxiety to make normative/ideological points about 'central encroachment' on 'local autonomy'. The standard histories, for example, cite the post-war loss of functions from local government to the nationalised industries and the health service as cases of 'central government' absorbing local functions.[61] In fact neo-pluralist theory immediately suggests the substitution of a trichotomous set of categories for analysing transfers of responsibilities within the state sector, between central departments, local authorities and quasi-governmental organisations. On this basis the major post-war trends in Britain have been:

- a loss of functions by local government to the quasi-state sector and QUAGOs when the post-war 'welfare state' and mixed economy were established;

- a progressive expansion and concentration of a regional tier in the quasi-state sector;

- the accretion of a sizeable number of new functions in local authorities;

- and finally, the expansion of local government services and the regionally organised health service relative to other areas of the state apparatus.[62]

But what neo-pluralist theory pinpoints most acutely is the very poor information base on which such judgments rest; there has been no systematic analysis of changes in the distribution and relative importance of functions between tiers and sectors in the British state. If there has not been any pronounced tendency towards organisational or spatial centralisation, however, neither has there been any very marked decentralisation of functions in the locality. In many ways the expansion of local government functions has denied the neo-pluralist claim of a fragmentation of power, by creating (and later reorganising in the 1962-74 'reforms') authorities with control over a very wide span of issues. Certainly, local political institutions in Britain are larger than in any other Western society, and their control over 'urban' issues is probably more extensive.[63]

With professionalism, there seem to be three different problem areas in central-local relations. First, the existence of a strong professional basis in British local government creates a conflict with the overt decentralisation which local authority management secures. There are very strong continuities between policies adopted in one authority and those pursued in another, continuities which are strengthened by the interchange of personnel between authorities and the mechanisms in the professional community which diffuse information and innovation across councils of different political complexions.[64] Furthermore, the inter-penetration of central departments and local authorities by the same occupational community may tend effectively to

125

integrate nominally separate tiers of government over and above the
formal and political balance of power between them.(65) Professionalism
then appears to pull in a contradictory direction from decentralisation,
orientating local administrators to a non-local occupational community
and tending to nationalise processes of local policy change. The
stronger the control of an issue area by the profession, the greater
the effective unification of policy which may be achieved despite overt
decentralisation; the contrasting patterns of local policy change on a
highly 'professional, technical' issue like high rise housing, and on a
more 'political' issue like the comprehensive reorganisation of secon-
dary education, are instructive examples.(66)

Second, professionalism in some areas of local government operates
at the public private sector interface, and the occupational
communities involved span not just different tiers of government but
also a private practice segment of the profession and professionals
employed by corporate sector firms.(67) In these circumstances the
professional community can become a channel for corporate influence
to structure or distort the development of public policy. Far from
protecting the public interest, the greater openness of the professional
community to pressure or influence from sectional interests may pose a
most serious threat to the autonomous formulation of public policy.(68)

Third, professionalism may become problematic not where it is too
strong or well developed, as in the points made above, but where it is
too weak or poorly defined. Johnson has argued that the distinctiveness of a professional identity independent of particular employee
roles may be called in question under conditions of 'corporate
patronage' (where professionals are employed as salaried staff by state
or private sector agencies) or where the state mediates professional
services to clients.(69) The conflict of professional and bureaucratic
roles may be one-sided where an occupation is distinctive to the state
sector, as with the numerous 'local government professions' with no
real counterparts elsewhere in society. These occupations seem heavily
bureaucratised, their technical bases developing towards 'localism'
(a pre-occupation with the specific needs of the employer organisation
rather than the independent pursuit of knowledge).(70) The danger in
this trend is that professional orientations become devalued,
increasingly indistinguishable from normal employee attitudes,
functioning primarily to undermine spatial and organisational
decentralisation without conferring any of the benefits of socialising
decision makers into an attachment to the public interest claimed by
neo-pluralist theory.(71)

Overall, therefore, neo-pluralist theory suggests a number of major
issues involved in central-local relations which have barely been
touched on effectively in existing work and go to the heart of much
contemporary liberal thought on the development of advanced industrial
society.

MARXIST ANALYSES

Marxist approaches offer a radically different interpretation of the
role of the state from those already surveyed. They differ from
pluralist and neo-pluralist accounts in denying the independence or
potential neutrality of the state. But they also contradict the

attempts by elite theorists to argue that the state apparatus is tied
into policy making in favour of dominant economic and social elites
by networks of personnel contacts, common social values and the actions
of individual decision makers.[72]   Notwithstanding the kind of
Marxist elitist analysis put forward by Miliband,[73] Marxist analyses
essentially deny that the integration of the state into a nexus of
class rule by the bourgeoisie can be established at an individual or
institutional level. Rather they point to the necessary functional
integration of the state in capitalist society into fostering the
continued accumulation of capital, on which both the overall level of
economic prosperity and the revenues of the state apparatus depend.[74]
Since the process of capital accumulation is seen as one in which
uncompensated labour is extracted by the bourgeoisie from the working
class, state policies are viewed as class specific in character,
sustaining a process of exploitation and directed to the interests of
an economically and socially dominant class at the expense of other
social classes. This original instrumentalist conception has, however,
been substantially modified by recent Marxist work which denies that the
state always or necessarily acts to sustain the accumulation of capital.
Structuralist accounts emphasise the 'relative autonomy' of the state
in its functional role, stressing the frequency with which the state
may need to intervene against the short-run interests of capital.[75]
On this view state intervention is directed as much to the maintenance
of a social formation within which capital is dominant, as it is
directed to specifically capitalist interests, a function which puts a
premium on the continuous legitimation of the social system. Thus
state intervention, far from being directly coercive or repressive in
character, as instrumentalist accounts often suggest, will be directed
to the alleviation of social unrest, the attenuation of social
conflicts and the incorporation of political struggles in the long run
interests of capital.[76] In this process the maintenance of an
appearance of political neutrality, of the state as 'an organisation
of power that pursues common and general interests of society as a
whole, allows equal access to power and is responsive to justified
demands', is vital.[77] If public policy remained very overtly or
totally subordinate to the interests of one dominant class, it could
not secure widespread consent and the political stability of capitalist
society would be called in question.

   Marxist analyses' rejection of individual level explanations means
that they do not accord any particular importance to institutionally
defined questions, such as that of central-local relations. Indeed
some writers place all institutional arrangements at the level of
appearances, behind which a properly theoretical analysis must penetrate
to underlying social relations.[78] This approach can lead to an
undifferentiated assimilation of all governmental agencies into an
apparently monolithic 'state apparatus', in which the central-local
distinction often disappears and local government is treated
simplistically as 'the local state',   a kind of microcosmic example of
Marxist analyses' general theory of the state.[79] But in a more
general and acceptable way Marxist accounts suggest that an abstract
consideration of central-local relations, justified only by the
intrinsic interest of institutional arrangements, can have little or
no validity. Instead central-local relations need to be analysed in
the context of explaining concrete processes of social change and state
intervention.

However, it is worth trying to give a synoptic picture of Marxist views of the relations between different institutions in the state apparatus, if only because it is so widely believed by non-Marxists that Marxists have no such view.

Marxist approaches are confronted with a number of problems in explaining social and political change in terms of centralisation/ decentralisation. Essentially these approaches offer radically different accounts of these trends, rather than viewing them in a uniform fashion as the accounts reviewed earlier in this paper tend to do. The maintenance of a local government system at all in Western capitalist societies presents an initial explanatory difficulty for Marxist approaches. One important strand of analysis points to the importance of local government in the early industrial phase of capitalism, in coordinating the provision of state services to regionally or locally dominant sections of capital. Divisions within the bourgeoisie, on this view, could be managed by the confinement of most service provision functions to local authorities directly controlled by the bourgeoisie.(80) The development of monopoly capital and the consequent withdrawal of the bourgeoisie in many areas from participation in local government coincided with a period in which the interests of capital were served by local government reforms and by the increasing standardisation of services and conditions across the country.(81) Yet both the liberalisation of the franchise and the attack on corruption opened up local government (in Europe at least) to capture by the early socialist parties. Local government in particular areas became a focus of working class action, and mobilisation and control of local Councils became an important weapon in the articulation of pressures for the alleviation of conditions of working class life.(82) In the contemporary period the disengagement of monopoly capital from overt political involvement at the sub-national level is seen as constituting a strong centralising imperative in which local authorities are increasingly by-passed by the central state because of their control by parties representing non-dominant classes, or non-dominant fractions of capital (such as small business).(83) The retention and relative importance of the local government tier in Western societies is seen as indicative of a legitimation constraint; the complete abolition or control of a democratically elected tier of government is seen as too politically dangerous for dominant class fractions. Rather the residual independence of local government is sapped by tightening fiscal controls and the progressive displacement of urban issues to non-local levels in the state apparatus. The growth of a regional tier of administrative agencies is seen as particularly important in by-passing local authorities in key areas, such as the organisation of economic life at a sub-national level.(84) Apart from its continuing ideological importance, the attenuated local government system is seen as fulfilling a minor role in coordinating the development of capital accumulation in a spatially differentiated manner, particularly in alleviating the most serious consequences of the uneven development which is a fundamental characteristic of capitalist urbanisation.(85)

In this view, then, the survival of a local government system is an unintended by-product of the development of liberal democracy which retains a potential for furthering social change favourable to working class interests. As Cockburn argues: 'The play within the structure of the state, needed to enable the coordination of the interests of a divided dominant class, also afford opportunities for working class militancy to win concessions'.(86) And Castells dwells on the importance of local political institutions for socialist and communist parties: 'The ability to impose a political change at the local level prior to obtaining national power can be seen as an essential stage in consolidating a relationship to the population in the long process of the transformation of societal structures.(87) The development of central-local relations on this view is an important dimension of a broader societal process, the attack by monopoly capital on democratic forms remaining as residual elements from earlier stages of economic development.

A very different picture is suggested by other strands in Marxist approaches, which draw attention to the nature of working class mobilisation into local government at the turn of the century and in the inter-war period. The central objective of movements such as Poplarism or municipal socialism emerged in the course of struggles over particular issues as unobtainable in the context of local government. The point of many of the disruptive uses of local political institutions was to force the displacement of issues from the local level, where implementation was clearly impossible on any extensive scale, to the national arena where working class militancy could ensure a properly funded and acceptable standard of service provision or administrative organisation. Undeniably the pressure of working class parties in the present century has basically constituted the redistributive politics which is widely credited with effecting the transfer of functions away from local authorities. Correlatively pressures for the maintenance of decentralised government in capitalist society can be traced back extensively to dominant social interests. For the bourgeoisie decentralised administration of collective consumption services, in particular, may be seen as functional in maintaining the vulnerability of fragmented local authorities to the pressure exerted by spatial movements of non-local capital.(88) To maintain an effective fiscal base and to protect the employment and prosperity in their areas, even socialist localities tend to be forced into conformity with the interests of capital, depressing local taxes, providing cheap sites or facilities and turning a blind eye to pollution hazards. This 'market discipline' enforced particularly by large non-local corporations differentially affects the depressed industrial areas and inner city zones of traditionally radical munipical politics, already the 'natural victims' of uneven development.(89)

For the non-dominant social classes outside the working class local political institutions seem to provide a distinctively important focus of political mobilisation, accentuating their alignment on a broad range of issues with the interests of capital. For intermediate or 'middle class' groups a fragmented local government system provides a key mechanism for enforcing 'social closure' and for distancing their social situation from that of the working class.(90) Thus, local politics absorb much of the political energies of owner-occupier groups and the differential political activism of non-manual classes means that local authorities can be important mechanisms by which these classes can resist and frustrate the implementation of policy concessions won by working class pressure at a national level.(91) In a broader way the spatial fragmentation of issues, and the consequent fracturing of political activity on locally handled issues, can be seen as functional for the maintenance of social cohesion in several respects. It tends to spatialise the issues involved, lending weight to the 'urban ideology' which interprets social problems as products of particular urban spatial environments or naturalistic corollaries of processes of technical change mapped onto a spatial plane.[92] It underplays the continuities of class experiences and situations, reinforcing the notion of 'community' in ways which reduce class consciousness and inhibit broader patterns of mobilisation.[93] And it can lead to the exclusion of certain issues altogether from the range of political issues, subtly converting them from potentially threatening redistributive issues into administrative-technical matters remote from the mainstream of public debate and political conflict. In this perspective then, centralisation is a goal of working class action, a prerequisite for effective articulation of issues and mobilisation along class lines. The maintenance of decentralised local governments is taken as indicative of the power of the bourgeoisie and similarly aligned non-dominant classes to impede and fragment the resolution of key issues under a cloak of democratic legitimacy and respect for local 'autonomy'.

Clearly Marxist approaches are fertile soil for the political sociologist looking for a broader characterisation of the issues involved in central-local relations, even if the approaches are themselves ambivalent in their characterisation of central-local conflicts. The bald summary given here anyway overstates this ambivalence, for all Marxist approaches agree on the necessity to locate a discussion of this kind in specific historical contexts, and in context many of the contradictory interpretations suggested can be resolved into a coherent picture. Above all the contradictions derivable from the same Marxist premises highlight large research areas left untouched by liberal studies and theories, and the implausibly individualistic explanations which are widely accepted as legitimate in British political science. Consider the 1962-74 local government 'reforms'. In the existing (predominantly pluralist) accounts of these changes much attention is paid to the politico-ideological debates which surrounded the reorganisations and to the activities and views of particular individuals and groups of elite decision makers.[94] But no account is offered of the background of socio-economic changes which underlay the 'reforms', of the class distribution of pressures for change, or of their political and distributive consequences. In fact, it has been shown that the provincial changes in England and Wales alone effected a massive transfer of some sixteen per cent of the population involved from potentially Labour (or at least two-party) county boroughs to over-whelmingly Conservative controlled shire counties, a change with critical implications for millions of working people, for levels of public expenditure and for the political viability of the Labour party. The 'reformed' local government system leaves some fifty-eight per cent of the England and Wales population living in areas of safe Conservative control at the most important local government tier (i.e. at the London borough, metropolitan district and shire county levels), with a Labour 'safe' population of less than twenty per cent of the total by comparison.[95] Whether or not an outcome of this kind can be shown to have been the conscious goal of any individual decision maker, it is difficult to imagine an outcome which could be more

functionally appropriate for the interests of capital in the current
British semi-continuous recession, as the history of local government
expenditure cuts and underspending from 1975 onwards bears eloquent
testimony. In shifting the focus of debate from the individual level,
Marxist approaches have a value which is not restricted to the direct
plausibility of their accounts of state intervention and public policy
change.

CONCLUSIONS

The central conclusion from this survey is that all the theoretical
approaches reviewed have much to offer an empirical researcher setting
out to analyse the issues involved in central-local relations in
Britain. Set against the hackneyed administrative conundrums and
ephemeral fashions in behavioural theory which seem to dominate so much
of the practitioner orientated literature in this area, these
substantive theoretical positions are clearly in a different category
of 'theory'. Unlike the management nostrums which come and go with
bewildering rapidity in allegedly 'policy relevant' research, these
positions go to the heart of major controversies and disputes in the
social sciences. Research into central-local relations from any of
these perspectives would serve to connect the issue area with the
mainstream of social scientific debates; whereas low level
redescriptions of phenomena in behavioural terminology, such as the
currently fashionable inter-governmental theory, leave it isolated
and stagnant, a backwater inhabited by issue - specific 'theories' and
ideas.

  Beyond this initial conclusion, research into central-local relations
should not only be theoretically based, i.e. drawing on the type of
substantive theory reviewed here, but should be multi-theoretical,
i.e. it should draw on several or all of the theories relevant to the
empirical questions examined, using them as sources of competing
hypotheses and interpretations to guide the research.

NOTES AND REFERENCES

(1)   This is a wholly rewritten and much shorter version of my paper
        to the SSRC Central-Local Research Panel entitled 'Theories of
        the State and Society and the Study of Central-Local Relations',
        written in September 1978. Copies of the full paper may be
        obtained from the author at the London School of Economics. I
        would like to thank Jim Sharpe, Geraint Parry, Chris Pollitt
        and Mark Pattison for comments and suggestions incorporated
        here.
(2)   D. Nicholls, The Pluralist State, Macmillan, London, 1975;
        C.B. Macpherson, 'Do We Need a Theory of the State?',
        European Journal of Sociology, Vol. 18, 1978.
(3)   A.H. Birch, Representative and Responsible Government, Allen &
        Unwin, London, 1964, and R.A. Dahl, A Preface to Democratic
        Theory, University of Chicago Press, Chicago, 1956.
(4)   S. Keller, Beyond the Ruling Class, Random House, New York, 1963.
(5)   R. Rose, Politics in England Today, Faber, London,1974; A.H.
        Birch, Representative, Pall Mall, London, 1971.

(6)   G.A. Almond and S. Verba, The Civic Culture, Little Brown, Boston, 1965.

(7)   A. King (ed.), Why is Britain Becoming Harder to Govern? BBC, London, 1976.

(8))   J.S. Mill, Utilitarianism, Liberty and Representative Government, Dent, London, 1910.

(9)   R.A. Dahl and E.R. Tufte, Size and Democracy, Oxford University Press, London, 1974.

(10)   W.A. Robson, Local Government in Crisis, Allen & Unwin, London, 1966.

(11)   Layfield, Committee of Inquiry into Local Government Finance: Report, HMSO, London, 1976.

(12)   A. Downs, An Economic Theory of Democracy, Harper & Row, New York, 1957.

(13)   D. Robertson, A Theory of Party Competition, Wiley, London, 1976.

(14)   J. Becquart-Leclerq, Paradoxes du Pouvoir Locale, Presses de la fondation nationales des sciences politiques, Paris, 1976.

(15)   P.J. Dunleavy, Urban Political Analysis, Macmillan, London, 1980, forthcoming;and I. Budge, I Crewe and D. Farlie, Party Identification and Beyond, Wiley, London, 1976.

(16)   P.G. Richards, The Reformed Local Government System, Allen & Unwin London, 1978, (Third revised edition).

(17)   R.A.W. Rhodes, 'A Model of Central-Local Relations in Britain', Paper to the Policy Studies Conference, INLOGOV, Birmingham, 7 June 1978.

(18)   L.J. Sharpe, (ed.) Decentralist Trends in Western Democracies, Sage, London, 1979.

(19)   J.A. Schumpeter, Capitalism, Socialism and Democracy, Allen & Unwin, London, 1954; and A. Downs, op. cit., and D. Robertson, op. cit.

(20)   K. Newton, Second City Politics, Oxford University Press, London, 1976.

(21)   P.J. Dunleavy, op. cit.

(22)   Ibid.

(23)   K. Prewitt and A. Stone, The Ruling Elites: Elite Theory, Power and American Democracy, Harper and Row, New York, 1973,; also V. Pareto, Pareto- Sociological Writings, (edited by S.E. Finer), Pall Mall, London, 1966; and G. Mosca, The Ruling Class, McGraw Hill, New York, 1939.

(24)   W.L. Guttsman, The British Political Elite, MacGibbon and Kee, London, 1963; and G. Parry, Elites, Allen & Unwin, London, 1969.

(25)   A. Giddens and P. Stanworth, Elites and Power in British Society, Cambridge University Press, London, 1974; and I, Crewe, (ed.) British Political Sociology Yearbook, Volume I: Elites in Western Democracy, Croom Helm, London, 1974.

(26)   K. Prewitt and A. Stone, op. cit.

(27)   T.R. Dye and L.H. Zeigler, The Irony of Democracy, Duxbury Press, North Scituate, Mass.: 1975.

(28)   R. Michels, Political Parties, Free Press, Glencoe, Illinois, 1915.

(29)   R.E. Pahl and J.T. Winkler, 'The Coming Corporatism', New Society, 10 October 1974.

(30)   W.L. Guttsman, op. cit.

(31)   C.W. Mills, The Power Elite, Oxford University Press, London, 1956.

(32)   B.J. Kleinberg, American Society in the Postindustrial Age, Merill, Columbus, Ohio, 1973.

(33) C.W. Mills, op. cit.

(34) G. Parry, op. cit.

(35) F. Hunter, Community Power Structure, Chapel Hill Books, Chapel Hill, N.C; 1953; and G.W. Domhoff, Who Rules America?, Prentice Hall, Englewood Cliffs, New Jersey, 1967.

(36) A. Giddens and P. Stanworth, op. cit.; W.L. Guttsman, op. cit.; and I. Crewe, (ed.) op. cit.

(37) I. Crewe, op. cit.; and G. Parry, op. cit.

(38) L.J. Sharpe, 'Whitehall: Structures and People', in R. Rose and D. Kavanagh (eds.), New Trends in British Politics, Sage, London, 1977, and J. Mackintosh, The Government and Politics of Britain, Hutchinson, London, 1974.

(39) T.J. Johnson, Professions and Power, Macmillan, London, 1972.

(40) P.J. Dunleavy, The Politics of High Rise Housing in Britain: Local Communities Tackle Mass Housing, D. Phil. Thesis, Oxford University, 1978, forthcoming from Oxford University Press as: The Politics of Mass Housing in Britain; and M. Pattison, 'Implementation Level Resistance and Intergovernmental Relations: the Case of Comprehensive Education in Britain', Oxford Bulletin of Education, forthcoming 1980.

(41) M. Kesselmann, The Ambiguous Consensus, Knopf, New York, 1967; and J. Becquart-Leclercq, op. cit.

(42) But see the dent in this picture given in J.A.G. Griffith, Central Departments and Local Authorities, Allen & Unwin, London, 1966.

(43) K. Young and J. Kramer, Strategy and Conflict in Metropolitan Housing, Heinemann, London, 1978; M. Pattison, op. cit., and P.J. Dunleavy, (see Note 39).

(44) R.V. Clements, Local Notables and the City Council, Macmillan, London, 1969; and D.S. Morris and K. Newton, 'The Social Composition of a City Council, 1925-66', Social and Economic Administration, 1971.

(45) P. Saunders, Who Runs Croydon? Power and Politics in a London Borough, Ph.D. Thesis, University of London, 1974, and 'They Make the Rules: Political Routines and the Generation of Political Bias', Policy and Politics, Vol. 4, pp. 31-58, 1974.

(46) P.J. Dunleavy (see note 14).

(47) See K. Newton, op. cit., especially chapters 3 and 4.

(48) F.F. Piven and R. Cloward, Regulating the Poor, Tavistock, London, 1972.

(49) Much of the grant funding under the Urban Aid Programmes has taken this form.

(50) D. Bell, The End of Ideology, Crowell-Collier, New York, 1961; and The Coming of Post Industrial Society, Basic Books, New York, 1973; also A. Etzioni, The Active Society, Free Press, New York, 1968; J.K. Galbraith, The Affluent Society, Penguin, Harmondsworth, 1962; and The New Industrial State, Penguin, Harmondsworth, 1969.

(51) A.F. Bentley, The Process of Government, Oxford University Press, London, 1967; and V.O. Key, Politics, Parties and Pressure Groups, Crowell, New York, 1964.

(52) B.J. Kleinberg, op. cit.

(53) D. Bell (1973), op. cit., T.J. Johnson, op. cit.

(54) D. Bell (1973), op. cit., and J.K. Galbraith (1969), op. cit.

(55) B.J. Kleinberg, op. cit., and P.J. Dunleavy, 'Demand Pressure and Structural Change in British Government', Paper to the Problems in British Politics seminar, Nuffield College, 1976.

(56) W.J.M. Mackenzie, D.C. Hague and A. Barker, (eds.), Public Policy and Private Interests: the Institutions of Compromise, Macmillan, London, 1975; and C. Hood, 'The Rise and Rise of The British Quango', New Society, August, 1973.
(57) B.J. Kleinberg, op. cit.
(58) A. Etzioni, op. cit.
(59) B.J. Kleinberg, op. cit., draws out this implication.
(60) G. Sartori, 'Will Democracy Kill Democracy? Decision Making by Majorities and by Committees', Government and Opposition, Vol. 10, 1975, p. 150.
(61) K.B. Smellie, The History of Local Government, Allen & Unwin, London, 1968.
(62) P.J. Dunleavy (1976), op. cit., presents a partial analysis of these trends.
(63) L.J. Sharpe, 'Reforming the Grass Roots: An Alternative Analysis', in D. Butler and A.H. Halsey, (eds.) Policy and Politics: Essays in Honour of Sir Norman Chester, Macmillan, London, 1978.
(64) P.J. Dunleavy (see note 14); and F. Musgrove, 'The Educational and Geographic Background of some Local Leaders', British Journal of Sociology, Vol. 1, 1961.
(65) Ibid.
(66) P.J. Dunleavy (see note 39) and M. Pattison (see note 39).
(67) P.N. Malpass, Professionalism in Architecture and the Design of Local Authority Homes, Newcastle upon Tyne University, M.A. Thesis, unpublished, 1973.
(68) M.McEwan, Crisis in Architecture, RIBA, London, 1975.
(69) T.J. Johnson, op. cit., pp. 63-86.
(70) T.J. Johnson, op. cit.
(71) P.N. Malpass, op. cit.
(72) E. Laclau, 'The Specificity of the Political: the Poulantzas-Miliband Debate', Economy and Society, Vol. 4, 1975, pp. 87-110.
(73) R. Miliband, The State in Capitalist Society, Weidenfeld & Nicolson, London, 1969.
(74) J. O'Connor, The Fiscal Crisis of the State, St. James Press, London, 1973; and N. Poulantzas, Political Power and Social Classes, Faber, London, 1973.
(75) M. Castells, City, Class and Power, Macmillan, London, 1978; and C.B. Macpherson, op. cit.
(76) J. Habermas, Legitimation Crisis, Heinemann, London, 1976.
(77) C. Offe, 'The Theory of the Capitalist State and the Problem of Policy Formation', in L.N. Lindberg, R. Alford, C. Crouch and C. Offe, Stress and Contradiction in Modern Capitalism, Lexington Books, Lexington, Mass:, 1975.
(78) N. Poulantzas, op. cit., expresses this Althusserian position.
(79) C. Cockburn, The Local State, Pluto Press, London, 1977.
(80) Ibid.
(81) J. Garrard, 'The History of Local Political Power', Political Studies, Vol. 25, 1977, pp. 252-69.
(82) P. Dickens, 'Social Change, Housing and the State: Some Aspects of Class Fragmentation and Incorporation', in M. Harloe (ed.), CES Conference on Urban Change and Conflict, York 1978, Centre for Environmental Studies, London, 1978; and B. Hindess, The Decline of Working Class Politics, MacGibbon and Kee, London, 1971.

(83) S. Biarez, C. Bouchet, G. de Boisberranger, C.G. Mingasson, M.C. Monzies and C. Pouyet, _Institution Communale et Pouvoir Politique: le cas de Roanne_, Mouton, Paris, 1973; and M. Castells and F. Godard, _Monopolville_, Mouton, Paris, 1974.

(84) Ibid., and Rowntree Research Unit, 'Aspects of Contradiction in Regional Policy: the Case of North-East England', _Regional Studies_, Vol. 8, 1974.

(85) D. Harvey, _Social Justice and the City_, Arnold, London, 1973.

(86) C. Cockburn, op. cit., p. 50.

(87) M. Castells, op. cit. p. 1.

(88) J. Lojkine, _Le marxisme, l'etat et la question urbaine_, Presses Universitaires de France, Paris, 1977.

(89) E. Lebas, 'Movement of Capital and Locality: Issues Raised by the Study of Local Power Structures', in M. Harloe, (ed.), _CES Conference on Urban Change and Conflict, York 1978_, Centre for Environmental Studies, London, 1978; and for a non-Marxist view of the same phenomenon see P.E. Peterson, 'A Unitary Model of Local Taxation and Expenditures in the United States', _British Journal of Political Science_, Vol. 9, 1979, pp. 289-314.

(90) F. Parkin, 'Strategies of Social Closure in Class Formation', in F. Parkin, (ed.), _The Social Analysis of Class Structure_, Tavistock, London, 1974.

(91) For examples see K. Young and J. Kramer, op. cit.; and M. Pattison, op. cit.

(92) M. Castells, _The Urban Question_, Edward Arnold, London, 1977.

(93) C. Bell and H. Newby, 'Community, Communion, Class and Community Action', in D. Herbert and R. Johnson (eds.), _Social Geography and the Study of Urban Areas_, Wiley, London, 1975.

(94) L.J. Sharpe, op. cit.; Lord Redcliffe-Maud and B. Wood, _English Local Government Reformed_, Oxford University Press, London, 1974; B. Wood, _The Process of Local Government Reform, 1966-74_, Allen & Unwin, London, 1976; J. Brand, _Local Government Reform in England, 1888-1974_, Croom Helm, London, 1974; F. Smallwood, _Greater London: the Politics of Metropolitan Reform_, Bobbs-Merrill, New York, 1965.

(95) P.J. Dunleavy (see note 14).

FURTHER READING

P. Anderson, _Considerations on Western Marxism_, New Left Books, London, 1976.

D. Ashford, 'The Limits of Consensus: the Reorganization of British Local Government and the French Contrast', in S. Tarrow et al., see below.

P. Bachrach, _The Theory of Democratic Elitism_, University of London Press, London, 1969.

C.D.P. _The Costs of Industrial Change_, The Home Office, London, 1977.

D.N. Chester, _Central and Local Government_, Macmillan, London, 1951.

J. Dearlove, _The Politics of Policy in Local Government_, Cambridge University Press, London, 1973.

B. Fay, _Social Theory and Political Practice_, Allen & Unwin, London, 1977.

R. Flynn, 'Planning and the State: A Discussion and Critique of Some Recent Marxist Writings', Paper to the Political Studies Association Annual Conference, 1978.

J. Gyford, Local Politics in Britain, Croom Helm, London, 1976.

F. Hunter, Top Leadership, USA, Oxford University Press, London, 1959.

S.M. Lipset, Political Man, Doubleday, New York, 1963.

D.H. McKay, 'Political Science and Urbanism in Europe: Some Lessons from the American Experience', European Journal of Political Research, Vol. 3, 1975, pp. 303-17.

W.J.M. Mackenzie, 'Local Government in Parliament', Public Administration, Vol. 32, 1954.

W.J.M. Mackenzie and J.W. Grove, Central Administration in Britain, Longmans, London, 1957.

K. Newton, 'City Politics in Britain and the United States', Political Studies, Vol. 17, 1969, pp. 208-18; and 'Community Performance in Britain', Current Sociology, Vol. 26, 1977.

G.C. Pickvance, 'Explaining State Intervention', Paper to CES Conference on Urban Change and Conflict, University of York, 1977; and 'Marxist Approaches to the Study of Urban Politics: Divergences among some Recent French Studies', International Journal of Urban and Regional Research, Vol. 1, 1977, pp. 219-55.

J.J. Richardson, A.G. Jordan and R.H. Kimber, 'Lobbying, Administrative Reform and Policy Style: the Case of Land Drainage', Political Studies, Vol. 26, 1978.

L.J. Sharpe, 'Innovation and Change in British Land Use Planning', in J. Hayward and M. Watson, (eds.), Planning, Politics and Public Policy, Cambridge University Press, London, 1975.

M. Stacey, Tradition and Change, Oxford University Press, London, 1960.

M. Stacey, E. Batsone, C. Bell, and A. Murcott, Power, Persistence and Change: a Second Study of Banbury, Routledge and Kegan Paul, London, 1975.

S. Tarrow, P.J. Katzenstein and L. Graziano, Territorial Politics in Industrial Nations, Praeger, London, 1978.

P. Thoenes, The Elite in the Welfare State, Faber, London, 1966.

P. Walton and A. Gamble, From Alientation to Surplus Value, Steed and Ward, London, 1972.

11 Measuring Decentralisation

Brian C. Smith

This essay is founded on the assumptions that decentralisation is a
variable and that it is necessary to devise a method of measuring it.
The concept of decentralisation refers to the geographical dimension
of state apparatus.(1) It is a broader concept of hierarchical
relationships than that associated with traditional ideas about
central-local relations. It encompasses all institutions that
constitute governmental arrangements for local communities.

THE PROBLEM OF DECENTRALISATION

The appeal of decentralisation is now so great that it is in
competition with democracy as the concept that no political theory,
ideology or movement can afford to eschew. It is a value embraced by
the left, whether revolutionary, utopian or reformist; by liberals;
and by the radical right.(2) It has become commonplace in
industrialised countries to deplore the over-centralisation of modern
government. As the pressures for larger organisation units, national
minimum standards and central planning capabilities mount so the
concern for local autonomy grows.(3) Modern society seems
characterised by concentration of power.(4) Individuals are seen as
threatened by large, remote and impersonal organisations.(5) Local
autonomy has been a major theme in discussions of UK central-local
relations.(6) In developing countries it is regarded as an obstacle
to development.(7)

  Decentralisation is commonly associated with a wide range of economic,
social and political objectives in both developed and developing
countries.(8) Yet it is not without its critics. To some it is
parochial, inegalitarian and unconcerned with the privileges and
exploitation built into local power structures.(9) It ignores the
possibility that the holders of economic power at the local level will
dominate local institutions and perpetuate hierarchy and oppression.
Critics note how decentralisation in liberal regimes has been used to
strengthen existing patterns of domination.(10) Even those sympathetic
towards decentralisation are often critical of its working in
practice.(11) It can produce inefficiencies and diseconomies(12) in
developed and developing states, capitalist and socialist
economies.(13)

  It thus becomes imperative to distinguish decentralisation as state
apparatus from its economic, political and ideological context.
Comparative analysis requires a common framework for evaluating
decentralisation as practised in different contexts. We must
hypothesize about decentralisation as a mean to an end, not dogmatise
about it as an end in itself.

VARYING DECENTRALISATION

It is necessary to investigate systematically the relationship between decentralisation and its effects on political life and public policy. Decentralisation is an intrinsically variable process.(14) It is not unusual to compare states in terms of their degree of decentralisation,(15) yet hardly any progress has been made in devising measures of decentralisation.(16) Different traditions in political science have neglected to treat decentralisation as a variable.

The historical-legal tradition in public administration emphasised the extent to which decentralisation is to be distinguished from local autonomy. The former is a function of the rules which delegate authority from one geographical level to another and is susceptible to manipulated change. The latter is a function of socio-economic aspects which may support or undermine the independence of a particular sub-national territory or community.

However, the historical-legal approach to decentralisation tends to neglect two important aspects of the centre-periphery relationship. First, there are the consequences for both political power and public policy of different degrees of decentralisation. The localisation of power is too readily seen as an end in itself, and policy studies have not been concerned with the effects of different levels of decentralisation on policy outputs. Secondly, different criteria have to be employed in measuring decentralisation according to the type of organisation involved, be they central department, local authority, or regional board. Decentralisation to an area is more complex than is assumed by conventional studies of central-local relations because the government of an area entails different structures of local administration, which cannot be evaluated by reference to a common standard. Public administration has concentrated almost exclusively on relationships between central government and local authorities. From the perspective of the local community the state is represented in many institutional forms. Measuring decentralisation means taking an area and analysing whether the power and discretion of its whole system of government has changed and if so in what direction.

The community politics approach to decentralisation has been almost exclusively concerned with identifying the location of power within communities. The level of decentralisation has been assumed to be a constant factor: decentralisation and autonomy have been confused and treated as a dependent variable.(17) Decentralisation needs to be distinguished from autonomy in order to assess the impact of variation in the organisational aspects of local autonomy. It is necessary to single out the man-made constraints over local autonomy emanating from the centre from those which originate in the socio-economic structure of the area.

THE MEASUREMENT OF DECENTRALISATION

To evaluate the political and administrative consequences of more or less decentralisation areas with different degrees of power delegated to them by the centre have to be compared and variations in the administrative and political experiences of those areas in terms of decentralisation accounted for. The measurement required cannot be a precise exercise; rough judgments will have to be made.

The first measure of decentralisation relates to governmental functions. The tasks assigned to area governments have to be analysed to distinguish between whole functions (e.g. education), part functions (e.g. primary education) and low-level policy making (e.g. school buildings). Distinctions have to be drawn between the structures of decentralised administration, since some functions can be assigned to either devolved councils or field officers. Purely central tasks (e.g. inspection and audit) performed at the local level have to be distinguished from executive functions which can be either devolved or deconcentrated.[18] Decentralisation can be measured by the distribution of expenditure between the centre and different forms of peripheral government. The more responsibilities are handled by devolved methods the more decentralised the system will be. Centralisation can thus be reduced by expanding the range of decision areas (or jurisdiction) of local governments.

The second measure relates to taxation. Areas and systems of decentralisation may be compared according to their powers of revenue raising. Two features need particular attention. One is the proportion of total state revenue which is raised locally.[19] The second is the extent to which local revenues are allowed to expand faster than the rate of inflation.[20] A considerably decentralised system of government would be one in which there is no legal restriction on the level of local tax rates and where there is a tax base which can expand in line with the growth of the economy and the rate of inflation.

Thirdly, it is necessary to measure the level of decentralisation within the field offices of central government, to enable a more precise estimate to be made of the greater centralisation involved in field administration than local government. The variables relating to field administration's contribution to the level of decentralisation include the number of levels in the field organisation's hierarchy; the responsibilities assigned to field personnel in terms of both tasks and varying degrees of autonomy within them (such as the approval of schemes under a certain cost); the form of inter departmental coordination used; the frequency with which field officers have to refer matters to headquarters for decision; the way conflict between generalists and specialists is handled; the policies of transferring personnel between headquarters and field stations and between the field districts; methods of communication between headquarters and the field and methods of headquarters control over field staff, such as review, reporting and inspection.

Fourthly, the amount of delegation to area political authorities can be measured by reference to three factors: local authorities with a 'general competence' can be regarded as more decentralised than those subject to the rule of ultra vires; the greater the number of local decisions which are centrally influenced rather than controlled, the greater the decentralisation; and whether central control tends to take the form of initiation or veto. It seems reasonable to assume that it is more, rather than less, decentralised to give area governments the statutory right to do whatever they judge to be in the best interest of their areas rather than be required to find statutory confirmation of the right to take a decision.

The extensive variation between states in methods of control and influence makes comparative analysis difficult. There is a need to assess the relative significance for decentralisation of different types of control, for example, approval of budgets vs. selective financial controls, and the motives behind such controls.(21) Each system of decentralisation presents a different pattern of controls and influences at the disposal of the centre, and their impact on the overall level of decentralisation has to be judged.

Fifthly, the methods of creating area governments and delegating power to them constitute a measure of decentralisation. Greater decentralisation is involved if area authorities have statutory powers and duties assigned by the legislature than if the same powers are first assigned to the executive which then delegates to area governments acting as agents of the centre. It is important to know whether local governments have a legal existence independent of the central executive.

Next, the level of total local expenditure as a proportion of total public spending may be used when the aim is to compare states or a single political system over a period of time. The greater the proportion of total public spending incurred by area governments the greater the decentralisation. This test has been used in the USA to compare state and local expenditures and is thus restricted to expenditure which could in principle be the responsibility of either the area or the centre (state). In a unitary state it may be necessary to exclude expenditure on items such as foreign affairs and defence, which could never be decentralised.

Seventh, there is next the question of whether the system of decentralisation entails a single tier structure of unitary authorities or a multi-tiered structure. So far there can be only speculation as to how far either pattern affects the level of decentralisation, since conflicting conclusions may be deducted from each arrangement. If there are many levels in the hierarchy there may be 'discretionary gaps' and 'leakages' of authority, thus increasing discretion at the lower levels.(22) On the other hand, a system may be regarded as more decentralised the more there is a strict coincidence of community area and governmental authority. So a simple, unitary system should be more decentralised than a complex, tiered system.

Eighth, the ratio of local government revenues to total government revenues may be used as a measure of decentralisation especially since the dominant view seems to be that as central funding grows so does central control. So the proportion of local revenues coming from central grants would seem an excellent indicator of decentralisation. However, the evidence often seems to run contrary to conventional wisdom. The viability of financial 'dependence' as a measure of decentralisation requires further investigation. It should certainly not be assumed a priori that variation in levels of expenditure equals decentralisation any more than uniformity equals centralised control(23) Also the method of administering grants as well as their size may be important to the centre-periphery relationship.(24)

Next, the personnel of local institutions need to be classified. Are they 'locals'.(25) Are they elected or selected locals? What proportion of the local public servants are the employees of central agencies and what of local governments? Adjustments need to be made to the central-local personnel ratio to take into account the labour intensity of local services.(26)

Lastly, larger authorities might be expected to have more autonomy on the grounds that they will have stronger revenue bases, more developed professional administrations, greater power when dealing with other institutions, including the centre, greater ability to deal with minority needs and greater experience at handling large scale operations than smaller authorities. So a legislative enactment creating fewer, larger area governments might be considered a decentralising measure. However, this argument must be approached with caution since the larger the units of decentralised government, the fewer for central government to control. Also, the hypothesis that smaller authorities submit and conform has not been verified. Further research is needed into the viability of this and the other measures of decentralisation.

DECENTRALISATION AND AUTONOMY

Formal relationships between centre and localities, including sets of positive controls, do not tell everything about central-local relations. We need also to know how far a potential for control is translated into action and, if it is not, why.

There is much evidence to suggest that central departments in Britain vary in their willingness to use the controls available to them. Central departments vary in their philosophies or attitudes towards local authorities, ranging from laissez-faire through regulatory to promotional.(27) Local authorities also vary in their ability to resist central control. There is great scope for bargaining, negotiation and initiative. Local authorities vary too in their responses to attempted centralisation. They differ in their docility and their willingness to use the resources, political, financial, legal and administrative, at their disposal to resist central control.(28) 'Interaction' is probably a better term than control when describing central-local relations.

Many political and organisational factors condition this interaction. Central agencies may not present a consistent policy to area authorities. There may be conflicting guidance from different departments on revenue raising, expenditure and service provision; 'From the point of view of local autonomy, incompatibility and obscurity are virtues'.(29) Statutory sanctions (e.g. over loans for capital expenditure) may be mediated by other decision making processes and inter organisation arrangements such as alternative sources of finance, the ability of area authorities to influence the centre's choice of projects or the tendency to reject only low priority projects.(30) Local authorities may be just as successful when in conflict with the centre over matters where statutory powers are available to it as when involved in conflicts where the centre has only administrative influence at its disposal.

Control may be a function of technology. The more effective the arrangements for keeping local units under the scrutiny of the centre, through reporting, inspection and record keeping, the more centralised the system. The better the communication between centre and locality the easier control becomes. Many technological developments increase the analytical capabilities of the centre and its power. The physical distance separating parts of an organisation may be relevant in this respect, especially in less developed countries. Discretion at the lower levels may grow beyond officially defined responsibilities if physical separation reduces supervision to intermittent contacts.

The conclusion is that it is important to distinguish changes to the machinery of government, to make the system more decentralised, from other aspects of an area, such as its wealth, resources, political system, demographic structure, geographical location, which may be more important in determining its autonomy. Varying decentralisation may not produce all that is expected of it. Political factors can operate to make a constitutionally decentralised system highly centralised. The political complexion of local councils compared with the national government will be an important mediating factor, as will the level of 'politicisation' of area governments. France is a good example of how localities can use the power of their deputies, mayors and other offices against the formal powers of the centre. In the USA, on the other hand, attempts have been made to counter Dillon's Rule by the introduction of 'home rule' provisions in state constitutions. The formally decentralist provisions seem to have had little effect on the overall balance of power between state and local governments. More decentralisation does not necessarily mean more autonomy, and vice versa.

THE CAUSES OF DECENTRALISATION

The reasons why states have to organise themselves at the local level are familiar: access, geography, primordial loyalties, needs and communication. It is one thing to know that local administration exists, and that in a variety of forms it is an inevitable organisational consequence of the modern state: it is another to know why there is more or less decentralisation to local institutions in one country, period, public service or region compared with another. It is, however, possible to formulate a number of hypotheses, though they are not all mutually compatible.

Less decentralised

(i) A system will be less decentralised if there is conflict within the regime to an extent which threatens the dominance of the current political leadership. Where the bureaucracy can be said to mediate between interests within the dominant class it will be reluctant to see alternative power bases constructed in the provinces.

(ii) A system will be less decentralised if an authoritarian regime is seeking ways to mobilise and incorporate the lower classes in support of the regime's policies without permitting the operation

of national political organisations which might threaten the
current political leadership. The instrument for this purpose
is likely to be some form of local council operating under close
central control. Such an instrument will be used to recruit
leaders who support the regime, as in the case of Pakistan's
Basic Democracies.

(iii) If the level of decentralisation coincides with that of
the field administration, then a regime concerned with maintaining
political stability will tend to adopt for political purposes a
prefectoral system and so operate a less decentralised form of
local administration.

(iv) The greater the relative competence of the officials of
central institutions, the less decentralised will be the overall
system.

(v) The more centralised and unified, ideologically and organisation-
ally, are the national political party or parties, the less the
decentralisation.

(vi) The more socially homogeneous the population, the less the
decentralisation. Decentralisation is often a response to the
centrifugal tendencies of ethnic, regional, racial, linguistic,
religious and economic cleavages. Decentralisation may be used
in contrasting ways, particularly in developing countries but also
historically in Europe. It may be used to destroy local and
regional centres of power hostile to the national regime, or to
incorporate them into the structure of a new state. Sometimes
existing and distinct cultural entities are recognised by the
system of decentralisation. Sometimes they are absorbed into
different, perhaps larger sub-national entities. Decentralisation
may have a primarily political objective, such as to foster local
interests or the predominantly administrative objective of serving
the national interest by ensuring that local decisions conform to
national plans, policies and standards. The level of decentralisation may be a delicate compromise between national and local
objectives, a compromise vital to the stability of the state.

(vii) The greater the involvement of the national government in the
economy, the less the decentralisation.

More decentralised

(viii) A system will be more decentralised if the dominant ideology
is pluralist. Local communities will be seen as pressure groups
in their own right. The local power structure will be regarded as
legitimate. The power of the state will be suspect. The dominant
political rhetoric will be populist but non-egalitarian except
with the franchise. Democracy will be defined exclusively in
terms of political participation within the existing state
institutions for which local authorities will be regarded as a
training ground. However, cultural factors such as the existence
of authoritarian attitudes and social relationships, or egalitarian
values applied to political institutions, will have a varying
impact on decentralisation. Developing countries in particular

may have to cope with mixed cultural attitudes towards political authority which may demand not only different structures of local government in different areas but also different degrees of decentralisation to them. This aspect is one reason why decentralisation should not be confused with the type of government established at the periphery. Tradition may demand a degree of autocracy within a local government setting which is nevertheless highly centralised.

(ix) As a prefectoral system becomes redundant and the administration turns to functional field administration, the system will become more decentralised.

(x) A system of local administration will become more decentralised as concern for political stability declines and as autonomous methods of political interest aggregation and articulation are developed. Political change of this kind may well be accompanied by the replacement of the prefectoral form of coordination with local governments meeting the need for geographical variation in policy.

(xi) In less developed countries strong devolution, the existence of self governing institutions, will not exist unless there is strong central control over local authorities. The argument is that as individual authorities prove their abilities, controls are relaxed on a selective basis. But the original devolution of power will take place only if the central government has 'covered' itself by way of central controls.

(xii) The larger the country, in territory and population, the greater the decentralisation. The delegation of power is often a response to geographical and demographical size, and it is often assumed that smaller states and other political entities tend to be more centralised.

(xiii) Finally, decentralisation may be strengthened by historical factors such as the existence of ancient cities or regions with political status predating the nation of which they form constituent parts. Alternatively the traditional political culture may be related hypothetically to decentralisation as in the mythology of American politics where the South is believed to be centralised while New England is thought to have a strong localised tradition.

THE CONSEQUENCES OF DECENTRALISATION

Some of the values conventionally attached to decentralisation imply a particular form of decentralisation. It is often assumed that the form of decentralisation will be devolution: that the areas into which the state is divided will have their own self-governing institutions. It is important to remember that the form of decentralised institutions is only one measure of the level of decentralisation in operation.

Another common assumption is that the form of devolution will be democratic. Many of the objectives of decentralisation are in fact the objectives of democratic decentralisation. But local self-

government is not inevitably democratic self-government. It is
logically possible and historically common to have a highly decentralised but non-democratic form of local self-government. The
democratic quality of a system of local government is no measure of its
level of decentralisation. Any form of community self-government, however autocratic, is more decentralised than administration by field
agents of the centre. How much power is delegated from the centre to
the periphery is a different question from how democratic the periphery
is in its decision making arrangements.

The main purpose of measuring decentralisation is to evaluate the
consequences of more or less of it. To do this we require hypotheses
about the likely effects of different levels of decentralisation. When
evaluating decentralisation it is important to apply the appropriate
tests to different political arrangements. This task may involve
piercing the facade of political rhetoric to see why a system of
decentralisation is not achieving its objectives. The system may be
not what it purports to be, that it is less democratic, say, than its
protagonists pretend. The level of decentralisation is thus not the
only significant variable when evaluation takes place. The level of
democracy may be as important when assessing how far a system of
decentralisation is achieving its objectives. From a democratic viewpoint a system of decentralisation may be achieving a great deal, as
measured by levels of citizen awareness and participation. From the
decentralist viewpoint, however, it may be achieving very little.
Democratic institutions may be functioning well, but within highly
constricted powers and responsibilities. The important question is how
important is the level of decentralisation for the achievement of
democratic goals. Will a more decentralised system of democratic
self-government help achieve the goals of democracy, or is this
objective dependent on the structure of institutions at the local
level and their environment, rather than the relationship between the
area and the centre? If power is decentralised to democratic forms of
government in the localities and the political goals of democratic
decentralisation are not realised, is it because of the level of
decentralisation or because of the nature of the political system of
the locality?

Assuming that communities or areas with self-governing institutions
are run according to democratic principles, possible consequences of
decentralisation may be divided into two groups of hypotheses:
political (i-ix) and administrative (x-xiii).

(i) The more decentralised a system of government the more equal
will be the distribution of power within the community. This
hypothesis translates the traditional expectation that decentralisation will promote liberty into a prediction that it will promote
a more equal distribution of power. The translation retains the
essence of the original idea that autocracy could be avoided by
dispersing power. It seems reasonable to ask how far decentralisation achieves a distribution of power among individuals by the
distribution of power among communities. The Layfield Committee's
report is the latest expression of this expectation. Local
authorities 'are the means by which people can take part in decisions
concerning the services and amenities in their own area. Local
government, therefore, has a value in its own right in promoting

democracy. By providing a large number of points where decisions are taken by people of different political persuasion and different background, it acts as counterweight to the uniformity inherent in government decisions. It spreads political power'.(31)

(ii) The more decentralised a system of government the more politically educated will people be. This hypothesis may sound paternalistic in Britain after a century of compulsory education and forty years of full adult suffrage,(32) but it is still of considerable interest as an objective of decentralisation in developing countries faced with great obstacles to political communication and consensus building. Of particular and lasting interest is John Stuart Mill's belief that political decentralisation would extend opportunities for political participation to the 'lower grades' of society. This notion links the political education hypothesis to the political equality hypothesis set out above.

(iii) The more decentralised a system of government the more stable it will be. This hypothesis is deduced from the idea that 'popular participation in public affairs at the local government level may stimulate commitment and thus loyalty to the government. Participatory (or autocratic) decentralisation is, therefore, often considered to be a significant tool in the work of nation building'.(33)

(iv) The greater the decentralisation, the closer government will be brought to the individual and the less remote, alienated and untrusting the citizen will feel in his perceptions of government.

(v) Decentralisation is a training ground for political leadership which is able to mobilize political activism and articulate interests. The more decentralised the political system, the more local recruitment there will be into the national leadership and the more open will access be to positions of leadership in different state institutions.

(vi) The greater the decentralisation, the higher will be the levels of participation as measured by such variables of activism as turnout in local elections, membership of political organisations and contested seats. But there is some evidence of relatively high levels of decentralisation being associated with low levels of participation in local politics.(34)

(vii) The higher the level of decentralisation, the greater will be the potential for political conflict. There will be conflict between the centre and the localities brought about by differential party control, the different social composition of political leaderships at the centre and the periphery and the independent political bases of local bureaucracies. Such conflict will be at two levels: between the national government and the governments of individual areas; and between national policies and the aggregate decisions of area governments.(35) There will be conflict within areas, because expectations will be aroused which limited resources cannot fulfil, because conflict is institutionalised by the provision of arenas for political decision making, and because the formation of organised pressures is encouraged.(36)

(viii) The greater the decentralisation, the less support there will
be for laissez-faire and the protection of private property rights
and associated interests. This conclusion arises from a study of
regulatory powers sought by local authorities in land use planning,
public health, consumer protection, public safety and public order
between 1946 and 1969. Decentralisation was not associated with
restricted governmental intervention. 'Local authorities act as
institutional pressure groups for extending controls to promote
what they see as the "public interest" while the central government
uses its powers to harness and restrain these pressures.'(37)

(ix) The greater the decentralisation the more accountable will be
local officialdom. This hypothesis must be taken to mean more than
that local decisions and policies will reflect the interests,
conflicts and compromises within the local community as articulated
by its political organisations and representatives. It also refers
to the efficacy with which grievances are redressed, inefficiencies
curbed, bureaucracies made answerable, maladministration is
disclosed and waste prevented. It is usually assumed that political
decentralisation is better at ensuring accountability than other
forms of local administration, but it remains to be investigated
systematically.(38)

(x) The greater the decentralisation the higher the level of
administrative efficiency. Self-government in the localities
prevents the overloading of government at the centre. It increases
efficiency in resource allocation by the identification of community
priorities in a way that reflects consumer preferences. This
hypothesis is already supported by empirical evidence in the USA
which suggests that 'a decentralised system seems to work on behalf
of service outputs'(39), i.e. the more decentralised the administrative system the greater the quality and quantity of public services
as measured by such indicators as the number of teachers per hundred
pupils, the mileage per capita of state administered roads, the
average welfare payment per recipient, and the number of physicians
per 100,000 population.

However, confidence in the efficiency of decentralised government
is not universal. Many advocates concede that initially at least
decentralisation will cause a decline in efficiency and an increase
in costs. These drawbacks are considered acceptable because of 'the
enhancement of the democratic character of individual citizens
through participation in decentralised organisational environments.
In short, if they had to make a choice they would rather have
inefficient decentralised government than efficient centralised
government.'(40)

(xi) The greater the decentralisation, the more responsive localised
administration will be to needs. Government will be more responsive
because decision makers will have greater knowledge of local
conditions and greater capacity to respond to local needs. Since
decentralised units are relatively small they are in close
geographical proximity to their clientele and so 'allow for more
equitable access for affected publics to policy making processes.'(41)
Citizens are also provided with advocates within public agencies
rather than just neutral administrators.

147

An alternative formulation of this hypothesis is that in as far as needs and interests are perceived by those experiencing them and immediately affected by them, then self-government is bound to be more responsive than an external governing agent. A self-governing arrangement for a community will more likely reproduce, in the perception of needs and the formulation of policies, the balance of power in a community, than an external agent.

(xii) The greater the decentralisation, the more innovation there will be in the development of services. 'The opportunities and incentives for innovation are limited in a centralised organisation concerned to apply policies uniformly.'[42] There is already some evidence modifying this hypothesis because of the high proportion of innovations which can be vetoed by other units in a decentralised system. Zald's work on welfare organisations suggested that the more decentralised an organisation, the more innovations are conceived and proposed but the fewer the number of innovations adopted.[43] However, this tendency may apply more to internal relationships within large organisations than to the geographical hierarchy of the state. The source of innovation and veto in centre-periphery relations remains to be explored.

(xiii) Political decentralisation produces problems of vertical integration with national policies and goals.[44] This consequence could be a deliberate objective of political decentralisation. Horizontal decentralisation is much less of a problem for area governments: it has been suggested that it is its major strength. It overcomes the problems which the convenience of administrative specialisation at the centre produces at the periphery. The required 'mix' of governmental functions when applied at community level varies from one area to another. If the package is to be based on subjective assessments of communities themselves rather than an externally imposed coordinator (a prefect or district commissioner) then area government is essential: 'there must be some coordinating agency which can gather together the separate services coming down from the centre and adjust their content and character to the particular needs of each community in relation to each other. In short to determine the appropriate mixture of services for each community.'[45]

Administrative decentralisation produces its own problems of coordination, especially if the prefectoral form is deemed inappropriate. The phenomenon of departmentalism in the field, with specialists working in their own functional area and looking to headquarters for policy guidance rather than to their opposite numbers in other area offices, is a widespread phenomenon. Thus the choice of a system of decentralisation will have its own impact on policies and programmes.[46]

This list does not claim to be an exhaustive set of the hypotheses which could be formulated about the consequences of decentralisation. Together with the arguments for and against decentralisation outlined in an earlier section of this essay, it indicates some of the directions which research might take.

CONCLUSION

Decentralisation is a complex subject with many dimensions. As a
variable factor in the design of governmental and administrative
machinery it needs to be measured. It should be treated as a matter
of formal organisational relationships, separable from the concept of
local or community autonomy. Only then can progress be made in the
evaluation of changes designed to alter the balance of power within
states between the centre and periphery. Variations in decentralisation can then be related to the political and administrative
factors which produce them and flow from them. Research motivated by
these conceptions of decentralisation will throw light on the problem
of regarding it as a variable element in the political structure of
modern states, though the use of measures of decentralisation is
inextricable from the business of testing their validity. It should
also clarify the importance of factors other than central-local
relationships for local or regional autonomy. It should strengthen
our understanding of the political, social and economic influences
on patterns of decentralised government and administration, and it
should enable realistic assessments to be made of changes to the
hierarchical and geographical structures of the state.

NOTES AND REFERENCES

(1)   James Fesler, 'Centralisation and Decentralisation', International
          Encyclopaedia of the Social Sciences, Vol. 2, 1968.
(2)   N. Furniss, 'The practical significance of decentralisation',
          Journal of Politics, Vol. 36, No. 4, 1974.
(3)   Y. Kuroda, 'Levels of government in comparative perspective.
          Conceptual and operational considerations'. Comparative
          Political Studies, Vol. 7, No. 4, 1975.
(4)   D.K. Hart, 'Theories of government related to decentralisation
          and citizen participation', Public Administration Review,
          Vol. 32, October 1972.
(5)   J.G. Van Putten, 'Local Government in the seventies',
          International Review of Administrative Sciences, Vol. 37,
          No. 3, 1971.
(6)   N. Boaden, 'Central departments and local authorities: The
          relationship examined', Political Studies, Vol. 18, No. 2,
          1970.
(7)   J.J. Heaphey, Spatial Dimensions of Development Administration,
          Duke University Press, Durham, N. Carolina, 1971.
(8)   W.B. Shepard, 'Metropolitan political decentralisation: a test of
          the life-style values model', Urban Affairs Quarterly, Vol. 10,
          No. 3, 1975; Dilys Hill, Democratic Theory and Local Govern-
          ment, Allen and Unwin, London, 1974; Arthur Maass (ed.), Area
          and Power, Free Press, New York, 1959; Van Putten, op. cit.
(9)   J. Fesler, 'Approaches to the understanding of decentralisation',
          Journal of Politics, Vol. 27, 1965.
(10) I. Katznelson, 'Antagonistic ambiguity: notes on reformism and
          decentralisation', Politics and Society, Vol. 2, No. 3, 1972.
(11) L.J. Sharpe, 'Reforming the grass roots: an alternative analysis'
          in David Butler and A.H. Halsey (eds.), Policy and Politics,
          Macmillan, London, 1978; B.C. Smith and J. Stanyer,
          Administering Britain , Fontana, London, 1976; R.K. Yin and
          W.A. Lucas, 'Decentralisation and alienation', Policy Sciences,

Vol. 4, No. 3, 1973; Boaden, op. cit.

(12) R.C. Wood, Metropolis Against Itself, Committee for Economic
      Development, New York, 1959; D. Yates, Neighbourhood
      Democracy; The Politics and Impacts of Decentralisation,
      D.C. Heath, Lexington, Mass., 1973, p. 3.

(13) B. Mukerji, 'Administrative problems of democratic
      decentralisation', Indian Journal of Public Administration,
      Vol. 7, No. 3, 1961; N.R. Lang, 'The dialectics of
      decentralisation: economic reform and regional inequality
      in Yugoslavia', World Politics, Vol. 27, No. 3, 1975.

(14) M. Aiken, 'Comparative cross-national research on sub-national
      units in Western Europe: problems, data sources and a
      proposal', Journal of Comparative Administration, Vol. 4,
      No. 4, 1973.

(15) The Layfield Committee of Inquiry into Local Government Finance,
      Report, HMSO, London, 1976; R.C. Fried, 'Politics, Economics
      and Federalism: Aspects of urban government in Austria,
      Germany and Switzerland'in T.N. Clark (ed.), Comparative
      Community Politics, Sage, New York, 1974; K. Newton,
      'Community decision makers and community decision making in
      England and the United States' in Clark, op. cit.; J.G. Grumm
      and R.D. Murphy, 'Dillon's Rule Reconsidered', Annals of the
      American Academy of Political and Social Science, Vol. 416,
      1974.

(16) Fesler (1965), op. cit.

(17) T.N. Clark, 'Community Autonomy in the National System:
      Federalism, Localism and Decentralisation' in Clark, op. cit.

(18) H. Maddick, Democracy, Decentralisation and Development, Asia
      Publishing House, Bombay, 1963; G.R. Stephens, 'State
      centralisation and the erosion of local autonomy', Journal of
      Politics, Vol. 36, Feb. 1974.

(19) Grumm and Murphy, op. cit.

(20) K.J. Davey, 'Local Autonomy and Independent revenues', Public
      Administration, Vol. 49, Spring 1971.

(21) H. Kaufman, Politics and Policies in State and Local Governments,
      Prentice-Hall, Englewood Cliffs, New Jersey, 1963; N.P.
      Hepworth, 'Public expenditure controls and local government',
      Local Government Studies, Vol. 2, No. 1, 1976.

(22) A. Downs, Inside Bureaucracy, Little, Brown & Co., Boston, 1967.

(23) C.D. Foster, R.A. Jackman and M.J. Osborn, 'Centralisation and
      local discretion in educational expenditure', Appendix 10 to
      the Layfield Committee Report, op. cit; J. Brand, 'Ministerial
      control and local autonomy in education', Political Quarterly,
      Vol. 36, No. 2, 1965.

(24) Grumm and Murphy, op. cit.

(25) C.M. Bonjean et al., (eds.), Community Politics, Free Press,
      New York, 1971.

(26) G.R. Stephens, op. cit.

(27) J.A.G. Griffith, Central Departments and Local Authorities,
      Allen & Unwin, London, 1966.

(28) G.W. Jones, 'Intergovernmental relations in Britain', Annals of
      the American Academy for Political and Social Science, Vol. 416,
      1974.

(29) R. Harris, 'Communications and the rate support grant process',
      Linkage, July 1978.

(30) R.A.W. Rhodes, 'Central-Local Relations' in Appendix 6 to the Layfield Committee Report, op. cit.
(31) Layfield Committee Report, op. cit.; Kuroda, op. cit.
(32) L.J. Sharpe, 'The role and functions of local government in Modern Britain', Appendix 6 of the Layfield Committee Report, op. cit.
(33) A. Leemans, Changing Patterns of Local Authorities, I.U.L.A., The Hague, 1970.
(34) M. Aiken, op. cit.
(35) Fesler, (1965), op. cit.
(36) D. Yates, 'Making Decentralisation Work: the view from city hall', Policy Sciences, Vol. 5, No. 3, 1974.
(37) H. Scarrow, 'Policy pressures by British local government: the case of regulation in the public interest', Comparative Politics, Vol. 4, 1971.
(38) B.C. Smith, 'The justification of local government' in L.D. Feldman and M.D. Goldrick, Politics and Government in Urban Canada, Methuen, Toronto, 1972.
(39) I. Sharkansky, 'Government expenditures and public policies in the American states', American Political Science Review, Vol. 61, 1967.
(40) D.K. Hart, op. cit.
(41) D.K. Hart, op. cit.
(42) Layfield Committee Report, op. cit.
(43) M.N. Zald, 'Decentralisation: myth vs. reality', in R.T. Golembiewsky et al., (eds.), Public Administration, Rand, McNally, Chicago, 1966.
(44) D. Porter and E. Olsen, 'Some critical issues in government centralisation and decentralisation', Public Administration Review, Vol. 36, No. 1, 1976.
(45) L.J. Sharpe, 'Theories of local government' in L.D. Feldman and W.D. Goldrick, Politics and Government in Urban Canada, op. cit.
(46) D. Porter and E. Olsen, op. cit.

Further reading

A.H. Birch, Political Integration and Disintegration in the British Isles, Allen & Unwin, London, 1977.
N. Boaden, Urban Policy Making, Cambridge University Press, London, 1971.
F. Cripps and W. Godley, Local Government Finance and Its Reform, University of Cambridge, Cambridge, 1976.
M. LeMay, 'Expenditure and non-expenditure measures of state urban polity outputs', American Politics Quarterly, Vol. 1, No. 4, 1973.
J. Milch, 'Urban government in France: municipal policy-making in the centralised state', Administration and Society, Vol. 9, No. 4, 1978.
D.S. Pugh, J. Hage and M. Aiken, 'Relationships of centralisation to other structural properties', Administrative Science Quarterly, Vol. 12, No. 1, 1967.
F. Sherwood, 'Devolution as a problem of organisational strategy' in R.T. Daland (ed.), Comparative Urban Research, Sage, New York, 1969.

12   Relations between Central and Local Government in Sweden: the Control of Local Government

Royston Greenwood

INTRODUCTION

Responsibility for managing the national economy pushes the central
government of any industrialised country to seek a measure of control
over the spending decisions of local authorities. In particular, the
centre seeks to manipulate the aggregate level of local government
expenditure. The proportion of the public sector given to local
government makes the objective inevitable. Nevertheless, in all
countries there are disagreements over the appropriate level and forms
of central influence.

The concern here is to review recent developments in Sweden. The
analysis explores some of the effects of the economic dislocation
experienced in recent years upon the pattern of interactions between
the centre (referred to in Sweden as 'the State') and municipal
authorities. It will be demonstrated that the quadrupling of oil
prices in the early 1970s created adverse economic conditions which in
turn prompted the State to attempt closer control over local government
expenditure. That pattern is not dissimilar to recent events in the
United Kingdom,[1] but the interesting difference between the two
countries is that whereas in the United Kingdom there has been
effective central government intervention, in Sweden the attempt at
closer control was relatively unsuccessful. One of the principal aims
of this paper will be to seek explanations for the relative inability
of the Swedish central government to obtain control.

The analysis is based upon interviews conducted between 1 April and
30 August 1978 with sixteen officers and councillors from three of the
larger municipalities: Stockholm (661,000), Uppsala (140,000) and Umea
(77,000). Each interview lasted between one and two hours. The small
sample of authorities is clearly insufficient to support general
observations of the local government system and the results obtained
must be regarded as tentative. Some attempt to broaden the data base
was made through a questionnaire distributed to the seventeen largest
municipalities, of which twelve replied.

The discussion takes as its starting point the economic context
within which local authorities operate and which shapes the nature of
their interactions with the State. It would be foolish to abstract
the patterns of interaction and influence between the State and local
government from prevailing financial circumstances. The interpretation

and explanation of events has a temporal base and some knowledge is evidently required of the significant features of the period studied (provided in the next section). Subsequent sections deal with the strategy adopted by the central government in an attempt to manage the economic context and the response of local government to that strategy. Finally an examination is made of the structure of local authority autonomy in Sweden.

THE ECONOMIC CONTEXT

Sweden, in common with all industrialised nations, faced difficulties after the quadrupling of oil prices. The rate of inflation increased from under four per cent in 1973 to over twelve per cent in 1977-8. The volume of exports fell over the same period, creating a serious deficit on the balance of payments. The rate of growth of manufacturing investment was less than anticipated, and the sluggish growth of the economy as a whole became increasingly worrying. The initial response of the government was not one of deflation. Despite the downward turn of international economic activity in late 1973 and early 1974 the Swedish economy was expanding rapidly and the government found it convenient to adopt an economic strategy designed to stimulate domestic demand in order to allow the strong upturn in industrial activity and production to continue:

> 'The intention ... was to bridge the international recession.
> It seemed reasonable to suppose that demand abroad would
> strengthen appreciably during 1976. Sweden would then be
> able to "jump aboard" with a strong expansion of exports,
> whereupon the growth of domestic demand could be retarded'
> (Preliminary National Budget 1977, p. 2).

Domestic expansion was to be achieved in two ways. Disposable household income would be increased through a package of tax reductions coupled with moderate increases in other taxes such as the local income tax.(2) The State was able to cut the rate of national income tax and successfully sought an agreement with local government authorities to limit the level of increases in rates of local income tax. Secondly, spending in the public sector would be increased. Expenditure by both central and local governments rose (in volume terms) by 5.5 per cent in 1974-5, a rate higher than the average annual increases of the previous four years (see Table 1)(3).

This stimulative policy, however, underestimated the international recession. Foreign demand did not pull out of its downswing either as consistently or as strongly as expected. Furthermore, the levels of price and wage increases within the economy made Sweden increasingly unable to compete internationally. Far from bridging the recession the government's policy helped the economy lose its share of international markets. A direct consequence was a deteriorating balance of payments, financed by borrowing abroad. And, by 1976, the 'comparatively favourable' position enjoyed by Sweden in 1974 had been largely dissipated. As a result the 1976 Budget Statement heralded a shift in direction. The principal need had now become the restoration of balance to current payments, which was to be secured:

> 'by conducting an expansionary economic policy which is

Table 1
Public Expenditure in Sweden:
1970/1 to 1977/8

	1970/1 %	1971/2 %	1972/3 %	1973/4 %	1974/5 %	1975/6 %	1976/7 %	1977/8 %
A. CONSUMPTION (Volume Changes)								
. Central Government	4.5	3.0	2.5	1.0	5.5	0.5	0.5	3.5
. Local Government	4.0	3.0	1.5	5.0	5.5	4.0	4.5	4.5
. Public Sector	4.5	3.0	2.0	4.0	5.5	3.0	3.0	4.0
B. CAPITAL INVESTMENT (Volume Changes)								
. Central Government	-3.0	12.5	-5.0	0.0	-7.5	-2.5	-2.5	3.5
. Local Government	-10.0	0.0	-11.0	-2.0	-2.0	-2.0	10.5	5.5
. Public Sector	-9.0	2.5	-10.0	-1.5	-3.5	-2.0	7.5	5.0
C. EMPLOYMENT (Volume Changes)								
. Central Government	.	4.0	4.1	4.0	2.9	2.8	2.3	.
. Local Government	.	6.0	4.1	7.0	6.0	5.3	6.1	.
D. PUBLIC SECTOR: % of GNP	2.9	32.1	29.5	30.9	31.9	.	.	.

(Source: Central Bureau of Statistics, Stockholm)

designed to boost exports. This requires a continuous
expansion of production capacity or in other words a
rapid growth in investments. It is only a strong
expansion of our capacity for producing goods, coupled
with unimpaired industrial competitiveness, that is
likely to combine the restoration of external balance
with the central goal of full employment' (1976 Budget
Statement p. 10).

The importance of this shift is considerable as it affected the
substantive content of central-local negotiations. The government's
policy since the early 1970s and until 1976 involved the restraint of
increases in taxation rates in order to stimulate spending by increasing
disposable household income. From the local authority's point of view
the government's attention was directed at limiting rises in the local
income tax but not necessarily in expenditure. The policy of mild
stimulation was not inconsistent with expansion of local government
expenditure. As long as expenditure growth did not entail tax increases
the central government was unconcerned. After 1976 this benign approach
to expenditure was discarded. From then on increases in local
government consumption were directly inconsistent with the government's
policy of switching resources from public into productive sectors of
the economy: 'domestic demand must be curbed in order to release
resources for the export industry and for the industries that compete
with imports' (Revised National Budget, 1977, p. 20). In summary, the
aim of the central government between 1973 and 1976 was to moderate
increase in local tax rates. During and after 1976 the aim was to
limit tax increases and to curb expenditure.

It is in the context of the economic situation and the government's
economic policies that we should seek to understand the relationship
between central and local government authorities. And it is with this
issue that following sections are concerned. Data are presented on how
the State attempted to restrain increases in tax rates and expenditure
as a preliminary to an assessment of how successful was the State in
those directions.

NEGOTIATIONS FOR RESTRAINT

Local income tax in Sweden is not subject to ratification by any
national authority. Nor are limits placed upon the level of taxation
that can be set (unlike in Norway where a ceiling is imposed). Indeed,
this freedom from central direction prompted Hjelmquist to acclaim the
local income tax as 'the foundation of local autonomy'.(4) How far
this claim is justified will become clear. What is evident is that in
1973 the State had to find some means of persuading local authorities
to limit their inclinations towards higher levels of taxation. It did
so by persuading the local authority associations to prevail upon their
members to restrain increases in local taxes. The first agreement was
announced to take effect in 1973:

'An essential element in the government's economic policy
is the agreement concluded in the spring of 1972 with the
Boards of the Association of Municipalities and County
Councils where the latter would recommend municipalities
and county councils to refrain from increasing their tax

rates for a two year period, 1973-4. The agreement stipulated
that an increase could be accepted only if it was absolutely
essential' (Swedish Budget Statement, 1973-4, p. 21).

Similar agreements were negotiated in the following years. In 1975
local authorities were to continue moderation with increases restricted
to cover absolutely essential growth in expenditure. In 1976 and 1977
the agreement was rather more precise:

'By the terms of an agreement with the Government in February
1975, the Boards of the Associations of Municipalities and
County Councils have recommended that the average local tax
rate should not be increased by more than one percentage point
in 1976 and 1977 combined' (Preliminary National Budget 1976,
p. 132).

The agreements were not one sided. In exchange for the support of
the associations the government was to provide financial compensation.
Thus, the agreement covering 1976 and 1977 was 'bought' by the
provision of 'an extra State grant totalling 600 million kronor in both
1976 and 1977' (Preliminary National Budget, 1976, p. 132). This
compensation was in lieu of the tax revenues that would be lost by
local authorities in the exercise of restraint over tax increases and
illustrates that the aim of the central government during this period
was less to curtail expenditure than to limit tax increases.

Table 2

Rate of Tax Increases: 1972 to 1978

	1972	1973	1974	1975	1976	1977	1978
'Agreement' (%)	'absolutely essential'				0.5	0.5	not known
Actual Rates of Tax Increases (%)	4	0.15	0.9	1.2	0.92	0.69	1.90

Source: Budget statements prepared by Economic Department of the
         Ministry of Finance and the National Institute of Economic
         Research, Stockholm.

The extent to which the agreements successfully affected local
authority tax increases may be gauged from Table 2 which compared the
average increases for local government as a whole with the negotiated
agreements struck with the associations. The figures indicate that the
annual average rise from 1973 onwards was significantly below that of
the years preceding (i.e. see 1972); and that the annual averages from
1973 onwards are not substantially above the agreed guidelines. Over
the two year period 1976-77 for example, when the agreement was for an
increase of no more than one percent, the actual increase was between
one and a half and one and three quarter per cent.

One might thus conclude that the attempt by the central government to
moderate average increases in local taxation met with some success. The
crucial statistic after 1976, however, was not the rate of tax increase,

but the volume of expenditure growth. As indicated earlier the
government was constrainted by previous agreements to work through the
tax rate in order to reduce expenditure, but the aim was to reduce
expenditure. How far the government achieved that aim is partly
indicated by the figures given in Table 1. Examination of those
figures should bear in mind that the average growth in local government
revenue consumption for 1960-65 was five per cent, and 3.9 per cent
for 1965-70. It is against the background of that decade of growth
that the experience of the 1970s should be assessed.

The striking observation is that the pressure upon local income tax
rates failed to curb the growth in expenditure. The growth rate from
1976-7 remained at approximately the same level as that experienced
in the early 1960s, and is almost certainly much higher than the level
desired by the State. Even more illuminating is that for two of the
four years from 1972-3 to 1975-6, whenthe principal economic aim was
one of tax restraint combined with a measure of mild stimulation, the
rate of expenditure growth was actually lower than the growth rates
of 1976-7 and 1977-8 when the aim was to reduce or at least curtail
expenditure.

In short, the evidence from Table 1 indicates that the State achieved
limited success in its campaign to curb expenditure. One other source
of evidence is available. The questionnaire distributed to the larger
municipalities asked them to indicate how the extra resources provided
by increases in their tax rate had been spent. The purpose was to
examine how far authorities were using additional resources to finance
the provision of new services. Thus, expenditure was classified in
terms of:

(1)   expenditure to meet increases in costs and salaries;

(2)   expenditure to meet the revenue consequences of previous
      capital investments;

(3)   expenditure to cover increased demands for existing
      standards of service (e.g. demands caused by population
      changes);

(4)   expenditure to cover the provision of new services.

Categories (1) and (2) represent 'committed' expenditures and reflect
an attempt to maintain existing services or to carry through policy
decisions taken in earlier years. Expenditure used to meet demands on
existing services, i.e. (3), similarly reflects an attempt to adhere to
previously taken policy decisions. By contrast, the fourth category of
expenditure represents the development of new policies. The use of
expenditure for this category reflects an unwillingness to avoid
increases in total expenditure. Therefore, the greater the number of
authorities that deployed resources on category (4), the lower was the
impact of the State's attempt to curb local expenditure.

In England, increases in the rate levy are now comparatively rarely
used to meet (4). Moreover, even expenditure falling into categories
(2), (3) and (4) may well have to be financed through displacement of
existing expenditures.(5) How far this development happens in Sweden

is shown in Table 3 which summarises the responses of the larger municipal authorities. In 1978 eleven of the twelve authorities replying to the questionnaire took decisions to initiate and finance new services. Despite the attempt by central government to curb

Table 3

Usage of Additional Resources by Type of Expenditure

Type of Expenditure	Number of Authorities
1. increases in costs and salaries	12
2. revenue consequences of capital investment	10
3. increased demands for existing standards of service	4
4. new services	11

expenditure the larger municipal authorities continued to improve the provision of local services thus necessitating growth in expenditure.

Summary

The rate of increase in local income tax slowed from 1972, and for local government as a whole the average annual increase was somewhere near the guidelines agreed between the State and the local authority associations. Whether the agreement itself had any direct influence upon the actions of local authorities is unclear but certainly the fiscal activities of local authorities were consistent with the initial (i.e. pre 1976) aim of the State. The ability of the central government to restrain local government expenditure, on the other hand, was limited. During the period studied the volume of local government expenditure rose annually by the order of four to five per cent. Only in 1971-2 and 1972-3 did the increases fall below four per cent. In the three years following the shift in national economic policy towards a concern with expenditure (rather than taxation rates) the annual growth rates were 4.0 per cent, 4.5 per cent, and 4.5 per cent. These expenditure increases are marginally greater than those experienced between 1965 and 1970. At worst, the evidence is that by the middle of 1978 the State had largely failed in its attempts to curb local expenditure.

The position is not static. From 1972 to 1978, and especially from 1976, local authorities were increasingly aware of the need to limit expenditures. By 1978 those interviewed were admitting the likely turn of the screw:

'There has been no stopping of services, but now there is some talk of it. The politicians are talking of cutting food in schools for children. But they have not done it yet ...' (Umea).

'There is some political haggling but so far we have always had the money. They have found the money to satisfy me. For

158

example, they gave us back the money to provide for supervision at school meals ... But the climate is changing.
They consciously put the (allocations)very low and I do not
know what will result this year ...' (Uppsala).

'Until last year we made things cheaper. Now we have to
make cuts in services ...' (Stockholm).

Local authorities are beginning to respond to pressures for restraint
even though the response has not begun to show through in the annual
statistics. Partly the increasing awareness of the need to curb
expenditure may be a response to the toughening approach adopted by the
State:

'They (the State) say that if we do not push expenditure
and taxes down they will cut the subsidies in the schools,
and so on. There are threats to this effect. We are all
aware of this ... I think that in Stockholm and the big
cities people are aware of this risk ... What the national
government says carries weight' (Stockholm).

'I have met State officials who threaten to move local
services out of the local government system if expenditure
does not stop' (Umea).

There are signs that the financial behaviour of local authorities may
change. As yet, the State has not curbed local expenditure. Unlike
England, where local authorities capitulated to central pressures,
Swedish municipalities have retained a greater measure of local
autonomy. Why has this retention been possible?

THE STRUCTURE OF LOCAL AUTONOMY IN SWEDEN

Why do local authorities in Sweden appear to enjoy a greater financial
freedom than their counterparts in England? What factors enabled
Swedish local authorities to resist attempts to influence levels of
local taxation and expenditure especially during the later (post 1976)
stages of the government's economic policy? There are four possible
explanations.

1. The local income tax

It is a commonplace to argue that the independence of any local government is partly dependent on a local and independent source of
revenue.(6) Swedish local authorities have such a source, namely the
local income tax, which supports the larger proportion of their
expenditure (see Table 4). English local authorities also have an
independent source of revenue, 'rates', which can be increased without
financial approval from elsewhere. The important advantage of the
Swedish income tax, however, which explains why it supports a much
higher proportion of municipal expenditure than does the English
rating system, is that it is a buoyant source of revenue. The Swedish
local authority can expect an increased yield from its income tax even
if the rate of tax is unchanged. Furthermore, essentially limited
increases in tax rates yield significant amounts of further income

Table 4

Sources of Swedish Local Government Revenue %

1971 - 1978

Proportion of Revenue from	1971	1972	1973	1974	1975	1976	1977	1978
A. Local Taxes and Fees	51	54	53	53	52	53	55	58
B. Grants	24	25	27	28	27	27	27	26
C. Other (including Borrowing)	24	19	18	18	19	18	16	16

Source: Budget Statements

prepared by Economic Department of the Ministry of Finance and the

National Institute of Economic Research, Stockholm.

Table 5

Yields from Alternative Increases in Tax Rates

1971 – 1978

	1971	1972	1973	1974	1975	1976	1977	1978
% Tax Increases	5	4	0.15	0.09	1.2	0.92	0.69	(1.90)
% Yield	16	21.5	9.5	11.00	14.5	19.0	28.5	(24)

Source: Budget Statement

prepared by the Economic Department of the Ministry of Finance and the

National Institute of Economic Research (NIER), Stockholm.

The figures for 1978 are in parentheses because they are estimates made

by the NIER from a survey conducted in late 1977.

(Table 5). For example, modest increases in 1973 and 1974 of less than half a per cent provided additional resources of the order of ten per cent: an advantage denied the local authority in England where the property-based rating system yields the same amount of revenue until the rate levy is increased. One of the fundamental advantages of the Swedish municipality, in other words, is its ability to support a substantial proportion of expenditure through a form of taxation which is both independent of central control and economically bouyant. The local income tax is one contributory factor towards an explanation of why the State failed to control local government expenditure.

2.   The pattern of grants

Grants from the State to the Swedish municipality are usually in the form of grants-in-aid for particular purposes. The law passed in 1970 forbidding the State from instituting regulations placing financial burdens upon the local authority without making provision for financial support has encouraged the extensive use of specific grants. Non-specific (or block) grants do exist. A form of tax equalisation to the less wealthy authorities is provided as a block grant. Tax compensation is also provided without reference to specific services. But the considerable emphasis in Sweden is towards the use of grants earmarked to support the provision of particular services.[7] In Britain the emphasis is in the opposite direction with local authorities receiving block grants unconnected to the provision of particular services. Admittedly, the calculation of the Rate Support Grant involves reference to specific services, and ministers are able to claim that they have successfully argued in the cabinet for inclusion within the Grant of resources for particular services. Nevertheless the Grant is actually spent, and is intended to be spent, as the local authority thinks fit. Authorities can allocate the Grant without reference to the aspirations and intentions of national politicians.

    The utilisation of specific grants has several effects each limiting the ability of the State to reduce the total level of grant. First, the process of dismantling specific grants would be administratively complex. It would be much less convenient to adjust the terms and conditions of multiple specific grants in order to achieve savings of a given total. The calculations required to curtail expenditure by a given aggregate through reductions in, and the removal of, a myriad of specific grants would be much more complicated than the calculations required in England over the total of a single block grant. The administrative complexity of the grant structure in Sweden may well be a disincentive for the State to operate through it as a control over local expenditure.

    Second, the network of grants relates money to political benefit. Specific grants inform politicians of the services yielded by items of expenditure. To cut that expenditure is to cease provision of the service. To have to make decisions on specific grants forces politicians to make choices between services for which they may well have expressed previous commitments. In Britain the block allocation of resources through the Rate Support Grant effectively allows the centre to argue for reductions in expenditure without the need to discuss in detail which service areas should be cut. The block grant system facilitates the pushing of unpopular political decisions onto a

162

different level of government. National politicians in England are
more able to divorce responsibility for the management of total
expenditure (how much should be spent) from responsibility for the
management of resource allocation (where it should be spent).
Politicians in Sweden, on the other hand, cannot pursue the goal of
expenditure restraint without understanding and legitimating the
benefits lost in terms of services reduced or withdrawn. They cannot
manage the economy at the centre and pass to the locality through
reductions in grant the unpopular responsibility for the cutting of
services. We would suggest that this feature is an important
motivational constraint upon the use of grants as a means to curb
local government expenditure.

3.   The constraint of initial actions and purposes

In any case, grants in Sweden support a much smaller proportion of
local expenditure than does the income tax. It makes much more sense
for the State to grasp control of the income tax than it does to curb
grants. One can thus identify a third important factor determining the
State's lack of success. In 1976 the State sought to control local
expenditure through control of income tax rates because of its previous
concern with tax rates as an end in itself. However, once the economic
aim had changed and control over tax rates become a means to expenditure
restraint the government was faced with the difficulty of changing an
existing machinery linking it with the local authority Associations.
The State found itself, in 1976, when its economic thinking began to
change, with an established agreement (negotiated in 1975) covering
local expenditure until the end of 1977. Part of the agreement, moreover, involved the payment of compensation. In short, the change in
policy was constrained by the existing machinery established to achieve
rather different economic aims. That machinery, moreover, was ill
equipped to meet the new, more pressing need for expenditure restraint.

4.   The cultural commitment to local government

The above are key factors that should be considered when tracing the
relations between local and central governments in Sweden. But they
hardly answer the more important questions. The existence of the local
income tax, providing the municipality with a buoyant and independent
source of local revenue, coupled with a grant structure based upon
specific rather than block grants, are advantages not enjoyed by the
English local authority and go some way towards explaining the relative
capitulation of English local authorities to central pressure and the
successful resistance experienced in Sweden. But, at the end of the
day, the Swedish central government could have seized control of the
income tax. It has the legal authority to dismantle the tax. Less
drastically, it could place ceilings upon either local expenditure
or the local income tax in a manner similar to what happens in
Norway.(8) Indeed, both of these alternatives have been openly
considered in Sweden, but have been rejected. Why? What stops the
State from taking steps to counteract the advantages outlined so far?

    To anyone familiar with the British system of government, and the
desultory support given to local government as an institution of
democracy, one noticeable and notable feature of Swedish society is the
widespread, openly admitted and enthusiastic commitment to the idea of

strong local government. Whether there is strong local government is
another matter. Marshall with his extensive knowledge of the English
system of local government was moved to remark that in Sweden:

> 'Local authorities have more independence than any others
> known to the writer, a feature of which they are justly
> proud. This autonomy is related to their financial
> position ...'.(9)

Anton, in contrast, with his experience of local government in the
United States, was less generous:

> 'Detailed national legislation obliges municipalities to
> carry out certain responsibilities (education, social services,
> housing and planning etc.) in specified ways ... The effect
> of these obligations and contributions is to remove much
> discretionary power from local authorities. More than 80
> per cent of the average local budget is devoted to these
> obligatory programs'.(10)

Anton's analysis is reinforced by Murray's assessment that only twenty
two per cent of local government expenditure is clearly under the control
of local government.(11) Our impression is that Swedish local
authorities are much more constrained by central regulations than are
English local authorities, at least for the services demanded by law.
For example, the education service is much more centralised in school
building design, classroom sizes, school organisation, and curricula.
But the local authority is able to ignore central guidelines (which
are attached to financial incentives) for those services such as
recreation and culture for which no legal obligation is placed upon the
authority. They can do so because of their option to raise resources
through the local income tax.

Of rather greater importance than the extent of municipal autonomy
over the provision of services is the commitment towards local autonomy
and the belief within Sweden that there should be strong local government. In Sweden, politicians and officers pay public tribute to the
value of local self government. Thus Hjalmar Mehr in his 1963 State
of the City Address to the Stockholm City Council could claim that:

> 'In depth, breadth, and significance, municipal self-
> government in our nation is unique, with its total
> sovereignty over essential community responsibilities.
> It trains women and men in responsibility; it anchors
> social consciousness and individual governing capacity
> in the citizenry; it is one of the cornerstones of
> Swedish democracy'.(12)

The same conclusion is found in rather simpler language in official
reports and publications. Thus, the Swedish Institute asserts that:
'Local self-government by means of municipalities is basic to Swedish
democracy'.(13)

Similar sentiments are found in Britain. Government publications
praise the importance of local government, and local politicians amplify
the benefits produced by service on the local council. What cannot be

culled from published sources, however, is the strength of commitment
behind them. Swedish public officials appear much more convinced about
local self government than do their English counterparts. Every person
interviewed paid testimony to the prevailing commitment to local
government: this commitment underlies the recent actions of central
government and their relative unwillingness to seize effective hold of
the local income tax. The local income tax symbolises the idea of an
independent, strong local government; and, in the context of the cultural
support for local government as an institution, the State is effectively
restrained from confronting that symbol. One chief officer captured
the dilemma:

> 'The problem of local autonomy is a holy cow in Sweden. All
> parties talk very proudly about the need for strong local
> government, and how we must decentralise ... Everyone is
> very frightened of interfering with the independence of local
> government. We are brought up from the cradle to believe
> in the importance of strong local government. All the parties
> are unwilling to interfere. The culture of an independent
> system is very strong'.

There exists in Sweden an expressed, deeply entrenched belief that
local government should be strong. This belief holds back the State
in its dealings with local government. Local authorities in Sweden
have the local income tax because of this cultural belief. It is not
the income tax itself that protects the local authority but the
supportive cultural context. English local authorities, it could be
argued, do not have the local income tax, and will not have it in the
foreseeable future, despite the analysis and recommendations of the
Layfield Committee, because there is insufficient commitment to the
idea of strong local government. Indeed, it could be argued that
local authorities in England are publicly regarded as wasteful and
inefficient. In Sweden local authorities are not subject to the same
measure of criticism and ill-will.

   The actions of central government in Sweden are understandable within
the cultural context. In order to moderate local income tax rates the
government sought 'agreements' with the local authority associations.
They made no attempt to impose fiscal and expenditure guidelines. The
distribution of anything equivalent to a white paper calling for severe
restraint without prior consultation with local government, as has been
the dominant practice in England, was not a serious possibility.
Similarly, the refusal of central government in England to discuss
the total level of public and local government expenditure (despite the
creation of the Consultative Council) has no parallel in Sweden. In
Sweden relations between the State and local government are characterised by negotiation, not by direction.

Conclusion

The position towards the middle of 1978 was that for some time local
authorities in Sweden had acted contrary to the expressed aims of the
State. Despite moderate growth in rates of local taxation the volume
of local government expenditure had continued to grow at an annual rate
in excess of four per cent. The evidence points clearly to a local
government acting contrary to the dictates of national economic policy.

This action is _possible_ because of two advantages built into the structure of local government finance: the existence of a buoyant and independent source of local taxation (the income tax), and a pattern of grants tied to particular services. A third advantage is based upon the shift in economic policy which was constrained by initial aims and actions. The _continuation_ of these advantages is a function of the cultural context. Underlying the specific actions of State and municipality between 1972 and 1978 was the cultural assumption that local authorities should be independent. That cultural assumption is symbolised by the existence of the local income tax and explains the unwillingness of the State to coerce local authorities in their use of that tax.

IMPLICATIONS FOR RESEARCH INTO CENTRAL-LOCAL RELATIONS

1.   The attitudinal and cultural context of central-local
     relations

A central argument presented above is that the autonomy of local government authorities is a function of an independent source of local revenue coupled with an unwillingness of the centre to intervene with use of that source. The analysis of Swedish experience demonstrates the crucial importance of the context of values within which govern-mental institutions work.

To understand the interactions of central and local government it is not enough to study the methods (e.g. the structure of local government financing) or the procedures (e.g. the existence of agencies such as the Consultative Council used in the United Kingdom) of central-local interaction. It is equally, and perhaps more, important to understand the attitudes and values which people bring to the use of those methods and procedures. To ignore attitudes and values is to misinterpret the factors which determine the configuration of central-local relations. That is, any attempt to study the relative dependence of local authorities upon the centre should not focus exclusively upon existing methods and procedures. Patterns of dependence cannot be traced to existing methods and procedures. Indeed, in one sense the prevailing procedures and methods are the expression of the pattern of dependence: but they are not the cause. The cause of dependence lies in the values which led to the development of those procedures and methods.

In one respect this argument smacks of an infinite regress. The researcher is urged to look for the cause behind the causes behind the causes and so on. However, our contention is that existing methods and procedures are the organisational structure supporting a prevailing set of attitudes and beliefs about what ought to be the relationship between tiers of government. Those attitudes and beliefs, the cultural context, are not necessarily articulated explicitly or acknowledged. Nevertheless, they exist and demand exploration. For example, the critical reaction of the civil service to the recommendations of the Layfield Committee tells more about values and beliefs within the civil service than they do about the merits and disadvantages of the local income tax.

Thus, there are several implications for research into local government relations with the centre:

- what are the attitudes and assumptions held by relevant
  personnel of the 'proper' relationship between centre
  and locality;

- how are these attitudes and assumptions reflected in the
  methods and procedures that structure interorganisational
  relations;

  and

- what are the determinants of these attitudes and assumptions.

2.   The pattern of grants

The common view is that block grants are more likely to increase local
autonomy than are specific grants. In various circumstances this view
is probably the case. Receipt of a sum of monies without detailed
specifications for its allocation provides the local authority with
scope for allocating resources between services according to local
circumstances. But there are circumstances where this thesis may be
incorrect. Thus, specific grants may <u>protect</u> local authorities during
times of financial restraint. It is relatively more difficult to <u>curb</u>
expenditure through use of specific grants than through the use of
block grants which <u>can</u> be used to curb total expenditure.

   The thesis was proposed from an admittedly limited study of Sweden.
The thesis made assumptions about the factors which shape and determine
the decisions and behaviours of central government personnel. But no
interviews were conducted with those personnel. Thus, we have an
unusual (perhaps even a perverse) hypothesis which, although it fits
available data and has a deal of plausibility, requires more empirical
appraisal. In order to understand the relationship between central and
local government an investigation should be launched into the effects
of alternative patterns of grant upon the decision options open to,
and attractive to, central government ministers and civil servants.
We need to get beyond the untested generalisations contained within the
textbooks that block grants increase local discretion. We need to learn
of how different grant arrangements (e.g. block grants v specific grants)
constrain the actions and decisions of central government over which
issues (total expenditure? spending in particular policy areas?) and
under what circumstances (e.g. resource growth: resource stability:
resource decline).

3.   The role of the associations

In Sweden the local authority associations appear to be accredited with
a greater measure of importance than are their British counterparts.
The accuracy of this impression   is simply assumed here although no
assumptions are made about the respective merits of the associations
within their systems of local government. This thought prompts a
general line of enquiry. The study of interorganisational interactions
has raised the importance of 'strategies' adopted by organisations in
their dealings with other organisations. One approach is to examine
the strategies of individual local authorities. Another line of enquiry
would be to examine the strategies of intermediary organisations such

as the associations and to relate those strategies to the importance
and effectiveness of those organisations. Thus, at first glance the
local authority associations in England appear to have adopted a
cooperative strategy towards central government (as has the over-
whelming majority of local authorities). This trend is reflected in
the comparatively willing provisions of information and attendance at
various centrally initiated bodies (e.g. Consultative Council). And
yet such a strategy can only be effective if the distribution of power
between organisations is not unduly imbalanced. It would seem that
given present behaviour there is a substantial imbalance of power
between centre and locality. Therefore, is the cooperative strategy
appropriate?

An interesting line of enquiry would be into the strategies adopted
towards the centre by the various local authority associations in
different countries. What are these strategies? Why are differences
to be found between countries? What are the effects upon central-local
relations? These are interesting lines of investigation hitherto
largely ignored in this country.

4.   The importance of specificity

In this essay emphasis has been upon the interactions between the
Swedish State and its municipal authorities over total local government
expenditure. Central-local relations can be expected to vary over
different issues. For example, it was intimated for Sweden that there
may well be substantial central control over the provision of specific
services, such as schooling, nursery education, etc. Such a pattern
of interactions contrasts with that put forward for control of total
expenditure during a time of financial restraint. Thus, research
into central-local relations should be specific about the substantive
decision arena, and the temporal context. General statements about
the nature of central-local relations may be unhelpful. What is
required is an examination of how (methods and procedures) and centre
interacts with local authorities (either directly or through
intermediary organisations) with what purpose (i.e. what is the
substantive issue) under what conditions (i.e. the prevailing economic
and political circumstances) and with what effects. The substantive
issue and the conditions are crucial variables determining the
relevance of methods and effects.

NOTES AND REFERENCES

(1)   R. Greenwood, C.R. Hinings, S. Ranson and K. Walsh, Patterns of
         Management in Local Government, Martin Robertson, London, 1979.
(2)   Local authorities in Sweden obtain resources from three principal
         sources: local taxation (the local income tax; fees for
         services such as the supply of gas and electricity); grants
         from central government; and borrowing.
(3)   Increases occurred in current (revenue) expenditure. Capital
         expenditure declined.
(4)   I. Hjelmquist, Lecture delivered at the Institue of Local
         Government Studies, University of Birmingham, 31 March 1976,
         p. 9.

168

(5)   R. Greenwood, C.R. Hinings, S. Ranson and K. Walsh, In Pursuit
       of Corporate Rationality: Organisational Developments in the
       Post - Reorganised Period, Institute of Local Government
       Studies Occasional Paper, 1976, and Greenwood et al. (1979),
       op. cit.

(6)   K. Davey, 'Local Autonomy and Independent Revenues', Public
       Administration, Spring. 1971; Layfield, Local Government
       Finance. Report of the Committee of Enquiry, HMSO, London,
       Cmnd. 6453, 1976.

(7)   This may change in the future. A government enquiry has critic-
       ally examined the array of specific grants and recommended that
       they be substantially replaced with block grants. For the
       moment, however, specific grants pervade the financial link
       between the State and local authorities.

(8)   S.D. Gold, 'Scandinavian Local Income Taxation: Lessons for
       United States?' Public Finance Quarterly, Vol. 5, No. 4,
       October 1977.

(9)   A.H. Marshall, Local Government Administration Abroad, Vol. 4,
       Report of the Committee on the Management of Local Government,
       HMSO, London, pp. 25-62.

(10)   T.J. Anton, Governing Greater Stockholm: A Study of Policy
       Development and System Change, University of California Press,
       Berkeley, 1975, especially V on 'The Structural Bases of
       System Performance', p. 26.

(11)   R. Murray, The Division of Responsibility between national and
       local government in Forvaltringsekonomiska Problem, B.C.
       Ysander, (ed.), Jurist-och Samhallsvetarforbundets, Stockholm,
       1970.

(12)   T.J. Anton, 'The Pursuit of Efficiency: Values and Structures in
       the Changing Politics of Swedish Municipalities'in Terry N.
       Clark, ed., Comparative Community Politics, Sage, New York,
       1974, p. 102.

(13)   Swedish Institute, Local Government in Sweden, Stockholm, 1976,
       p. 1.

An earlier version of this chapter appeared in Public Administration,
Winter 1979.

13   Centre-Periphery Relations in France

Howard Machin and Vincent Wright

THE TRADITIONAL ANALYSES

The debate on centre-periphery relations in France has always been, and continues to be, dominated by the agency model (rather than the partnership model). In other words, research has focussed on the extent and nature of centralisation, rather than on elements of local autonomy. It will be made clear, however, that the various approaches have not been free from internal contradiction as a result of starting from a centralisation viewpoint.

   The 'Jacobin' or 'Napoleonic' analysis of centre-local relations has been approached in three basic different ways.(1)

The legal-juridical approach

The finest examples of this approach were to be found in the writings of constitutional lawyers and professors at the law faculties. These works were dominated by an exposition of the purely legal situation. The authors placed emphasis upon the 'Napoleonic' or 'Jacobin' conception of relations between Paris and the provinces. They stressed the importance of tutelle (legal tutellage) exercised by State appointed officials on behalf of their hierarchical superiors in Paris over all actions taken by elected local councils.

   Others who shared this approach included senior civil servants (notably from the Council of State), many of whom also taught in the law faculties and, more recently, in the Instituts d'études politiques. Since these lawyers, law professors and senior civil servants dominated the examinations systems in law, political studies and civil service recruitment they were able to demand, and in practice to impose, their approach upon most research. Though no longer required, it is revealing that many mémoires de stage at the Ecole nationale d'administration reflected, and a majority of doctoral theses still reflect, the juridical approach. Notable examples of the legalistic approach are

AMET Jean, L'Evolution des attributions des préfets de 1800 à
   nos jours, Thèse, Droit, Paris, 1954.
LUDWIG Robert, Le Rôle du préfet en matière économique et sociale:
   Théorie et réalités. 3 vols., Thèse, Droit, Strasbourg, 1963.
DAWSON G., L'Evolution des structures de l'administration locale
   en France, Paris, 1969.
LAMARRE J., Les Structures internes des préfectures depuis la réforme
   du 14 mars 1964. Mémoire, Paris, D.E.S., Droit, 1969.
LATOURNERIE M-A., La Coordination administrative sur le plan
   départemental, Mémoire, ENA, Paris, 1965.

BOVLOVIS J., 'L'Organisation administrative des collectivités
   locales', Revue du Droit Public, Nov.-Dec. 1971, pp. 1337-1357.
BONNAUD-DELAMARE Roger, Les Attribution juridiques des préfets et
   et sous-préfets, Monaco, 1951.
BELORGEY Gérard, Le Gouvernement et l'administration de la France,
   Paris, 1967.
DETTON Hervé & HOURTICQ Jean, L'Administration régionale et locale
   de la France, Paris, 1968 (5th ed.)
PIQUEMAL Marcel, L'Administration territoriale. Le département,
   Paris, 1975 (La Documentation française).
MOREAU Jacques, Administration régionale, locale et municipale
   Paris, 1972.
GAILLARD Gilbert, Les pouvoirs de police du préfet, Thèse, Droit,
   Grenoble, 1977.

The 'opportunistic' approach

The highly centralist model is frequently adopted in the public
declarations and writings of those people actively involved in centre-
local relations for largely opportunistic motives. These actors in the
system include:

a.   local notables, especially mayors and members of departmental
      councils,
b.   state officials in prefectures and local field services,
c.   national politicians.

Although, as will be made clear below, many within these groups
privately admit that in practice centre-local relations are more
complex and flexible than their public statements imply, all the groups
have in interest in propagating the myth of the 'one and indivisible
Republic' ruled from Paris. The myth is useful for both local and
national politicians as a device for institutionalised hypocrisy: it
enables them to attribute blame for their own short-comings to the
'system'. On the other hand, in an attempt to legitimise their
position, State officials employ this myth when bargaining with local
politicians. Analyses of these 'opportunistic' approaches are given in

MENY Yves, Centralisation et décentralisation dans le débat
   politique français, 1945-69. Paris, 1974.
GREMION Pierre & WORMS Jean-Pierre, Les Institutions régionales
   et la société locale, Paris 1968.

The 'political' approach

This approach has been adopted by observers who, for a variety of
reasons and motives, believed in the existence of the over centralised
State. Within this broad approach three distinct strands may be
discerned:

The critique of the inefficacy of the over centralised State apparatus,
a view which has been taken by several groups:

a.   the technocrats, notably those involved directly in planning,
      regional development and administrative reform. For examples
      see

BAECQUE F. de, 'Pour une Politique cohérente de décentralisation', Revue française de science politique, 17 (1), 1967, pp. 5-27.
MONOD J. & CASTELBAJAC P. de, L'Aménagement du territoire, Paris, 1971.
VIOT P., 'Les Aspects régionaux du IVe Plan', Revue administrative, 14/84, 1961, pp. 597-602.
GUICHARD O, Aménager la France, Paris, 1965.

b.   the political liberals, who favoured the radical decentralisation of authority: the best examples are

SERVAN-SCHREIBER Jean-Jacques, Le pouvoir régional, Paris, 1973.
PISANI Edgard, La région, pour quoi faire? Paris, 1969
ROCARD Michel, Décoloniser la province, Paris, 1967.
PARTI SOCIALISTE, Citoyen dans sa commune, Paris, 1977.

c.   the 'State renovators', of whom the most prominent was de Gaulle himself, who expressed his basic ideas in a famous speech at Lyons in 1968, and reiterated them in his Mémoires d'Espoir (2 vols. Paris, 1970 , 1971).

This same idea of renewing and restoring the State through decentralisation may be found in some academic writings. See, for example

DEBBASCH Charles et al., La décentralisation pour la rénovation de l'Etat, Paris, 1970 (the papers of a colloquium organised by Aix-en-Provence law department).
CLUB JEAN MOULIN, L'Etat et les collectivités locales, Paris, 1967 (the papers of a colloquium).

The anti-Paris critique, which is a negative response to the demographic, economic, social, intellectual, cultural and political domination of the French provinces by the capital. The best expression of this approach is to be found in

GRAVIER Jean-François, Paris et le désert français, Paris, 1972, 2nd ed.
GRAVIER Jean-François, La question régionale, Paris, 1970.

The regionalist demand is a more positive response to centralisation, even if it remains implicitly rooted in a 'colonial' model of centre-periphery relations. This view emphasises the need to resuscitate the dying economies and cultures of the provinces and to release the unused energies and dynamism of the provincials. Many eloquent spokesmen of this standpoint are defenders of Brittany and 'Occitania':

PHLIPPONEAU Michel, La gauche et les régions, Paris, 1967.
LAFONT Robert, La révolution régionaliste, Paris, 1967.
LAFONT Robert, Décoloniser la France, Paris, 1971
MARTRAY Joseph, La région pour un Etat moderne, Paris, 1970.
FOUGEYROLLAS P. Pour une France fédérale, Paris, 1968
FRONT REGIONALISTE CORSE, Main basse sur une île, Paris 1971.
GLAYMAN G., Liberté pour les régions Bretagne et Rhône-Alpes, Paris, 1971.

As noted, all these traditional analyses (the traditional, the 'opportunistic' and the 'political') of centre-local relations were based on variations of the agency model, namely that local government institutions can only carry out orders and instructions made in Paris. This view is still frequently repeated in public declarations by opposition politicians and in the writings of regionalists. It was also given some considerable publicity in the immensely successful recent book by Alain PEYREFITTE (today Minister of Justice): Le Mal français (Paris 1976).

RECENT RESEARCHERS

There are many different schools. Although the idea of the highly centralised State provides the axiomatic point of departure, most present research highlights the complexity of centre-local relations.

The Crozier team

From the early 1960s, the extremely talented group of scholars of the Centre de sociologie des organisations (CSO), led by Michel Crozier, undertook a number of studies which concentrated on the behaviour and attitudes of those directly involved in local government. The main scholars in the CSO team were: Michel Crozier, Erhard Friedberg, Catherine Grémion, Pierre Grémion, Jacques Lautman, Jean-Claude Thoenig and Jean-Pierre Worms.

The work of this group was rooted in a broad analysis of French cultural traits: Crozier's own works, and in particular Le phénomène bureaucratique (Paris, 1963), La société bloquée (Paris, 1970), (with FRIEDBERG Erhard) L'Acteur et le Système (Paris 1977), serve as the foundation stones for this research. Some of the results of these studies were radically to revise thinking on centre-local relations. The most important publications of this group are:

'L'administration face aux problemes du changement', Sociologie du travail, 3/66, July-September 1966 (special issue)
Où va l'administration française? Paris, 1974.
PEYREFITTE Alaine et al., Décentraliser les responsabilités. Pourquoi? Comment? Paris, 1976.
GREMION Pierre & Worms Jean-Pierre, Les institutions régionales et la société locale, op. cit.
THOENIG Jean-Claude & FRIEDBERG Erhard, La création des directions départementales d'équipement, Paris, 1970.
GREMION Pierre, La structuration du pouvoir au niveau départemental, Paris, 1969.
GREMION Pierre, Le pouvoir périphérique, Paris, 1976.
GREMION Pierre, 'L'administration des villes et l'administration des champs', Projet, 77, July-August, 1973 pp. 771-784.
GREMION Pierre 'Introduction à une étude du système politico-administratif local', Sociologie du Travail (1), 1970, pp. 51-73.
GREMION Pierre 'L'Etat et les collectivités locales', Esprit, March, 1970, pp. 533-44.
GREMION Pierre 'La théorie de l'apprentissage institutionnel de la régionalisation du Vème Plan', Revue Française de Science Politique, XXIII (2), April 1973, pp. 305-320.

GREMION Pierre, Pouvoir local, pouvoir central: essai sur la fin de
l'Administration républicaine, Paris, Université René Descartes,
Thèse de doctorat d'Etat, 1975.
GREMION Pierre, THOENIG J-C, Worms J-P, 'Administration et pouvoir
économique', Esprit, (1), 1973, pp. 51-70.
GREMION Pierre & WORMS Jean-Pierre, 'La concertation régionale:
innovation ou tradition?', in Annuaire Française d'Aménagement
du Territoire, Paris, Documentation Française, 1968, pp. 35-60.
GREMION Pierre & WORMS Jean-Pierre, Les institutions régionales
et la société locale, Paris, 1968.
GREMION Pierre & WORMS Jean-Pierre, 'L'expérience française de
régionalisation au cours des années 60', Rencontre de Rome, Paris,
1972.
CROZIER Michel & THOENIG Jean-Claude, 'The Regulation of Complex
Organised Systems', Administrative Science Quarterly, 21 (4),
December, 1976, pp. 547-570.
THOENIG Jean-Claude, L'Ere des technocrates, le cas des Ponts et
Chaussées, Paris, 1973.
THOENIG Jean-Claude, French bureaucracy and collective decision
making at the local level. Unpublished manuscript, Paris, 1975
THOENIG Jean-Claude & DANSEREAU F., La société locale face à une
institution nouvelle d'aménagement du territoire: le cas de la
métropole d'équilibre lorraine. Paris, 1968.

The Marxists

Very little of the work of the marxist scholars has focussed
specifically on centre-periphery relations, but there has been
considerable study of the nature of local power, especially in medium
sized or large towns. Much of this research is dominated by the search
for evidence of class conflict and the workings of State monopoly
capitalism. These studies have been valuable in contributing to the
knowledge of the mechanisms whereby centre and periphery are linked,
especially in the area of town planning. Marxist researchers have
dominated a number of Paris based teams, notably the Centre d'etude
des mouvements sociaux (which includes Lojkine and Godard), the
Centre de sociologie urbaine and the Mission de recherches urbaines.
Many members of the CERAT group have also taken marxist approaches.
The most interesting marxist works include:

HUET A., et al., Urbanisation capitaliste et pouvoir local, Paris
1977.
Urbanisme monopoliste, urbanisme démocratique, Paris 1974
(colloquium organised by the Centre d'Etudes et de Recherches
marxistes).
CASTELLS Manuel et al., Sociologie des mouvements sociaux
urbains, Paris, 1977
POULANTZAS Nicos, La Question urbaine, 3rd ed., Paris 1975.
POULANTZAS Nicos (ed.), La Crise de l'Etat, Paris 1976
(see articles by Manuel Castells and Renaud Dulong).
CASTELLS Manuel & GODARD Francis, Monopolville: l'entreprise,
l'Etat, l'urbain, Paris, 1974.
LOJKINE Jean, La politique urbaine dans la région lyonnaise,
Paris, 1974.
BIAREZ Sylvie et al., Institution communale et pouvoir politique,
le cas de Roanne, Paris, 1973.

SOUCY, C., Contribution à une sociologie des centres urbains. Reconstruction et développement. Les centres de Caen et du Havre. Paris, 1970.

JOBERT B., Planification urbaine et institutions politiques, Unpublished paper, CERAT, Grenoble, 1973.

GODARD F., Sur la notion d'équipements urbains collectifs, (Paper to ECPR urban politics workshop) Strasbourg, 1974.

BIAREZ S, et. al., Les Elus locaux et l'aménagement urbain dans l'agglomération genobloise, Unpublished paper, CERAT, Grenoble, 1974.

... Prendre la ville, Paris, 1977.

BIAREZ S, et al., 'Le traitement politique de l'aménagement urbain par l'institution communale'. Espaces et Sociétés, 8, February 1973, 105-122.

CASTELLS Manuel, La Question urbain, Paris, 1972.

The historians

From the mid 1960s a number of historical works began to question the validity of the Tocquevillian model which posited the early and inexorable growth and consolidation of the centralised State, and they began to place emphasis on the existence of areas of local autonomy and independence. These works include:

GOUBERT Pierre, L'Ancien régime, Vol. II: les pouvoirs, Paris, 1973.

RICHET Denis, La France moderne, l'esprit des institutions, Paris, 1974.

TUDESQ Andre, Les grands notables en France (1840-1849), Etude historique d'une psychologie sociale, 2 vols. Paris, 1964.

TUDESQ Andre, Les Conseillers Généraux en France au temps de Guizot, Paris, 1967.

LE CLERE Bernard and WRIGHT Vincent, Les Préfets du Second Empire, Paris, 1974.

ZELDIN Theodore, France 1848-1945, Vol. I, Oxford, 1973.

WEBER Eugene, Peasants into Frenchmen, London, 1977.

FURET Françoise and RICHET Denis, The French Revolution, New York, 1970.

AUBERT Jacques et al., Les Préfets en France: 1800-1940, Geneva, 1978.

Provincial groups

There are small teams of researchers, usually linked to Instituts d'etudes politiques and law departments in provincial universities. The most notable of these are:

the CENTRE DE RECHERCHE ADMINISTRATIVE, Aix-en-Provence, (which includes Charles DEBBASCH),

the CENTRE DE RECHERCHE ADMINISTRATIVE, Nice (including Jean-Paul GILLI) and

the CENTRE D'ETUDE DU DROIT DE L'ADMINISTRATION ET DES COLLECTIVES LOCALES, Rennes (including Yves Mény).

There are also small groups, mainly composed of law professors involved in local government research in the universities in Toulouse, Lille, Strasbourg, Perpignan, Amiens and Montpellier.

The two most important provincial research groups are those at

Grenoble and Bordeaux. In Bordeaux, linked to the Institut d'études politiques, is the Centre d'étude et de recherche sur la vie locale (CERVL) led by Albert Mabileau, Jacques Lagroye, and more recently, Jean-Claude Thoenig (from the Crozier team). The major publications of the CERVL team are:

MABILEAU Albert et al., Les facteurs locaux de la vie politique nationale, Paris, 1972

LAGROYE Jacques, Société et politique. Chaban-Delmas à Bordeaux. Paris, 1973.

LAGROYE Jacques, LORD Guy et al., Les Militants politiques dans trois partis française, Paris, 1976

FAVREAU B., Georges Mandel, un clémentiste en Gironde, Paris, 1972.

BOUSQUET-MELON J., Louis Barthou et la circonscription d'Oloron 1899-1914. Paris, 1972.

In Grenoble is the slightly older and larger group, the Centre d'étude et de recherche sur l'administration économique et l'aménagement du territoire (CERAT), which has included Lucien Nizard, Michel Longepierre, Fran ois d'Arcy and J-P. Quermonne. The CERAT keeps an up to date card catalogue of all publications and research in local government and organises the annual publication of Aménagement du territoire et développement régional, a large collection of research articles in this area. Other CERAT publications include,

L'administration traditionelle et planification régionale, Paris, 1964.

ARCY François d', Structures administratives et urbanisation: la Société centrale pour l'équipement du territoire. (SCET), Paris, 1968.

LONGEPIERRE Michel, Les Consillers généraux dans le système administratif français, Paris, 1971.

BIAREZ S., et al., Institution communale et pouvoir politique: le cas de Roanne, op. cit.

The Institut français des sciences administratives (IFSA)

Created in 1965 under the guidance of Rene Cassin (of the Council of State), the IFSA is a voluntary association which organises meetings and publications in which all aspects of public administration are examined. Recently, as a result of the work of Guy Braibant (also from the Council of State), regional sections of IFSA have been created and these now organise meetings in their respective regions. The importance of the IFSA conferences lies in the fact that they bring together academics, high-ranking civil servants, and national and local politicians. Whilst the resulting publications are often disappointing some are extremely valuable. A number of these Cahiers de l'IFSA are useful for the study of centre-local relations.

No. 1 Le régionalisme en pratique, Paris, 1967.

No. 10 Les aspects administratifs de la régionalisation, Paris, 1975

No. 11 La gestion déconcentrée des finances de l'Etat, Paris, 1974.

No. 14 L'administration des grandes villes, Paris, 1977.

No. 15 Vers la réforme des collectivités locales, Paris, 1977.

No. 17 La région en question, Paris, 1978.

Parisian research groups

Some research relating to centre-local relations is carried on in the law departments of the main Paris universities, and at the Centre de Recherches administratives of the Fondation nationale des sciences politiques where Jean-Luc BODIGUEL and Marie-Christine KESSLER have produced a number of studies (see below).

The Ecole nationale d'administration has also been responsible for some work in this field, both through the organising of seminars and through the drafting by every student (until 1971) of a mémoire during his year long stage in a provincial prefecture. Although many of these mémoires are legalistic, some are interestingly indiscreet about the reality of links between prefects, field services and local councils. In 1965 the ENA students in the prefectures carried out a group study for the Ministry of Administrative Reform:

ENA, PROMOTION STENDHAL, Application de la réforme administrative étude des arrêtés de délégation pris par les préfets, Paris, 1965.

Finally, a number of other bodies which occasionally collaborate in research in this area should also be noted. These are:

the Ecole pratique des hautes études (which often collaborates with the IFSA in organising meetings on historical problems).
the Maison des sciences de l'homme where several researchers are based.
the Institut technique des administrations publiques, which is especially concerned with problems of introducing new administrative methods.

Official research

A number of ministries and central government agencies have become directly involved in research in pursuit of more detailed information about either their own operations or about public reactions to their work. In many cases the research work has not been carried out by civil servants but studies have been commissioned from existing research teams (notably from the Crozier team, the CERAT at Grenoble and the CERVL at Bordeaux). The main commissioning bodies have been the Ministry of the Environment (formerly Equipement), the Planning Commissariat, the DATAR and the Ministry of Administrative Reform.

In some cases, however, groups of civil servants have themselves carried out the research work. Notable examples of such studies include the unpublished report drawn up for Michel Debré by an Inspecteur général de l'administration (Bardon) on the difficulties of relations between prefects and field services, the conclusions of the study group of senior civil servants which observed the experimental departmental reorganisation and regional reforms from 1961 to 1964, the investigation of local leaders' views of the 1969 regionalisation proposals and the 1977 study of mayors' reactions to the Guichard Report (which involved sending questionnaires to all France's 36,000 mayors). A number of senior civil servants (together with several Deputies and Senators) also take part in the work of the government's permanent advisory board on administrative reform, the Comité central

d'enquête sur le coût et le rendement des services publics, which
drafts regular reports. See
 Rapport général 1971 à 1975. Comité central d'enquête sur le coût
  et le rendement des services publics, Paris, 1976

 The most important results of the official research have included,
  Politiques urbaines et planification des villes, Paris, 1974 (the
  proceedings of a colloquium at the Equipement ministry).
 COMMISSION DE DEVELOPPEMENT DES RESPONSIBILITIES LOCALES, Vivre ensemble
  Paris, 1976 ('The Guichard Report').
 PEYREFITTE Alain et al., Décentraliser les responsabilités, Pourquoi?
  Comment? Paris, 1975 ('The Peyrefitte Report').

There have also been a number of studies carried out by individual
civil servants or small groups on their own initiative and these
sometimes produce some useful results. Two noteworthy examples are

 MAYER R., Féodalités on démocratie?, Paris, 1968
 La fonction préfectorale et la réforme administrative, Paris, 1961
  (Written and published by the Association du corps préfectoral).

Finally a number of civil servants (notably prefects) have related
their experiences in local government. See, for example:

 BURGALAT Yves, 'La région et la régionalisation vues par un Préfet
  de département', Administration, 68, 1970, pp. 37-45.
 CHADEAU Andre, 'L'Evolution du rôle du préfet depuis 1964',
  Administration 68, 1970, pp. 47-53.
 PELISSIER Jacques, 'La réforme administrative en pratique: l'exemple
  de la région du Languedoc-Roussillon', in Le Régionalisme en
  pratique, op. cit.
 BERNARD Paul, Le Grand tournant des communes de France, Paris, 1969.
 MONOD Jérôme, Transformation d'un pays pour une géographie de
  la liberté, Paris 1974.

FINDINGS OF RECENT RESEARCH: THE CENTRALIST CASE

Most research continues to place emphasis on central domination and is
concerned with exploring its sources. The major sources of continued
centralisation have been identified as follows.

The inefficacy of existing local authorities

It is argued by many observers that the existing local authorities
were designed for a rural age, and that they are now too small and too
numerous to carry out the tasks involved in industrial and urban
planning. Moreover, lacking both financial resources and technical
professional personnel they are seen to be ill equipped to deal
effectively with the rich and powerful prefectures and the local field
services of Paris ministries. On this problem, see:

 BOURDON Jacques, Le personnel communal, Paris, 1974.
 AUBERT Jacques, Le devenir de l'institution: demain, les communes,
  Paris, 1965.
 GUICHARD Olivier, Vivre Ensemble (Rapport de la commission de

développement des responsabilités locales), op. cit.

ROUSSILLON Henry, Les Structures territoriales des communes - réformes et perspectives d'avenir, Paris, 1972.

JOLLIVET M, & MENDRAS H., Les Collectivités rurales françaises, Paris, 1971.

LABORIE J-P., & LUGAN J.C., Le Système politique des petites villes françaises, Toulouse, 1975.

Administrative tutelle

Traditionally administrative tutelle has meant that local councils could not act without the legal ratification of their decisions by the prefect or sub-prefect. It is now generally recognised that prefectoral tutelle has been reduced to ineffectiveness (notably by the decrees of January 1959 and November 1970) and that in practice, since the Third Republic, political considerations may have effectively neutralised this tutelle. Nonetheless, the tutelle remains a source of irritation as a symbol of central government domination of local politics. See:

PIERRE Christine, L'Evolution récente de la tutelle administrative sur les collectivités locales, Mémoire, IEP, Aix-en-Provence, 1977.

RASERA Michel, Evolution de la tutelle communale, Thèse, Doctorat, Droit, Paris 2, 1975.

Central financial control

It has been strongly argued by several authors that prefectoral legal tutelle has been replaced by a financial tutelle which is more effective. This view is emphasised in the Livre blanc sur les finances locales (Paris, 1976), which was published by a group of mayors of major cities, and is also voiced in numerous complaints at the IFSA meeting on L'administration des grandes villes (see above). There is a considerable literature which examines this central financial control.

GUERRIER P. & BAUCHARD D., L'Economie financière des collectivités locales, Paris, 1972.

Rapport de l'intergroupe du Commissariat au Plan sur les finances locales, Paris, 1971.

DUCROS J-C., 'Politique et finances locales', Analyse et prévision, July-August 1966, pp. 499-518.

KOBIELSKI Josué, L'Influence de la structure des communes urbaines sur leurs dépenses de fonctionnement, Thèse, doctorat, sciences économiques, Rennes, 1974

ASHFORD Douglas, The Limits of Consensus: local reorganisation in Britain and the French Contrast, Western Societies Program Paper no. 6, Cornell University, July 1976.

ASHFORD Douglas, 'French Pragmatism and British idealism: financial aspects of local reorganisation', Comparative Political Studies, Vol. II (1), 1978, pp. 231-254.

DUPLOUY J., Le Crédit aux collectivités locales, Paris, 1967.

FREVILLE Y., 'L'évolution des finances des grandes villes depuis 1967', Revue de science financière, 4, 1973, pp. 725-758.

MONSEL R., 'Pouvoir monopoliste et finances des collectivités locales', Economie et politique, 198, January 1971, pp. 3-18

BERNARD Paul, 'A propos des incitations financierès aux regroupements de communes', Revue du Droit Public, 1967, No. 83, pp. 245-287.

HOURTICQ Jean, 'La réforme du régime des subventions d'investissement
de l'Etat aux collectivités locales', Revue administrative, 26,
January-February 1973, pp. 65-69.
PALLEZ G. & FOUQUET C., 'La réforme des finances locales', Analyse et
prévision, I, 1966, pp. 103-109.

Finally, there are several useful publications by La Documentation
française on this subject:

La Caisse des Dépôts et des Consignations, Paris, 1973.
Le Conseil Municipal, Paris, 1971.
La Réforme de la fiscalité locale, Paris 1968.
Les Inégalités de ressources des collectivités locales, Paris, 1968.
Les Finances locales, Paris, 1970.

None of the literature, however, really considers the central
question: does increased financial dependence on the State necessarily
involve a loss of local autonomy? As has been argued elsewhere, an
increase in State aid might, paradoxically, increase local autonomy by
widening the choice of possible policy options.

Technical supervision of the local authorities by the local field
services

Financial control of the local authorities is combined with the
technical control exercised by corps such as the ingénieurs des ponts-
et-chaussées and the ingénieurs des mines (now grouped in the directions
départementales d'équipement). All major construction and urban
planning projects involve their constant intervention (or interference
according to the critics), and the locally elected officials are
technically ill-equipped to challenge them. See

THOENIG Jean-Claude, L'Ere des technocrates, op. cit.
FRIEDBERG E. and DESJEUX D., 'Fonctions de l'Etat et rôles des
grands corps: le cas du corps des mines', Annuaire International
de la fonction publique, Paris, 1971.
ARCY F. d' and JOBERT B., La Planification urbaine en France,
unpublished, Grenoble (CERAT), 1973.

New forms of central control

The administrative tutelle exercised by the prefects, the technical
control of the specialised corps and the financial control of the
trésoriers-payeurs généraux over local authorities are traditional and
continue to be exercised. However, new forms of control, it is argued,
have emerged during the post war period. New State agencies of economic
planning and regional development have proliferated and have helped to
transmit the will of the State to the provinces. These agencies
include:

the Planning Commissariat,
the Caisse des Dépôts et Consignations,
the Délégation à l'aménagement du territoire et a l'action
régionale (the DATAR),
the Organisations regionales d'Etude et d'Aménagement d'une aire
métropolitaine or OREAM. (Regional offices of the DATAR),

the various regional funding linked to the Ministry of Economy,
the Missions (administrative bodies established to deal with
  specific areas) such as the Mission interministérielle
  d'aménagement touristique du Languedoc-Roussillon and the Mission
  d'aménagement du littoral d'Aquitaine,
the commissariats (politico-administrative organisations created to
  deal with specific problems) such as the commissariat général du
  tourisme and the commissariat de montagne,
the contrats de pays and the contrats de villes moyennes which are
  medium-term plans for economic and urban development agreed
  between the State and local officials, and whose effective
  implementation is heavily dependent upon financial inducements
  offered by the centre,
the programmes d'action prioritaires (or PAPs) which are a series
  of specific proposals affecting the provinces which are outlined
  in the late (i.e., Seventh) Plan.

The literature on this section is considerable: amongst the more
important works are:

LACOUR Claude, Aménagement du territoire, Paris, 1973.
DELMAS C., L'Aménagement du territoire, Paris, 1962
MONOD Jérôme et CASTELBAJAC de P., op. cit.
ROCHEFORT M. et al., Aménager le territoire, Paris, 1970.
HAYWARD Jack and WATSON Michael (eds.), Planning, Politics and
  Public Policy, Cambridge, 1975.
LANVERSIN Jacques, L'Aménagement du territoire et la régionalisation,
  Paris, 1967.
VIOT Pierre, Aspects régionaux de la planification française,
  Commissariat du Plan, Paris, 1966.
Aménagement du territoire et Développement régional, several volumes
  published by the CERAT of Grenoble (Paris, 1964).
POUYET B., La Délégation à l'Aménagement du territoire et à l'Action
  Régionale, Paris, 1967.
MANIGAUD Jean Sylvain, La DATAR, exemple d'une administration de
  mission dans le cadre du système administratif traditionnel,
  (thèse, Paris University I 1976).
POPLU Pierre, Les Sociétés de développement régional, Paris, 1973
GREMION Pierre, 'La théorie de l'apprentissage institutionnel et
  la régionalisation du Ve Plan', Revue Française de Science
  Politique, XXIII (2), April 1973, pp. 305-320.
ASTORG Michel, art. in PAGE Jean-Pierre, et al., Profil Economique
  de la France - structures et tendances, Paris, 1975.
MORVILLE Michèle, L'Intervention de l'Etat dans les équipements
  touristiques: le Languedoc-Roussillon, Paris, 1976.
LYONNET Alain and MENARD Luc-Alexandre, Recherches sur l'administra-
  tion de mission dans la vie locale, Paris, 1969.
ARCY François d' and GREMION Pierre, Les Services extérieurs du
  Ministère des finances dans le système de décision départemental,
  Paris, 1969.
DUPORT J-P., 'L'expérience des contrats de plan'. Bulletin
  International de l'Administration Publique, Vol. 25, January-March
  1973, pp. 161-175.
QUERE Henri, Une participation à l'aménagement d'une ville: le
  contrat ville moyenne Alencon (DES Mémoire, Caen, 1977).
ASTORG Michel, 'La régionalisation du VIème Plan', Bulletin de

liaison et d'information de l'administration centrale du ministère de l'Economie et des Finances, No. 60, July-September 1975, pp. 22-55.

CUISENIER J., BARRICHON G., and LAUTMAN J., Intervention de l'Etat et aménagement local..., Paris 1969.

New territorial structures

Since 1958 a number of major changes affecting local authority structures have taken place. The first changes involved the creation of the regions and regional bodies, and the second involved the elaboration of means to meet the so-called problem of the proliferation of small communes. There is a substantial literature on both areas:

Regions

BOURJOL Maurice, Les Institutions régionales de 1789 à nos jours, Paris, 1969.

Régions et Régionalisme en France du XVIIIème siècle à nos jours, Paris, 1977.

BOURJOL Maurice, Région et Administration régionale, Paris, 1973

BRONCNIART Ph., La Région en France, Paris, 1971.

FLORY Th., Le Mouvement régionaliste français, Paris, 1966.

QUERMONNE J.L., 'Vers un régionalisme fonctionnel', Revue Française de Science Politique, 13 (4), 1963, pp. 849-876.

MOREAU Jacques, Administration régionale, locale et municipale, Paris, 1972.

GOUREVITCH Peter, 'Reforming the Napoleonic State: the creation of regional government in France and Italy', in TARROW Sidney et al., Territorial Politics in Industrial Nations, London, 1978, pp. 28-63.

GREMION Pierre et WORMS Jean-Pierre, La mise en place des institutions régionales, op. cit.

HOURTICQ J., 'La loi du 5 juillet 1972 portant création et organisation des régions', Revue Administrative, No. 25, November-December 1972, pp. 635-639.

'La Région' (special issue of Les Cahiers Français, Nos. 158-159, Paris, 1973).

Les Aspects Administratifs de la Régionalisation, Cahier de l'IFSA, Paris, 1974 (contains good bibliography).

ABRIAL P., 'La Réforme régionale', Notes et Etudes Documentaires, No. 4064, February 1974, pp. 1-58.

BAGUENARD J., 'L'Organisation régionale', Revue de Droit Public, No. 89 (6), November-December 1973, pp. 1405-1466.

La Réforme régionale et le référendum du 27 avril 1969, Cahier de l'IEP, de Grenoble, Paris, 1970.

HAYWARD Jack, 'Presidential suicide by Plebiscite: de Gaulle's exit', Parliamentary Affairs, XXII, August 1969, pp. 289-319.

BLANC-GONNET P., L'Administration régionale en Basse-Normandie, Paris, 1969.

Les Nouvelles institutions régionales en Picardie 1973-1975, (Centre universitaire de recherches administratives et politiques de Picardie), Amiens, 1976.

PHILIP Christian, 'Les deux premiers budgets régionaux...' Actualité Juridique, 1976, Vol. I, pp. 4-19

Communal mergers and grouping and new towns

MADIOT Yves, Les fusions et regroupements de communes. Problèmes posés par la réforme des structures communales, Paris, 1973
'La Réforme Communale' special issue of Bulletin d'Informations of the Ministry of the Interior, March 1972, No. 4.
BOURJOL Maurice, Les districts urbains, Paris, 1964.
BOURJOL Maurice, La Réforme municipale, bilan et perspectives, Paris 1975.
BERNARD Paul, Le Grand tournant des communes de France.
BODIGUEL Jean-Luc and KESSLER Marie-Christine, 'Les Communautés urbaines' Revue Française de Science Politique, XVII (2), April 1968, pp. 257-277.
BODIGUEL Jean-Luc and KESSLER Marie-Christine, Le Regroupement Communal dans les agglomérations, Paris, Fondation Nationale des Sciences Politiques, 1968 (unpublished).
HERMAN Nadine, Contribution à une étude des fusions de communes dans une perspective de science administrative, (thèse, Univ. Paris, 1977).
BODIGUEL Jean-Luc et al., L'Expérience française des villes nouvelles, Paris, 1974.
CHATIN C., Neuf Villes Nouvelles, une expérience française d'urbanisme, Paris, 1975.
SCHMITT Charles, 'Le Regroupement des communes en France' Revue juridique et politique, No. 22, 1968, pp. 739-756
ROUSSILLON Henri, Les Structures territoriales des communes: réformes et perspectives d'avenir, Paris, 1972.
BRISSY Y., Les Villes Nouvelles, Paris, 1974.
LYONNET Alain and MENARD Luc-Alexandre, op. cit. (notably pp. 81-153).
MAURICE, R., Les syndicats de commune, Paris 1976.

The effects of the various reforms of territorial structures are the subject of a lively controversy. Some have argued, for example, that the consequence of the regional reforms was paradoxically, to reinforce the traditional departmental authorities. See the various works of GREMION Pierre, and MACHIN Howard (The Prefect in French Public Administration, London 1977), WRIGHT Vincent and MACHIN Howard, ('The French Regional Reforms of July 1972: a Case of Disguised Central-isation?', Policy and Politics, Vol. III (3), March 1975, pp. 3-28), and BODIGUEL Jean-Luc, ('Les Commissions de développement économique régional: composition, bilan et perspectives: L'exemple des Pays de la Loire', Revue Française de Science Politique, XVI (3), 1966, pp. 472-492).

It has also been claimed that either the territorial reforms were inspired by the need to increase central control (by reducing the number of local authorities to be consulted, bargained with or bought off) or, whilst the intention may not have been such the consequence was. On the controversy see,

SFEZ L., et al., L'Objet local, Paris, 1977.
WRIGHT Vincent and MACHIN Howard 'The French Regional Reforms...' op. cit.
VIOT P., 'De la planification régionale à la région politique et administrative en Europe', Bulletin de l'Institut International d'Administration Publique, No. 9, 1969, pp. 31-54.

Le Régionalisme en pratique, Cahier de l'IFSA, Paris, 1967.

KERVASDOUE Jean de, et al., 'La loi et le changement social: un
diagnostic. La loi du 16 juillet 1971 sur les fusions et
regroupements de communes', Revue Française de Sociologie, XVII,
1976, pp. 423-450.

KNAUB G., 'De l'incidence de regroupements de communes sur leur
autonomie financière', Revue de Droit Public, Vol. 87, 1971,
pp. 1113-1128.

GREMION P., and WORMS J-P., 'L'Etat et les collectivités locales',
Esprit, January 1970, pp. 20-35.

MEDARD J.F., 'Les Communautés urbaines: renforcement ou déclin de
l'autonomie locale', Revue de Droit Public, Vol. 84, 1968,
pp. 737-800.

VENEZIA J.C., 'Les regroupements de communes: bilan et perspectives',
Revue de Droit Public, Vol. 87, pp. 1061-1112.

At the heart of the debate about centre-local relations there is a
deep seated reluctance to accept any model which precludes State
dominance and malevolence. Thus, it is argued, on the one hand, that
becuase of the extreme fragmentation of the communal system (there are
too many communes and they are too small) the centre is able to crush
the periphery. Yet, on the other hand, when the State attempts to
reduce the number and increase the size of communes this is interpreted
as merely a means of strengthening its control. In short, there is a
constant presumption in favour of central duplicity and culpability.

FINDINGS OF RECENT RESEARCH: THE EXISTENCE OF LOCAL AUTONOMY

Some recent research (often by foreign scholars) has timidly suggested
that the manichean view of centre-periphery relations in France may not
correspond to the total reality, and whilst rejecting the partnership
model nevertheless suggests that there exist considerable areas of local
initiative and autonomy. This autonomy is the result of a number of
factors.

The importance of the role played by local notables and
especially by the mayors

This pouvoir notabiliaire has been analysed at length in the works of
the Crozier team (notably by Jean-Pierre Worms, Jean-Claude Thoenig and
Pierre Grémion) and of the historians quoted above.

The role and power of the mayors has been studied in a number of
works:

SCHMITT Charles, Le Maire de la commune rurale, 3rd ed. Paris, 1972.
(good analysis of functions).

KRYN Jacques, Lettre d'un maire de village, Paris, 1971.
(autobiographical, full of useful insights).

SOUCHON Marie-France, Le Maire élu local dans une société en
changement, Paris, 1967 (useful description)

KESSELMAN Mark, The Ambiguous Consensus, New York, 1966. (a systematic
approach by a political scientist to the powers and power of rural
mayors).

JOLLIVET Marcel and MENDRAS Henri, Les collectivités rurales françaises, Paris, 1972.

and

DEGREMONT, Eric, Les Maires ruraux, leur autorité, Mémoire IEP, Paris, 1965. (sociological approaches).
KUKAWA P., et al., Recherche sur la structure du pouvoir local en milieu urbain, Centre d'Etudes et de recherches sur l'administration économique et l'aménagement du territoire, Grenoble, 1969.
HOSS Jean-Pierre, Argenteuil et Bezons, Paris 1969.
BECQUART-LECLERCQ Jeanne, Paradoxes du Pouvoir local, Paris 1976. (a study of local government in selected communes in the North-East). For summary of main arguments in English, see 'Relational Power and Systemic Articulation in French Local Polity', in KARPIK Lucien, (ed.), Organisation and Environment, London, 1978, pp. 253-292.
GILLI Jean-Paul, 'Le Maire et l'exercise de ses fonctions dans le département des Alpes-Maritimes', Revue Française de Science Politique, 18 (3), 1968, pp. 467-507 (study of mayors in a département).
VERDES-LEROUX Jeannine, 'Caractéristiques des maires des communes de plus de 2,000 habitants', Revue Française de Science Politique, 20 (5), 1970, pp. 974-990.
The important role of the mayors of Rennes (Fréville), Grenoble (Dubédout) and Nice (Médecin) is highlighted in case studies in L'Administration des grandes villes, op. cit. Other important studies of powerful mayors include those of
LAGROYE Jacques op. cit.

and

BELL David, The Politics of Marseilles and the role of Gaston Defferre 1945-1973, Oxford, D. Phil. 1979.
For an interesting, yet largely self-justificatory, personal account of the role of an important mayor, see FREVILLE Henri, Un acte de foi, 30 ans au service de la cité, 2 vols., Rennes, 1978.
On other local notables see LONGEPIERRE Michel, Les Conseillers généraux... op. cit.
MARCHAND M., Le Conseillers généraux depuis 1945, Paris 1970

The existence of extra-juridical linkages between centre and periphery

This is achieved through the phenomenon of cumul des mandats (the holding by the same person of many offices) often both national and local. The Député-maire or Sénateur-maire are the most familiar manifestations of the phenomenon. The cumul des mandats enables local elites to penetrate decision centres in Paris. For details see:

THOENIG Jean-Claude, 'La Relation entre le centre et la périphérie en France', Bulletin de l'Institut International de l'Administration publique, No. 36, October-December 1975, pp. 77-123
ASHFORD Douglas, 'Are Britain and France "unitary"?', Comparative Politics (9), 1977, pp. 483-499.
HAYWARD Jack and WRIGHT Vincent, 'The 37,708 microcosms of an Indivisible Republic: the French local elections of March 1971',

<u>Parliamentary Affairs</u>, XXIV (4), Autumn 1971, pp. 284-311.

The extensive complicity in the rural areas between State
officials in the provinces and the mayors and local councillors

This complicity is finely analysed in the now celebrated article by
Jean-Pierre WORMS, 'Le Préfet et ses notables', <u>Sociologie du travail</u>,
III, July-September 1966, pp. 249-275, and has been accepted by the
rest of the Crozier team (see above). See also

  GEROME Noëlle, 'Sur l'administration académique et son environment',
    <u>Sociologie du Travail</u>, 1969 (2), pp. 145-163.

Local political élites are often able to enlist the support of the
prefects in combatting the reform of local government structures, for
the prefects are already convinced that such reforms merely weaken
their already fragile power. See

  MACHIN Howard, 'The French Prefects and Local Administration',
    <u>Parliamentary Affairs</u>, XXVII (2), Spring 1974, pp. 237-250.

  COLLIARD A. & GROSHENS J-C., 'La sous-préfectorisation des préfets
    des départements', <u>Revue du droit public et des sciences</u>
    politiques, 1, 1965, 5-30.

Alternatively they enlist prefectoral support to combat the
'technocratic' projects of the technical field services. See

  THOENIG J-C. and DANSEREAU F., <u>La Société locale face à une</u>
    <u>institution nouvelle de l'amenagement du territoire</u>, Paris
    (GSO), 1968.

The ability of local political elites to exploit divisions between
local State bureaucrats and between Paris officials dealing with
local affairs

Increasing State interventionism in economic and urban planning led to
the proliferation of State agencies dealing with local affairs, and
these agencies were not always agreed on the ends and means of their
policies. See:

  THOENIG Jean-Claude and FRIEDBERG Erhard, 'Politiques urbaines
    et stratégies corporatives', <u>Sociologie du Travail</u>, (4)
    October-December 1969, pp. 387-412.
  THOENIG Jean-Claude, L'Ere des technocrates, op. cit.
  ARCY François d', <u>Administration et urbanisme. La Société centrale</u>
    <u>pour l'équipement du territoire</u>. Paris, 1968.
  ROIG Charles, 'L'Administration traditionnelle devant les
    changements sociaux', <u>Administration et Planification</u>, Paris,
    1964.
  TARROW Sidney, 'Introduction' in TARROW <u>et al.</u>, <u>Territorial</u>
    <u>Politics in Industrial Nations</u>, New York, 1978.

The emergence of big towns

Many of these have some degree of financial leeway, increasingly

competent technical personnel and political leaders who wield considerable political influence. A recent article (by JOBERT P., and SELLIER
M., 'Les grandes villes: autonomie local et innovation politique',
Revue Française de Science Politique, 27 (2), April 1977, pp. 205-227)
makes the distinction between three types of big town:

the bureaucratic type dominated by a powerful bureaucrat wedded
  generally to the status quo;
the technocratic type, dominated by technocrats who are sensitive
  to central economic norms;
the municipalité innovatrice which, in certain circumstances, is
  able 'to defend its own specificity'.

On the autonomy of big towns, see

THOENIG Jean-Claude, 'La rélation...' op. cit.
TARROW Sidney, in Introduction to TARROW et al., Territorial
  Politics in Industrial Nations, op. cit.
MILCH Jerome, 'Influence as Power: French Local Government
  Reconsidered', British Journal of Political Science, (4), 1974,
  pp. 139-162.

The existence of policies which require cooperation and reciprocal
bargaining and concessions between central government and local
authorities

This area has received very little research attention, although
accounts of local council meetings (at regional, departmental and
municipal level) indicate that central and local officials are
locked in a permanent consultative process.

The existence of policies where there is broad agreement between
national and local elites, and where differences are related to
details or about the financial implications

The 'modernisation' of the big towns serves as an admirable example:
thus Jean Lojkine, La politique urbaine... op. cit., argues that the
ruling élite in Lyons willingly accepted the urban policies elaborated
by the State apparatus.

FINDINGS OF RECENT RESEARCH: CONCLUSION

Centre-local research is a major area of research, and it is carried
out by State agencies (e.g. the Ministry of the Environment, the DATAR),
by specialised teams (e.g. CERVL at Bordeaux and CERAT at Grenoble),
or by individuals in university law departments or Instituts d'Etudes
Politiques.

The tradition Jacobin or Napoleonic model is under attack, although
its intellectual appeal is still apparent in most recent research.

The existence of some degree of local autonomy is now accepted
(often begrudgedly), although it is invariably considered in the
context of a centralised framework. Local autonomy is either derided
as unimportant, or rationalised in terms of a general theory of central

State domination.

Marxist models of centre-local relations are implicit rather than explicit; they arise logically out of studies of the nature of local power (see 5. Biarez et al., op. cit. and J. Lojkine, op. cit.). Local actors are either viewed as 'objective' agents of State monopoly capitalism or as élites who are conceded a certain initiative by central authorities for purely political purposes.

The Crozier team model takes broadly three forms, all of which posit the general dominance of the centre:

the 'parallel powers' model of Crozier himself. In this model Crozier argues that because of fundamental French cultural characteristics (fear of face to face relations etc.) a rigid hierarchical bureaucratic system has been created. Given its rigidity, the only way the system is made to work is by the secretion of 'parallel powers', a network of unofficial and flexible relations which completely bypass the official model. In this model, local élites who belong to the unofficial network are perceived basically as the prisoners of 'the centralising logic'. (For a summary of the main arguments see Michel Crozier and Jean-Claude Thoenig, 'The Regulation of complex organised systems', op. cit.).

the 'resistance' model which may be found in the writings of Jean-Pierre Worms, Pierre Grémion, Mark Kesselman and Sidney Tarrow who insist upon the existence of a veritable 'pouvoir périphérique', and upon the 'functional autonomy of the local politico-administrative systems'. This model rests upon a theory of permanent complicity between local political élites and certain State bureaucrats (notably the prefects) who may combine to resist Paris, and especially in the area of local government reform (which might involve some diminution of their power). See notably

GREMION Pierre, 'Résistance au changement de l'administration territoriale: le cas des institutions régionales', Sociologie du travail, III, July-September 1966, pp. 276-295.

MAWHOOD Philip, 'Melting an iceberg: the struggle to reform communal government in France', British Journal of Political Science, Vol. 2, No. 4 October 1972, pp. 501-515.

MACHIN Howard, 'Local Government change in France - the case of the 1964 Reforms', Policy and Politics. Vol. 2, 1974, pp. 249-265.

MACHIN Howard, 'All Jacobins Now? The Growing hostility to local government reform', West European Politics, I (3), October 1978, pp. 133-150.

TARROW Sidney, Between Center and Periphery: grass roots politicians in France, London 1977.

TARROW Sidney, 'Local Constraints on Regional Reform: A Comparison of Italy and France', Comparative Politics, Vol. 7, No. 1, October 1974, pp. 1-36.

GOUREVITCH Peter, 'The Reform of Local Government: a political analysis', Comparative Politics, Vol. 10, No. 1, October 1977, pp. 69-88.

the 'honeycomb' model elaborated by Jean-Claude Thoenig which is the most sophisticated of the Crozerian school models. This model emphasises the importance of the local levels of decision making for the entire politico-administrative system, and is embedded in a general theory about the 'intermeshing' of local and national élites. As a possible theoretical framework for future research, the Thoenig model probably comes closest to that of Rhodes. For a recent exposition in English of the Thoenig model, see his 'Local Government Institutions and the contemporary evolution of French Society' in

LAGROYE Jacques and WRIGHT Vincent, <u>Local Government in Britain and France: Problems and Prospects</u>, London, forthcoming.

Scholars who support the 'tempered' or 'attenuated' centralisation 'school' are reluctant to elaborate any single general theoretical framework. Whilst recognising that final decisions are formally made in Paris, they reject the notion that all decisions are made by Paris (see the early articles of Roig Charles [e.g. 'Théorie et réalité de la décentralisation', <u>Revue Française de Science Politique</u>, (16), 1966, pp. 445-471)). They highlight the strategic role played by local <u>notables</u> (especially those holding national office) who are able to exploit a series of factors analysed briefly in this paper.

ANNEX I

A brief research guide

(i)   Present research and researchers into local government are in a considerable state of flux, as interests shift and as research teams break up and are re-formed. Any British scholar would be well advised to check the state of past research in the annual accounts published by the <u>Revue française de science politique</u>, and the position of present research projects with either Professor Georges Dupuis of the University of Paris or Professor Albert Mabileau of the <u>Institut d'Etudes Politiques</u>, Bordeaux. Both men are extremely well informed and very helpful.

(ii)   The <u>Fondation Nationale des Sciences Politiques</u>, rue Saint-Guillaume, Paris, is an admirable place to do research, since it has excellent newspaper files and takes all the journals.

(iii)   The CERAT at the IEP Grenoble has a detailed card catalogue of all past and present research carried out for the DATAR, its own press cuttings files, and an excellent library. The CERVL at Bordeaux has similar facilities.

(iv)   Scholars working on the history of local government would do well to contact Monsieur Guy Thuillier of the <u>Cour des Comptes</u> and Madame Jeanne Siwek-Pouydesseau of the <u>Centre National de la Recherche Scientifique</u>.

(v)   Certain publications are very important:

(a)   The annual report of the Délégation à l'Aménagement du
      territoire et à l'action régionale.
(b)   the Revue Administrative which contains useful articles
      and a section on 'Vie des collectivités locales'.
(c)   Aménagement du territoire et développement régional,
      the large annual collection of research articles
      published by the CERAT (see above).
(d)   the Cahiers de l'Institut français des sciences
      administratives (of which the most important are
      listed above).
(e)   the Bulletin de l'Institut international d'administra-
      tion publique (Paris, since 1967) which frequently
      includes useful research articles.
(f)   the Revue internationale des sciences administratives,
      published in Brussels.
(g)   Administration (Paris), the publication of the
      Association du corps préfectoral, which often includes
      accounts of the practical experiences of those in
      local government and administration.
(h)   Le Journal Officiel, for all laws, decrees and
      parliamentary debates.
(i)   La Vie urbaine, published by the Institut d'urbanisme
      de l'université de Paris.
(j)   Départements et communes, the journal of the Association
      des maires de France.
(k)   Etude des problèmes municipaux, published by the Service
      d'information et de documentation des maires et
      conseillers généraux of the ministry of the interior.
(l)   Espace et Sociétés, which is the source of many
      Marxist studies on urban problems.
(m)   Le Moniteur des travaux publics which contains some
      very useful information on locally financed public
      works projects.
(n)   Sociologie du Travail, for the work of various
      sociology groups (note particularly issues of 1966 (3)
      on 'L'Administration face au changement', and of 1969
      (4) on 'Politique urbaine'.)

(vi) A number of useful bibliographies are available:

(a)   GOURNAY Bernard & LANCELOT Marie-Thérèse,
      L'Administration française II les administrations
      locales, Paris, 1967.
(b)   BODIGUEL J-L., & KESSLER M-C., Guide de recherches.
      L'Administration française, Paris, 1970.
(c)   Bulletin du CEDERCOL. Collectivités locales, Paris,
      since 1969.
(d)   La recherche administrative en France, Paris, 1968
      (Cahier de l'IFSA, no. 3, op. cit.).
(e)   LAGROYE Jacques, Présentation de quelques travaux et
      publications sur le pouvoir local en France.
      Unpublished paper. CERVL, Bordeaux, 1974.
(f)   Histoire de l'Administration, Cahier de l'IFSA, Paris
      1972.
(g)   CHAZEL Lise, 'A Bibliography on local politics in
      France', Newsletter, ECPR work group on local

government and politics, No. 4, September 1976,
pp. 1-28, and No. 8, September 1978, pp. 1-8,
(deals mainly with urban studies).

(h)   A number of useful papers were given in a colloquium
on community power at the Centre de recherches
sociologiques, University of Toulouse, in October 1976.
These are available from Prof. Raymond Ledrut.

(i)   FRIEDBURG Erhard & GREMION Pierre, La Recherche sur
l'administration publique en France et en Allemagne.
Paris, 1975.

(j)   MEDARD Jean-François, La Recherche sur la vie politico-
administrative locale en France. Manuscript, 8th
IPSA September 1970.

(k)   La Région en Question, Paris, 1978 (Cahier de l'IFSA,
No. 17, op. cit.).

ANNEX II

Recent student research dissertations in the major universities

See also above under Section II. The name of the research supervisor
is given in parenthesis.

(i)   Aix-en-Provence

JOUBERT Madeleine, Le Conseil général, son rôle et son avenir
dans la région, Mémoire, IEP, 1972 (R. de Morant).
CASTA Jean-François, La bidépartementalisation de la Corse,
Memoire, IEP, 1973.
CONIBLIO Vincent, Problème et pratique de la centralisation
et de la décentralisation, Mémoire, IEP, 1973 (C. Debbasch).
BALL Didier, La Commission départementale. Aspects,
juridiques et politiques. Le Var 1968-74, Memoire, IEP,
1974 (M. Laligant).
MARCHETTI Martine, La nouvelle réforme régionale et les
réactions des élus locaux à la loi du 5 juillet 1972,
VINCENTY Christian, La Regionalisation française depuis 1968,
Mémoire, 3 vols., IEP, 1977 (M. Laligant).

(ii)   Lille

MAYEUX Annick & SALOME Martine, Les Maires dans
l'arrondissement de Béthune, Mémoire, Maitrise, Histoire,
Lille 3, 1977.
MARIEN Pierre, L'OREAM Nord, Mémoire, DES, Science politique,
Lille 2, 1975.

(iii)   Lyons (under A. Demichel)

CHAMERAT-LEBAS Noëlle, La Commune est-elle un service public?,
Mémoire, DES, Droit, Lyon 2, 1973
ENJOUVIN Bernard, La région du pouvoir et le pouvoir de la
région, Memoire, DES, Droit, Lyon 2, 1977.
FABRY Alain, La Planification imprévue. L'amélioration du

processus de pianification et le développement des
institutions régionales; Thèse, Doctorat, Droit, Lyon
2, 1977.
MALHIERE Pierre, La Collaboration entre collectivités locales,
These, Doctorat, Droit, Lyon 2, 1977

(iv)　　Rouen

BERTHAUD Alain, La Mission d'études pour la Basse-Seine,
Mémoire, DES, Droit, 1974.

(v)　　Amiens (under J. Chevallier)

CALVI Gerard, Régionalisation et participation: l'exemple
de l'application de la réforme régionale du 5 juillet
1972 en Lorraine et en Champagne-Ardennes, Thèse, Doctorat,
Administration publique, 1977.
BINAND Jean-François, Le Conseil général de la Somme et
l'administration préfectorale, Mémoire, DES, Droit, 1975.
DESESQUELLES Giles & HOLLEVILLE Giles, Le Poids des
fonctionnaires locaux dans les affairs municipales,
Mémoire, DEA, Administration publique, 1977.

(vi)　　Paris

DEVES Claude, Les Sociétés d'aménagement régional: entreprises
publiques locales ou démembrements fonctionnels de d'Etat,
Thèse, Doctorat, Droit, 1976 (Paris XIII: P. Gaugher).
BOUDIN Franck, Le Conseil général de la Seine-Saint-Denis,
Mémoire, DEA, Etudes politiques, Paris,1977 (G. Burdeau).
BRENET Bernard, Les Fusions des communes dans le département
de la Haute-Marne, Mémoire, DES, Science Politique,
Paris 2, 1977 (R. Drago).
TOMELIN Mario, Le Processus décisionnel dans la centralisation
et la décentralisation, Thèse, Doctorat, Science Politique,
Paris 2, 1974 (L. Sfez).
DORGET Manoël, L'Etat et les collectivités locales face à
l'urbanisation, Thèse, Doctorat, Droit, Paris 2
(A. de Lanbadère).
VEVER Bruno, La Réforme communale sous la Ve Républicque,
Mémoire, DES, Droit, Paris X, 1973 (P. Soubourin).

(vii)　　Strasbourg

KAUFMANN Jean-Luc, Les Adjoints au maire d'une grande ville,
Mulhouse, Mémoire, IEP, (R. Herzog).

(viii)　　Poitiers

MARSAUD Jacques, La Concertation Etat et collectivités
locales en matière de planification urbaine, Mémoire, DES,
Droit, 1972 (R. Savy).

(ix)　　Nice

LAGNIEZ Denis, Le Système de gestion d'une administration

départementale, Thèse, Doctorat, Droit, 1977 (X. Boisselier).

DAVID P., Le Personnel régional, Mémoire, DES, Droit, 1973 (J-P. Gilli).

FRANCESHI M., L'Evolution du concept régional sous la Ve République, Mémoire, DES, Droit, 1973 (J-P. Gilli).

STAGNARA V., La Région corse et ses problèmes, Mémoire, DES, Droit, 1973 (J-P. Gilli).

(x) Grenoble (important centre)

Several local politics theses have been published: amongst unpublished

AUGOYARD Anne-Marie, Les Elus locaux, l'action culturelle et le changement social, Mémoire, IEP, 1974 (B. Gilman).

(xi) Toulouse (under the direction of J-A. Maxeres)

BELAVAL Anne, Le problème du regroupement des communes, Mémoire, IEP, 1972.

HUMILIERE Michel, Le GREMIP (Groupe régional d'etudes Midi-Pyrénées) OREAM toulousain, Mémoire, DES, Science politique, Toulouse, 1975

ALAUX Gerard, Les Rapports entre le préfet et les chefs des services extérieurs; la réforme du 14 mars 1964 dans le département du Tarn, Mémoire, IEP, 1974

BERLESE Marilene, Le Regroupement communal dans l'arrondissement de Condom, Mémoire, IEP, 1974.

SOTOM, J., Le Regroupement des communes dans les arrondissements d'Auch et de Mirande, Mémoire, IEP, 1974.

(xii) Bordeaux

BIROLLEAU Patrick, Construction sociale et politique du logement. L'exemple de l'Office public d'HLM de la Communauté urbaine de Bordeaux, Mémoire, IEP, 1974 (J. Dumas).

THOMAS Louis C., Les Pouvoirs du maire, Thèse, Doctorat, 1973 (J. Lamarque).

LAMBERT Pierre, Les Conseillers généraux de la Corrèze: 1945-70. Mémoire, IEP, 1977 (J. Lagroye).

BASSO Jacques, La Tradition politique localiste dans les Alpes-Maritimes 1860-1968, Mémoire, IEP, 1971 (A. Mabileau).

COUDEVYLLE Andrée, Le Démembrement de l'administration départementale, Mémoire, DES, Science politique, 1974 (J-L. Maitres).

DUMAS J., Les Activités industrielles dans la communauté urbaine de Bordeaux, Thèse, Doctorat d'Etat, 1977.

(xiii) Rennes

MARTIN Jean-Paul, Le Rôle des élus locaux dans l'élaboration du SDAU du district de l'agglomération rennaise, Mémoire, DES, Droit, 1975 (J-P. Chandet).

ANNEX III

The Thoenig Model

The System of Regulation in French Inter-Governmental Relations

Elected Officials Channel   Administrative Channel

President of the Republic

                                                        The Ministry of
                                                        Finance and other
                                                        central agencies

The members of the Parliament
and influential socio-economic
leaders at national level

                                                        The Prefects and other
                                                        heads of State
                                                        agencies at the level
                                                        of the département

The General Councilmen and
local socio-economic leaders

                                                        Sub-prefects and other
                                                        heads of State agencies
                                                        at the level of the
                                                        cantons or
                                                        arrondissements

The Mayors

Local Councillors

Jean-Claude Thoenig, State Bureaucracies and
Local Government in France (Berkeley,
California, University of California, Dept.
of Political Science, mimeo., March 1975),
p. 36.

194

NOTES AND REFERENCES

(1)   The Jacobins were amongst the more radical Republican elements
at the time of the Revolution, and are associated with the
highly centralised and hierarchical system of government which
they advocated and partly created. Their centralising work
was completed by Napoleon. Thus, the highly centralist model
of centre-local relations is frequently referred to as either
'Jacobin' or 'Napoleonic'.

Index